STATE AND LOCAL
PENSIONS

STATE AND LOCAL
PENSIONS
WHAT NOW?

ALICIA H. MUNNELL

BROOKINGS INSTITUTION PRESS
Washington, D.C.

Copyright © 2012
THE BROOKINGS INSTITUTION
1775 Massachusetts Avenue, N.W., Washington, D.C. 20036
www.brookings.edu

Library of Congress Cataloging-in-Publication data

Munnell, Alicia Haydock.
    State and local pensions : what now? / Alicia H. Munnell.
        p.   cm.
    Includes bibliographical references and index.
    "Provides a broad look at the challenges facing U.S. pension plans and concludes that while some plans are in trouble, many are functioning reasonable well, but still face potential pitfalls, and proposes solutions that preserve the main strengths of state and local pensions while promoting reforms"—Provided by the publisher.
    ISBN 978-0-8157-2412-4 (hardcover : alk. paper)
    1. State governments—Officials and employees—Pensions—United States. 2. Local officials and employees—Pensions—United States. 3. State governments—Officials and employees—Pensions—Law and legislation—United States. 4. Local officials and employees—Pensions—Law and legislation—United States. I. Title.
    JK2474.M864 2012
    331.25'291352130973—dc23   2012028125

9 8 7 6 5 4 3 2 1

Printed on acid-free paper

Typeset in Adobe Garamond

Composition by Cynthia Stock
Silver Spring, Maryland

Printed by R. R. Donnelley
Harrisonburg, Virginia

Contents

Acknowledgments

The author thanks the Center for State and Local Government Excellence for supporting much of the research that made this book possible. The center's foresight allowed for the development of the expertise needed to understand the state and local pension sector at an opportune moment. The center's support also resulted in the creation of the *Public Plans Database,* a unique resource for researchers and practitioners.

My name appears in this book as the sole author, but Jean-Pierre Aubry, Laura Quinby, and Josh Hurwitz were my co-authors and full partners at the Center for Retirement Research at Boston College (CRR) on much of the original research. They brought to bear their unparalleled quantitative skills, keen insights, and tireless effort. Andrew Eschtruth exceeded his usual high level of substantive and editorial comment and virtually managed the production of the manuscript, which was extremely challenging as the state/local pension world was constantly changing between drafts. Without my colleagues at the CRR, there would be no book.

The author would also like to thank all who generously gave their time to read and comment on all or part of the first draft of this book. They include Jeffrey Brown, Keith Brainard, Frank Caine, Peter Diamond, Joshua Franzel, Jeremy Gold, Gene Kalwarski, Elizabeth Kellar, Anthony Laden, Gina Raimondo, and Michael Travaglini. These individuals, who come from a variety of disciplines, offered unique insights and perspectives on different aspects of this complex topic. Their comments, criticisms, and suggestions were invaluable; they not only reduced the number of errors, but produced a much richer story.

At the Brookings Institution Press, Christopher Kelaher helped get the book on its way, while Janet Walker and Larry Converse shepherded the book through its editing and production routine; Janet Schilling Mowery expertly edited the manuscript; Inge Lockwood proofread the typeset pages, and Sherry Smith provided a comprehensive index.

1

Introduction

Vallejo, California (2008), Prichard, Alabama (2010), and Central Falls, Rhode Island (2011) have filed for bankruptcy, with commentators citing pension promises to public employees as a major cause (see box).[1] A Googling of the words "state," "pension," and "crisis" found more than a twentyfold increase between 2000 and 2011 (see figure 1-1). The Governmental Accounting Standards Board (GASB) has promulgated new standards that could dramatically change how pension liabilities and costs are reported. Many states have substantially reduced benefits for new employees and increased employee contributions across the board. Yet the majority of states should be able to recover from the devastating impact of the 2008 financial crisis. What is going on here? How did the states and localities facing serious problems get into trouble? How did the others avoid problems? And where problems exist, what changes should be made that would be both effective and fair?

This book tells the story of state and local pension plans over the past three decades. The late 1970s and early 1980s is a good place to start. In 1978, the

---

1. Although press accounts link Vallejo's bankruptcy with pension costs (see Greenhut 2010; Scheer 2008; and Weber 2011), one reviewer of an earlier draft of this book disagrees. He contends that even though CalPERS (California Public Employees' Retirement System) was the city's largest single creditor, the cost of servicing the city's required pension contribution was not a major factor in its bankruptcy. Rather, the bankruptcy was the result of a collapse of the city's revenue base. This story sounds quite similar to that for Stockton, Calif., which filed for bankruptcy in June 2012. Stockton's financial problems stemmed more from extensive borrowing and the collapse of its real estate market than from pension pressures.

Figure 1-1. *Total Number of Google News Citations Using the Terms "State," "Pension," and "Crisis," 2000–11*

Number of citations

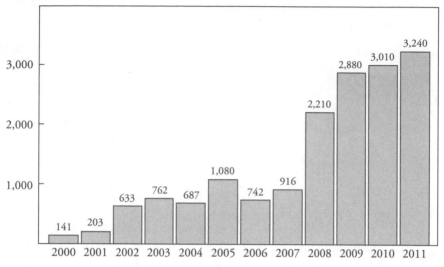

Source: Google News 2012, database search, March 1.

first comprehensive survey of state and local plans, mandated by the Employee Retirement Income Security Act of 1974, awarded public plans a grade of D:

> In the vast majority of public employee pension systems, plan participants, plan sponsors, and the general public are kept in the dark with regard to a realistic assessment of true pension costs. The high degree of pension cost blindness is due to the lack of actuarial valuations, the use of unrealistic actuarial assumptions, and the general absence of actuarial standards.[2]

It was also a period when the author served as a member of the Massachusetts Retirement Law Commission and witnessed the "Wild West" up close. The then chair of the commission later pleaded guilty to state and federal charges that he engaged in a scheme to defraud the Massachusetts retirement systems.[3]

From the perspective of the late 1970s and early 1980s, the management of state and local plans has improved dramatically. Plans began to put aside assets

2. U.S. Congress (1978), p. 4.
3. Business Wire (1994).

Cities That Have Filed for Bankruptcy

Vallejo, Calif., population 115,942, filed for bankruptcy in May 2008, the second largest municipal bankruptcy in California history behind Orange County in 1994.

—Bankruptcy was attributed to excessive compensation for police and fire union members; salaries and benefits accounted for nearly 80 percent of the city's budget.

—In August 2011, Vallejo was cleared to emerge from bankruptcy protection after agreeing to restructure nearly $50 million in debt by reducing pension benefits for new employees, cutting payments for retiree health care, raising contributions for current workers, and creating a rainy-day fund.

—Since 2008, the police department workforce has been slashed by nearly 50 percent, the firefighter workforce has been slashed by 42 percent, and three of eight fire stations have been closed.

Prichard, Ala., population 22,659, filed for bankruptcy in October 2010. The city's decline began in the 1970s as its population shrank by 40 percent and its tax base dwindled.

—Bankruptcy was attributed to the legislature sweetening benefits of the municipal plan over time without paying for them.

—Prichard had been warned since a 2004 actuarial review that continuous underfunding created the risk of default.

—Prichard stopped paying monthly pension checks to its 150 retired workers in September 2010, breaking a state law that requires pension benefits to be paid in full.

—Prichard filed for bankruptcy one month later in response to a lawsuit from retirees; the case was dismissed and is currently being appealed.

Central Falls, R.I., population 19,376, filed for bankruptcy in August 2011. With an unemployment rate near 15 percent, Central Falls is one of Rhode Island's poorest communities.

—Central Falls filed for bankruptcy after failing to negotiate significant concessions from the unionized workforce, which would have required reductions in pension benefits by as much as 55 percent.

—Central Falls faced $80 million in unfunded obligations and projected $5 million deficits for the next five years (its annual budget was about $17 million).

—A receiver negotiated new agreements with the unions and retirees, which reduced pensions by 50 percent. The cuts eliminated the operating deficit and are projected to produce balanced budgets through fiscal year 2016. Bondholders were protected.

to pay for future benefits. Assets started to be managed professionally. Plan sponsors began to provide regular actuarial reports. And many public plan officials became subject to the same fiduciary standards that apply to the private sector. In fact, the preface to a 2001 comprehensive study of public plans from the prestigious Pension Research Council at the Wharton School of the University of Pennsylvania, of which the author is a member, awarded state and local plans at least an A–: "State and local plans in the United States have impressive levels of assets backing their liabilities, they provide reasonable replacement rates to retirees, and they invest in a manner not too different from that of private pension managers."[4]

Two financial crises later—the bursting of the dot.com bubble in 2000 and the collapse of the entire equity market in 2008—it became clear that some state and local pensions were seriously underfunded. The ensuing recession, which decimated state and local budgets, precluded additional contributions to compensate fully for the drop in asset values. States and localities began to cut benefits for new employees, raise employee contributions, and, in some cases, shift to defined contribution or hybrid plans.

The economics profession followed with "I told you so." The issue, among the many complex questions surrounding the provision of pensions in the public sector, that economists pounced on was the rate used to discount obligations. Following the standards established by GASB, state and local plans have used the expected long-run rate of return on plan assets as the discount rate. But finance theory dictates that the appropriate rate should reflect the riskiness of the obligations; the expected long-run return backing those obligations is irrelevant. Using the economists' approach, unfunded liabilities turned out to be $2.1 trillion in 2008 rather than $507 billion. Divide the new figure by the number of residents and the problem looks insoluble.[5]

Some problems could have been avoided by discounting obligations *for reporting purposes* by the appropriate rate. For example, California's plans would not have appeared overfunded in the 1990s, and the legislature might not have expanded benefits dramatically. And breaking the link between expected returns and the discount rate might have resulted in lower holdings of equities. But the discount rate is a narrow prism through which to view the hard questions public plan sponsors face.

At the other extreme, a number of governors identified public sector unions as the source of the problem. Wisconsin eliminated collective bargaining for public employees except police and firefighters. Michigan passed legislation that

---

4. Mitchell and Hustead (2001), p. vii. By the time a more recent Pension Research Council study was published (Mitchell and Anderson 2009), it was clear that conditions had changed.

5. Novy-Marx and Rauh (2011a).

required each collective bargaining agreement to include a provision that allows an emergency manager appointed under the local government to reject, modify, or terminate the collective bargaining agreement. Oklahoma decided that municipal governments are no longer required to bargain, except with police and firefighters. And Ohio abolished the right to strike—a provision that was subsequently defeated by a referendum. Legislation to limit collective bargaining is currently under consideration in many other states.[6]

Unions, like the discount rate, are too narrow a focus for understanding the complex situation facing state and local governments. Consider Illinois, a highly unionized state with generous benefits. Three of its four large state-administered plans are in terrible shape; one is much better off. Why? The answer lies largely in the fact that the sponsors of the plan for municipalities made their annual required contributions each year, whereas the state legislature failed to make the required contributions for the three other plans.

Thus, plans have a number of dimensions, including the generosity of benefits and the extent to which those benefits are funded. But more important, pension benefits are part of the compensation package used to attract and retain a skilled public sector workforce. The risk at this point is that state legislatures will cut benefits too much for new employees, so that public schools and universities, without compensating wage increases, will not be able to compete with the private sector for skilled workers. In order to make good decisions about public plans going forward, it is important to understand them in their full complexity and be able to answer a range of questions:

—How did states and localities get into their current situation?

—Why are some plans in trouble, others not?

—How do pension commitments affect state and local budgets?

—Are public sector workers appropriately compensated?

—Do defined contribution plans have a role in the public sector?

—How can public plans fairly distribute the pain in the case of unsustainable benefit promises?

The answers to these questions matter because public pensions have a significant economic effect on every state, city, and town in the nation: these plans hold about $2.8 trillion in assets, cover 15 million working members (about 11 percent of the nation's workforce), and provide regular benefits to 8 million annuitants.[7]

6. For example, legislative proposals in Alaska (HB 134) and Rhode Island (S 409) would make both right-to-work states, whereby public employees can choose whether or not to join a union and cannot be penalized for not joining. Bills in South Carolina (H 4194) and New Hampshire (LSR 2114) would prohibit collective bargaining completely for public employees.

7. U.S. Census Bureau, *State and Local Public-Employee Retirement Systems* (2010); and U.S. Board of Governors of the Federal Reserve System, *Flow of Funds Accounts* (2011).

Organization of the Book

This book offers a comprehensive overview of the health of state and local pension plans, outlines the major challenges they face, and proposes solutions that preserve their main strengths while promoting needed reforms. By adopting a broad perspective, the book captures the core issues that should drive the policy debate, rather than more narrow concerns that produce much heat, but little light.

The story of state and local pensions is big and complicated. It cannot be reduced to a single mantra such as discounting obligations by the riskless rate of return or limiting union power. It is a story of plan sponsors with unique histories, resources, and political cultures. The main theme is that many states and localities have provided reasonable benefits and set aside money to pre-fund their commitments, but a few have simply behaved irresponsibly. Whatever differences existed before 2008 were magnified by the financial crisis. However, even the good states face challenges: scaling back their investments in risky assets, maintaining adequate compensation to attract talented workers, and obtaining the flexibility to alter benefits for current workers.

Chapter 2 sets the stage by first discussing the recent history of state and local pensions, from the late 1970s to the present. During the 1980s, most plans dramatically improved their funding and investment practices. But they also increased their holdings of equities in the 1990s and engaged in benefit improvements and funding holidays during the bull market. As a result, they were thrown seriously off course by the twin economic crises of the 2000s. By 2010, the reported funded level for state and local plans was 76 percent; estimates for 2011 suggest a level of 75 percent.[8] The chapter next provides a broad picture of the state and local plan universe, highlighting its breadth and diversity. The U.S. Census identifies 3,418 retirement systems that are sponsored by a government entity. State-administered plans, which often cover many local government workers as well as state employees, account for a tiny fraction of all plans but almost all of the participants and assets. While local plans are generally small, they hold more assets per active employee than state plans, likely because they cover police and firefighters who retire earlier and therefore have more expensive benefits. The final section discusses retiree health plans, the other major retirement benefit offered to state and local workers. Most of these plans are unfunded, so they represent a serious claim on future budgets. But due to their complexity and data constraints, retiree health merits a separate study and falls outside the scope of this book.

8. Center for Retirement Research at Boston College (2012a).

Chapter 3 covers the thorny issue of how best to account for the liabilities of public plans for reporting purposes and whether this choice should also influence investment and funding decisions. What may appear as an arcane issue has generated a white-hot debate among economists, actuaries, and practitioners. At issue is how best to measure future benefit promises made to current employees and the corresponding liability to the government.

As noted, most plans, following guidelines established by GASB, discount their obligations by the expected long-term return on the assets held in the pension fund, currently about 8 percent (although plans are beginning to lower their assumed rate of return). Economists argue that because pension benefits are guaranteed under most state laws, the appropriate discount factor is a riskless rate. The economists' approach would produce much higher liabilities than those currently reported by states and localities, and the unfunded liability would triple.

The argument is compelling that the obligations of public plans should be discounted by a riskless rate—for purposes of reporting. Such a change is not only theoretically correct, but would also deter plans from offering more generous benefits during periods when they appear to have "excess" assets and allow plans to reduce their holdings of risky assets without affecting their reported liabilities. And it would improve confidence in the stability of public plans among private sector observers.

The argument about the discount rate pertains to *reporting*; investing and calculating contributions are separate issues. Discounting obligations by a riskless rate does not imply that plans should hold only riskless assets. A number of considerations suggest that state and local plans should continue to invest in equities. If the returns on these equities resemble their long-run historical performance, then, for any given level of contributions, plans' unfunded liabilities would be paid off more quickly than if funds were invested in bonds.

Determining contributions is a trickier issue. Academic models suggest that the calculation should use the riskless rate. But contributing based on the riskless rate and investing in equities produces ever growing funding levels and declining contributions for each successive generation. These outcomes have political ramifications in the real world. Calculating contributions based on the expected rate of return is probably the least bad option and does not conflict with using the riskless rate for reporting purposes.

Building on chapter 2's discussion of the diverse pension universe and chapter 3's perspective on quantifying plan liabilities, chapter 4 analyzes the current funded status of plans to determine why some plans are in trouble while others are not. The discussion identifies the factors that lead plan sponsors to make their full annual required contribution (ARC) and the factors that, given the ARC payment, result in more or less funding. It then explores whether public employee unions have driven up plan costs, a concern expressed by many governors.

Three major conclusions emerge from the funding analysis. First, the notion that all public plans are in trouble is simply not correct. Before the two financial crises of the past decade, most plans were in reasonably good shape. And in the wake of the crisis, plan finances have begun to stabilize. Second, sponsors of seriously underfunded plans, such as those in Illinois, Kentucky, Louisiana, New Jersey, and Pennsylvania, have behaved badly. They have either failed to make their required contributions or used inaccurate assumptions so that their contribution requirements are not meaningful. An equally large number of states—Delaware, Florida, Georgia, Tennessee, and North Carolina—have done a good job of providing reasonable benefits, paying their required contributions, and accumulating assets. Third, it is impossible to identify a link between the poorly funded plans and the two factors others have highlighted as the source of the problem: (1) discounting obligations by the long-run expected return instead of the riskless rate; or (2) the collective bargaining activities of unions. The poorly funded plans did not come close to surmounting the lower hurdle associated with a high discount rate; raising the hurdle is unlikely to have improved their behavior. And union strength simply did not emerge as a significant factor in any of the empirical analyses. Pension funding is simply a story of fiscal discipline.

Chapter 5 puts the funding discussion in a broader perspective by assessing pension expenses as a share of state and local revenues. The important policy question is whether pension spending will squeeze out other priorities. The trade-offs here have become more challenging in recent years given both short-term fiscal pressures and more systemic factors driving up overall spending commitments. States and localities are still struggling to emerge from the budgetary strains that accompanied the financial crisis and Great Recession. Government revenues declined sharply as the economy deteriorated and took several years to begin to recover. At the same time, spending pressures resulting from the downturn have exacerbated structural budget challenges such as health care cost inflation.

Against this backdrop of ongoing fiscal challenges, it is particularly important to understand the burden that state and local pensions represent for their government sponsors. In 2009, overall pension contributions were about 4.6 percent of total state and local revenues. They will account for more in the future. How much more depends crucially on how much sponsors earn on plan assets. If they earn the expected return of 8 percent, pension spending will rise only modestly to 5.1 percent of revenue. If they earn only 6 percent, the share will grow to 9.5 percent. With a 4 percent return, pension contributions will account for 14.5 percent of revenue.

The future budget burden of pensions varies enormously by state. Well-run plans will see little increase in the share of their revenue devoted to pensions.

States that have avoided funding, such as Illinois, will see pension costs soak up a huge share of future revenue. Illinois may end up exhausting its pension assets and reverting to pay-as-you-go funding. New Jersey would have been in a similar position without its 2011 reforms. But the question remains whether New Jersey will stick to its new funding commitments. Both Illinois and New Jersey have issued pension obligation bonds in the past as a response to shortfalls, but this approach offers no real solution, as it may simply increase financial risk in states that are ill-equipped to handle it. California and New York are special cases; they have not been persistently bad actors, but their pensions are very generous and place an enormous burden on the state and its participating localities. Again, for states facing hard challenges, neither changing the discount rate nor curbing union power provides a solution. The path forward is clear: they will have to make tough decisions to distribute pain among current retirees, current employees, future employees, and future taxpayers.

Given the overall budget challenges facing the public sector and the acute pension problems in some jurisdictions outlined in chapter 5, it is not surprising that many proposals have emerged to cut pension benefits. A common presumption in these discussions is that pensions are "too generous." To gauge the accuracy of this presumption, chapter 6 explores total compensation—wages and benefits—in the state/local sector and compares the results with private sector compensation. It also addresses the related question of whether public employees end up richer or poorer than their private sector counterparts in retirement.

In assessing total compensation, one point on which most researchers agree is that wages for workers with similar levels of education and experience are lower for state and local workers than for those in the private sector. Pension and retiree health benefits for public sector workers roughly offset the wage penalty so that, taken as a whole, compensation in the two sectors is generally comparable. But this parity hides enormous variation by wage levels. State and local workers in the lowest third of the wage distribution are paid somewhat more than their private sector counterparts, those in the middle roughly comparable amounts, and those in the top third significantly less. Outcomes at retirement are related to lifetime employment patterns. Those who spend *most of their career* in the state/local sector end up with more wealth and higher replacement rates than their private sector counterparts. Short-term state/local workers actually end up with less wealth and lower replacement rates than similarly situated private sector employees.

The bottom line is that, for the nation as a whole, the difference between state/local and private sector compensation is modest. The implication is that policymakers need to be cautious about making massive changes without carefully studying the situation in their particular state or locality. This caution is particularly relevant for teachers, who make up more than half of the state/

local workforce and earn significantly less than private sector workers with similar education.

Chapter 7 explores how, in the wake of the financial crisis, some public plan sponsors have looked beyond cutting pension benefits or raising contribution rates toward structural change. Such changes would move from the traditional defined benefit system toward a system that includes a defined contribution component, akin to the 401(k) plans that now dominate the private sector. Is this type of shift good or bad? A complete answer to this question requires an understanding of the strengths and weaknesses of both types of pension plans and the rationale for shifting from sole reliance on defined benefit plans. The core issues here are how much risk plan participants should bear compared to plan sponsors and taxpayers and how the structure of benefits should treat short- versus long-service employees.

The main conclusion that emerges is that defined contribution plans have a role to play in the public sector. While defined benefit plans provide the most predictable retirement income for long-service employees, sole reliance on these plans in a political arena puts states and localities at considerable financial risk and creates a reward structure that provides little for shorter-term workers. At the same time, however, the 401(k) experiment in the private sector suggests that a wholesale shift to such plans would transfer too much risk to public sector workers. In order to balance risks and to provide some benefits for mobile workers, some combination of defined benefit and defined contribution plans would enhance the benefit structure in the public sector. The options extend beyond simply cutting back on the defined benefit plan and adding a 401(k)-type plan. Sponsors can consider modified defined benefit plans, such as a cash balance plan or one based on indexed career average earnings, the introduction of explicit risk sharing among plan sponsors, current employees, and retirees, or a "stacked" approach with a robust defined benefit base topped by a 401(k)-type plan.

Chapter 8 proposes solutions to the broad challenges facing all plans as well as the specific problems of severely troubled plans. These suggestions are not simple or painless, but they are feasible and would help ensure the health of the public pension sector for many decades to come.

All plans face three key challenges: the share of their assets allocated to risky assets; the implications of recent cuts in pension benefits for new employees; and legal constraints in adjusting future benefits for current employees. First, many plans have too much of their portfolio in risky assets, almost two-thirds in 2011. This policy undermines funding over time because strong investment returns often lead to pressure for benefit expansions, rather than being set aside to offset future fallow periods. Reducing equity holdings will mean lower returns and the need for higher taxes or lower benefits over the long term, but it will make plans more secure.

The second challenge for plan sponsors is maintaining compensation packages that will attract the best candidates for public sector jobs. This goal has been jeopardized by large cuts in pension benefits for new employees. Such cuts reduce total compensation, making the public sector a less attractive employer. Many of the benefit changes reflect good policy, such as extending the age for full benefits, but they need to be offset by higher wages to avoid eroding the public sector's ability to compete in the labor market.

The third challenge is to alleviate the legal constraints that make it very difficult for plan sponsors to change *future* benefits for current employees. Change is more feasible than generally thought given that in most states the protections are in statutes or derived from case law; they are not established in the state's constitution. The goal should be for public sector workers to have the same protections as private sector workers—namely, benefits earned to date cannot be taken away, but sponsors can amend the plan going forward.

For more troubled plans, a major reform effort is needed to address severe underfunding. A successful reform strategy must be fair. The need for benefit cuts for public employees or retirees must be broadly understood; and the burden imposed by these cuts needs to be distributed equitably among public employees. The responsibility for bringing the system into balance also needs to be distributed fairly between employees and taxpayers. Rhode Island provides a recent example where a fair process brought dramatic reform and moved the system toward a permanent solution.

Finally, even if states and localities solve their pension funding issues, public plans will remain a source of controversy. They simply provide more retirement income than do 401(k) plans in the private sector. However, the goal should not be to bring public sector workers down to the inadequate standards of the private sector, but rather to enhance the retirement system for private sector workers. The public sector pension infrastructure might provide a way to help achieve this goal.

2

State and Local Pensions: From the 1970s to Today

This chapter has three purposes. The first is to explain how we got where we are today in terms of state and local pension finance. The second is to describe the current pension landscape and to introduce the *Public Plans Database,* which serves as the basis for much of the empirical material covered in subsequent chapters. The final purpose is to tip our hat to the other major component of retirement benefits for public sector employees—namely, retiree health insurance. The unfunded liabilities for state-administered retiree health plans amount to about one-fifth of those for state-administered pensions.

The discussion proceeds as follows. The first section provides a brief history of public sector pensions and the evolution of their governance. The focus is on the three decades since the findings of a 1978 congressionally mandated study, which include the resulting efforts to impose federal legislation, the substantial improvement in pension plan administration and funding during the 1980s, increased investment in equities and benefit expansions during the 1990s, and the impact of the twin stock market crashes of the past decade. The second section shifts from the three-decade trends in governance and funding to an overview of today's pension structure. It also includes a brief discussion of the *Public Plans Database.* The final section offers a bird's eye view of retiree health plans to provide some sense of the total retirement liabilities facing state and local governments.

The conclusions that emerge from this chapter are threefold. First, state and local pensions have come a long way in implementing responsible management since the days of the "Wild West." Second, what remains is an extremely heterogeneous array of plans, where the benefit provisions and funded status vary not only across states but also within states. Anyone who says "all state and local plans are in trouble" or "all are doing well" has to be wrong, because plans differ so dramatically. Finally, states and localities are committed not only to paying pensions for their workers but also to providing retiree health. Most retiree health insurance plans are unfunded, so the employer share of premiums represents a serious claim on future budgets. But given that comprehensive reporting requirements only became effective in 2007 and that the provisions of these plans are complicated, the topic merits a separate study. The retiree health commitment should simply be kept in mind as the pension discussion proceeds.

History in a Nutshell

The first state or local plan dates from 1857, when New York City provided lumpsum benefits to policemen injured in the line of duty.[1] Many municipalities created plans during the last half of the nineteenth century, including a number of systems for teachers. In 1911, Massachusetts developed the first state system to cover its general government employees (that is, employees engaged in activities other than teaching or public safety). But the major expansion of coverage came in the wake of the 1935 federal Social Security legislation. During the 1930s and 1940s, nearly half of the large state and local plans were established or significantly restructured (see figure 2-1). By the early 1960s, most states and localities had established their pension systems.

State and local government employment roughly doubled between the early 1960s and the mid-1970s, resulting in an enormous growth in the population covered by state and local pension plans. This growth, combined with interest in private plan reform that culminated in the 1974 passage of the federal Employee Retirement Income Security Act (ERISA), focused attention on public pensions. Originally, both government and private plans were included in the legislative proposals, but by the time ERISA was passed, public plans had been exempted. Instead, Congress mandated a congressional study of retirement plans at all levels of government to determine: (1) the adequacy of existing levels of participation, vesting, and financing; (2) the effectiveness of existing fiduciary standards; and (3) the need for federal legislation.[2]

1. See Bleakney (1972).

2. According to the Congressional Research Service, several factors contributed to the decision to undertake a study rather than include state and local plans in ERISA. First, Congress found itself with a dearth of information on public plans. Second, no flow of complaints had been heard from participants of public plans similar to that from dissatisfied participants in private plans. Third, Congress had its hands full simply tackling the problems in the private sector. Fourth, it was unclear whether Congress could properly set standards for state and local plans that federal plans could not reasonably achieve. Finally, some legislators were unsure whether it was constitutional for the federal government to regulate the pension plans of states and localities. See Schmitt (1976).

Figure 2-1. *Percentage of Large State and Local Retirement Systems That Were Established or Significantly Restructured, by Date*

Percent

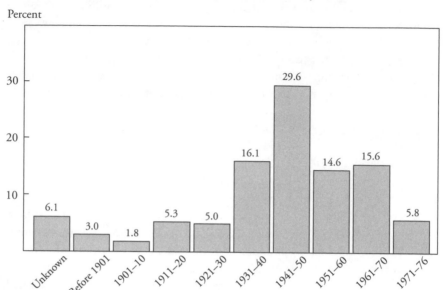

Source: U.S. Congress (1978).

Pension Task Force Report: 1978

The results of the ERISA-mandated congressional study were released in the spring of 1978 as the *Pension Task Force Report on Public Employee Retirement Systems*. The study concluded that serious problems existed at all levels of government in reporting, disclosure, fiduciary, and funding standards for public pension plans and that federal regulation was necessary and desirable.

With regard to reporting and disclosure, the task force noted that many plan participants were not informed about basic plan provisions and vested benefits, leading to unnecessary forfeitures. In addition, many plans were not operating in accordance with the generally accepted financial and accounting standards commonly used in the private sector. Further, lack of oversight opened up the possibility for abuse. And, importantly, many sponsors and taxpayers did not understand the full cost of these plans because of the lack of regular actuarial valuations.

With regard to benefit provisions, the study acknowledged that benefits were generally higher in the public sector than in the private and would easily meet ERISA's participation and benefit accrual requirements. On the other hand, the public sector had much more stringent vesting requirements than were allowed under ERISA. And most systems would not satisfy ERISA's requirement that

5 percent interest be paid to a terminated employee upon return of mandatory contributions. Finally, public sector employees would benefit from ERISA's provision requiring joint-and-survivor annuities.

On the funding front, the finding was that many plan sponsors had no idea about the true cost of their pensions because they did not have regular actuarial valuations. While some plans were accumulating assets as required under ERISA, many more were seeing rapidly rising pension costs due to the lack of funding. And 17 percent of plans were operating on a pay-as-you-go basis. Finally, even in those instances where assets were being accumulated, the unpredictability of the revenue stream, sometimes based on a stipulated allocation of state insurance premium taxes, federal revenue sharing monies, or special levies, often hindered proper funding.

The final issue was plan control and fiduciary responsibility. The management and control of plan assets were frequently found to be inadequate. The absence of statutory guidance or plan documents in some cases opened the door to abuse. Moreover, state and local plans had no uniform requirement that fiduciaries manage and invest pension assets prudently and for the exclusive benefit of plan participants or that such fiduciaries be held responsible for any losses resulting from a breach of their duties. The absence of safeguards, the study noted, had led to conflicts of interest and abuse, often resulting in loss of revenue. For example, some public pension funds were investing in the securities of their state or locality, despite the low-yield, non-tax nature of such securities and the tax-exempt status of the government. At the same time, numerous restrictive investment practices imposed by statute or policy, such as "legal lists" that precluded investment in equities, limited the ability of plans to earn full investment returns.

Based on its assessment of state and local plans, the task force concluded that federal regulation was necessary and desirable and that adequate constitutional authority existed for regulating most aspects of public plans. Because of the potential constitutional conflict and because many experts believed that funding decisions were more appropriately made by the sponsoring state and local governments, the legislative proposals for regulating public plans that emerged in the wake of the task force report were limited to reporting, disclosure, and fiduciary standards. (See appendix 2A for a discussion of the constitutional question.)

PEPPRA and Other Proposals: Early 1980s

Some form of public plan legislation was introduced in each of the next four Congresses. The one that received the most attention was the Public Employee Pension Plan Reporting and Accountability Act of 1982 (PEPPRA). While certain earlier versions of the legislation called for the establishment of a new federal agency to administer pension law in both the public and private sectors, this provision was later dropped.

While reporting, disclosure, and fiduciary standards may sound dull and routine, the proposed federal regulation met with passionate opposition during its long legislative history. Groups such as the National Association of Counties, the National League of Cities, the Municipal Finance Officers Association, and the National Conference of State Legislatures strongly opposed any form of federal intervention.[3] They maintained that most public employees were covered under large state systems that were generally well managed and that, where problems had existed, the states had made great strides in improving plan practices. Moreover, these groups argued that public plans had not seen the plan terminations or the flood of participant complaints witnessed in the private sector, and hence no compelling national interest for federal oversight or regulation of public plans existed.

Supporters of the legislation contended that major reporting and disclosure deficiencies still existed. Moreover, they argued that problems would probably persist since a conflict of interest often existed between the goals of elected officials and sound financial management of public plans. In the absence of adequate reporting and disclosure, public officials could grant generous benefit increases and shift the costs to future taxpayers.[4] Taxpayers could control such practices only if they had accurate information about the cost of benefit increases and the extent to which assets are put aside to cover future plan commitments. And they would need to know how their fund was doing relative to other funds of similar size. Only federal regulation could ensure that comparable information on state and local pension plans would be reported to a central agency on a regular basis.[5] Moreover, with respect to the control of plan assets, while little evidence of outright dishonesty had surfaced, the interests of the plan and its participants had often been subordinated to the broader concerns of the sponsoring agency.[6] Hence, federal fiduciary standards would have a salutary effect.

The two sides battled it out for several years but, in the end, no legislation was enacted for federal regulation of state and local plans. All the attention did, however, lead to improvements in disclosure and funding.

Public Plans Clean Up Their Act: 1980–2000

Sunshine often leads to reforms, and that was certainly the case for state and local pensions. The accounting profession turned its attention to these plans, policymakers lifted restrictive investment provisions, and a twenty-year stock market boom moved plans toward solid financial footing.

---

3. See statements from 1980 congressional hearings before the House Committee on Education and Labor in U.S. Congress (1980).
4. See statement by Schotland (1978).
5. See statement by McGill (1978).
6. Kohlmeier (1976).

IMPROVED REPORTING AND DISCLOSURE. In 1980, the Financial Accounting Standards Board (FASB)—the organization that provides accounting guidance for the private sector—issued Statement No. 35, "Accounting and Reporting by Defined Benefit Pension Plans," which was intended to apply to state and local government plans as well as private plans. However, the National Council of Governmental Accounting, which provided guidance in the public sector, argued that public sector plans were different from private sector plans and was successful in delaying the new statement's application to public plans.[7]

Shortly thereafter, in 1984, the Governmental Accounting Standards Board (GASB) was established specifically to set standards of accounting and reporting for state and local governments.[8] In 1986, GASB issued Statement No. 5, "Disclosure of Pension Information by Public Employee Retirement Systems and State and Local Governmental Employers." One important requirement was that plans report their benefit obligations and pension fund assets using uniform methods, to allow observers to make comparisons across plans. But the method that the accountants required for computing benefit obligations was very different from the approach most plan actuaries had adopted for establishing funding contributions. As a result, when users needed information about a plan's funded status and funding progress, they used information based on the plan's funding methodology.

Over the next few years, GASB undertook an extensive review of public sector accounting and disclosure that culminated with the issuance in 1994 of Statements No. 25 and 27, which became effective in 1996 and in 1997, respectively.[9] GASB Statements No. 25 and 27 contained a key innovation: they allowed sponsors that satisfied certain "parameters" to use the numbers that emerged from the actuary's funding exercise for reporting purposes.[10] Among others, these

7. For example, the council argued that benefits in public plans cannot be "settled" at any point in time by the sponsor and that state and local governments have a much lower risk of bankruptcy than private plan sponsors, so the FASB provisions, designed to provide a snapshot of the plan's finances at a given point in time, have much less relevance in the public sector.

8. GASB was established by agreement of the Financial Accounting Foundation and ten national associations of state and local government officials.

9. Statement 25 is entitled "Financial Reporting for Defined Benefit Pension Plans and Note Disclosures for Defined Contribution Plans." Statement 27 is entitled "Accounting for Pensions by State and Local Governmental Employers."

10. This arrangement is very different from what occurs in the private sector, where the actuary is required to make two valuations. For a single employer plan, the actuary must produce: (1) an actuarial valuation to determine funding according to the methodology prescribed by the Pension Protection Act of 2006, where the annual contribution required to cover benefits accrued that year (the target normal cost) and the amortization of any unfunded obligations are all based on benefits accrued to date; and (2) a valuation as stipulated by the accounting profession for reporting purposes that determines assets, liabilities, and the sponsor's annual pension expense, to be

parameters defined an acceptable amortization period, which was originally up to forty years and was reduced to thirty years in 2006, and an annual required contribution (ARC), which would cover the cost of benefits accruing in the current year and a payment to amortize the plan's unfunded actuarial liability.[11]

GASB provides the rules, but plans are not required to follow them. GASB, like its private sector counterpart FASB, is an independent organization and has no authority to enforce its recommendations. Many state laws, however, require that public plans comply with GASB standards, and auditors usually require state and local governments to comply with GASB standards to receive a "clean" audit opinion. In addition, most bond raters consider whether GASB standards are followed when assessing credit standing.[12] Thus, financial reporting requirements probably had considerable impact on the transparency of public plan finances and, by including a specified amortization period and the ARC as parameters, on the funding of public plans. As discussed in chapter 3, GASB's 2012 changes will reduce funding discipline in the future.

IMPROVED FUNDING. Although the GASB guidelines forced plans to focus on funding, three underlying developments also played a role. The first is that plans with meaningful amounts of assets in the early 1980s were probably overfunded, because the actuaries were assuming a discount rate of 6 percent while Treasuries were earning double-digit returns. That is, actuaries were discounting obligations by less than the riskless rate, a pattern in sharp contrast to today's practice of discounting by a rate far in excess of the riskless rate. Accumulated assets in excess of promised benefits provided a good foundation for funding.

The second factor was a move to expand investment options by substituting a general standard of prudence for the more restrictive "legal lists." These legal lists were a selection of eligible investments that states and localities established for institutions such as insurance companies and savings banks. Most included low-risk, low-volatility investments designed for investors in institutions where safety of principal was the major concern. In many states, these lists were also applied to the public pension plans, thereby limiting their ability to invest in equities. By the end of the 1980s, virtually all the legal list restrictions were significantly

---

reported on the financial statements of the sponsor and the plan. While actuaries attempt to keep assumptions as consistent as possible across these valuations, the discount rates used to value future obligations, a critical variable, can differ considerably (The Pension Protection Act of 2006; FASB 87; and FASB 158).

11. This amortization period applied to both the plan's "initial" underfunding and any subsequent underfunding created by benefit increases attributed to "past service" or experience losses.

12. U.S. Government Accountability Office (2008).

Figure 2-2. *Percentage of State and Local and Private Pension Fund Assets Invested in Equities, 1970–2011*[a]

Percent

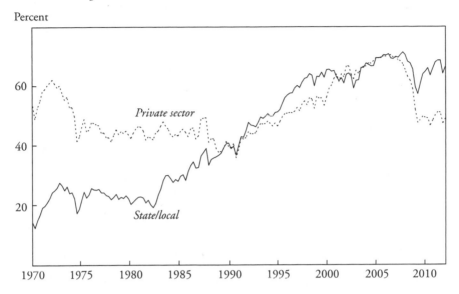

Source: Author's calculations from U.S. Board of Governors of the Federal Reserve System, *Flow of Funds Accounts* (1970–2011).
a. Assumes that equities account for 80 percent of assets held in mutual funds. Before 1984, private sector pension funds included both defined benefit and defined contribution accounts.

relaxed. The movement to a prudence standard allowed public plans to increase their holdings of equities, and their allocations quickly rose to roughly the same level as private plans (see figure 2-2).[13]

The third factor was the two-decade run-up in the stock market, during which the broad-based Wilshire 5000 rose from 1,000 in 1982 to 14,000 in 2000. The combined effect of increased investment in equities, a market boom, and GASB guidance was a more than doubling of assets per worker at both the state and local levels. As noted in the introduction, most observers of public plans at the turn of the century determined that they were in pretty good shape.[14]

13. Interestingly, the geometric mean of returns on equities (8.0 percent) and long-term government bonds (6.4 percent) did not turn out to be very different over the period 1980–2010. See Ibbotson Associates (2011).

14. Mitchell and Hustead (2001). One exception was Gold (2000), who argued that calculating contributions to public plans based on expected returns represented a one-way intergenerational transfer of cost/risk.

Figure 2-3. *State and Local Pension Funded Ratios, 1994–2010*

Percent

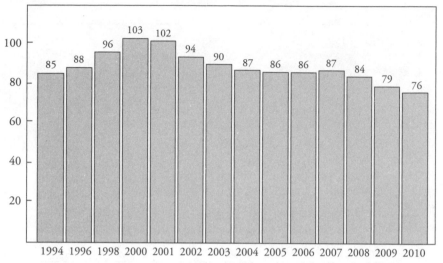

Source: Center for Retirement Research at Boston College (2012a).

The Collapse of the Equity Market: 2000–11

The funded ratio is frequently used to describe the financial health of public plans. A plan is fully funded when its assets equal its liabilities, producing a funded ratio of 100. In fact, in 2000 the actuarial value of assets amounted to 103 percent of liabilities, measured according to GASB reporting standards (see figure 2-3). But then the tech bubble burst, leading to a drop in funded levels as market losses replaced market gains from the 1990s. Funding then stabilized with the run-up of stock prices, which peaked in 2007. But the collapse of asset values in 2008 once again led to declining funded ratios. The aggregate ratio of assets to liabilities for state and local plans dropped from 84 percent in 2008 to 79 percent in 2009.

Critics of GASB's valuation procedures characterized the funding situation as much more dire.[15] According to finance theory, obligations should be discounted by a rate that reflects their riskiness. Since public pension benefits are virtually guaranteed, they should be discounted by a riskless rate. Discounting by the riskless rate produced funded ratios close to 50 percent.[16]

15. Biggs (2010); Novy-Marx and Rauh (2008); and Rauh (2009).
16. Novy-Marx and Rauh (2011b); and Center for Retirement Research at Boston College (2012a).

Regardless of how underfunding is measured, states and localities did not have the resources to close the funding gap. The collapse in asset values was followed by the Great Recession, which decimated state and local revenues and increased the demand for public services. Many public plan sponsors did not have the ability even to pay their full annual required contribution.

Instead, plan sponsors resorted to increasing employee contributions and reducing benefits for new employees—primarily by raising the age for full benefits. These changes cut future costs but had no effect on the current funded status of plans. Nine states reduced or suspended the cost-of-living adjustment (COLA) for current retirees, which immediately lowered liabilities and improved funding. Since most states have constitutions or statutes that preclude changing either current or future benefits for current employees, the COLA suspensions were challenged in court. In four cases—Colorado, Minnesota, New Jersey, and South Dakota—the suspensions were upheld, primarily because the COLA was not considered a core benefit protected by the legal provisions. The changes made by plan sponsors in the wake of the financial crisis and their efforts, in some cases, to restructure their plans as hybrids with a defined benefit and defined contribution component are discussed in more detail in chapter 7.

As of 2010, using GASB discounting of obligations, plans in the aggregate were 76 percent funded. But the funded status of plans varied widely across states and even within states. Explaining this variation is the task in chapter 4, and how the funded status will affect state and local budgets is discussed in chapter 5.

Pensions, however, involve more issues than their funded status. They are an important component of the compensation package of state and local workers. It matters whether the plans are designed to foster the management goals of the sponsor and whether, together with wages, they offer compensation comparable to that in the private sector. These topics are discussed in chapter 6.

Before proceeding to the heart of the analysis, the following section provides a brief overview of the public plan universe and describes the *Public Plans Database* (PPD), which underlies all the empirical work.

Characteristics of State and Local Retirement Plans

The U.S. Census Bureau volume *State and Local Public-Employee Retirement Systems* identifies 3,418 retirement systems that are sponsored by a government entity.[17] This information on the vast universe of plans not only provides a use-

17. Since 1992, the data have been updated every year with a survey administered to a subsample of the population. The 3,418 retirement systems cover more than 90 percent of the total assets held by state and local retirement plans according to the Federal Reserve's *Flow of Funds Accounts of the United States*. The definitions used in Census statistics about governments can vary considerably

ful overview of the public sector retirement landscape but also offers a standard against which to assess the comprehensiveness of the PPD.

Plans, Participants, and Assets by Level of Government

The Census identifies plans by the level of administration—state or local. Most local plans are administered by municipalities and townships, the remainder by counties, special districts, and school districts. The state systems usually cover general state government employees and teachers; locally administered systems often cover police and fire as well as general municipal employees. But the structure varies enormously. Some states (Maine and Hawaii) have a single system covering all types of employees, while other states (Florida, Illinois, Michigan, Minnesota, and Pennsylvania) have more than a hundred systems.

The stylized fact that emerges from the data is that state-administered plans account for a tiny fraction of the plans but for almost all the participants and assets (see figure 2-4). Specifically, state-administered plans account for only 6 percent of the systems, but represent 88 percent of the active members and 83 percent of assets. On average, in 2010, state plans held $10 billion in assets, while local plans held $0.1 billion. Of course, every generalization has notable exceptions. Six locally administered plans held over $10 billion each; leading the list were New York City Employees with $40 billion and New York City Teachers with $30 billion.[18]

While local plans on average tend to be small, they hold substantially more assets per active employee than state-administered plans—$263,000 versus $172,000. The most likely explanation is that local plans often cover police and firefighters, who have physically demanding jobs and are allowed to retire at earlier ages and require more extensive disability protection.

While the Census data provide a basic picture of the universe of public plans, they contain no information on benefit design or liabilities. That information must be collected from actuarial reports and comprehensive annual financial reports for each plan.

Public Plans Database

Using the individual plan reports, the PPD core sample incorporates data on 111 variables for 126 plans (107 state-administered and 19 locally administered)

---

from definitions applied in standard accounting reports. Most plans covering fewer than ten individuals or with less than $3 million in assets are excluded. With respect to plan type, the Census data almost exclusively cover defined benefit plans.

18. The other large locally administered plans are Los Angeles County Employees ($31 billion), New York Police ($20 billion), Los Angeles Fire and Police ($12 billion), and San Francisco City and County Employees ($12 billion). See U.S. Census Bureau (2010).

Figure 2-4. *State-Administered Plans as a Percentage of Total State and Local Plans, Active Members, and Assets, Fiscal Year 2010*

Percent

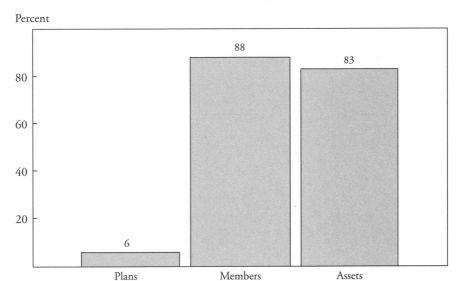

Source: Author's calculations from U.S. Census Bureau, *State and Local Public-Employee Retirement Systems* (2010).

over the period 2001–10. It supplements the basic data with two surveys of locally administered plans. A comparison of the PPD with the Census data shows that the state sample covers 97 percent of both assets and workers relative to the totals reported by Census (see figure 2-5). The sample of locally administered plans represents 59 percent of local plan assets and 55 percent of local workers. This outcome is to be expected given that state-administered plans are few and large, while locally administered plans are many and often small.[19]

Appendix 2B reports, for each of the 126 plans in the PPD core sample, the funded ratio, the percentage of ARC paid (2005–10), the normal cost and its division between employee and employer, and the percentage of each plan's portfolio in risky assets. Risky assets are defined as all assets that are not held in bonds or cash. Because this mass of numbers is difficult to interpret, an index—even if crude—seemed like a good idea. The plans were ranked from 1 to 126 on each of the four criteria presented; those in the lowest quartile were given a 1, second quartile a 2, third quartile a 3, and fourth quartile a 4. Each plan's quartile ranking was summed so that a plan with a high funded ratio, high percentage of

19. In total, Census data list 222 state-administered and 3,196 locally administered systems, compared to 109 and 17 in the PPD samples, respectively. See U.S. Census Bureau (2010).

Figure 2-5. *Public Plans Database Sample as a Percentage of Total Assets and Members, by Level of Administration, 2010 (State) and 2006 (Local)*

Percent

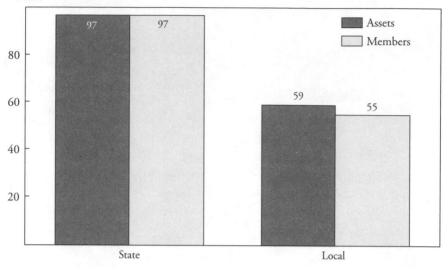

Sources: Author's calculations from U.S. Census Bureau, *State and Local Public-Employee Retirement Systems* (2006, 2010); *Public Plans Database* (2010).

ARC paid, low normal cost, and low percentage of assets in risky investments could receive a score of 16. If a state had more than one plan in the sample, the state ranking was a weighted average of the individual plans. The state ranking according to this crude index is presented in figure 2-6. The rankings may not be perfect, but it is not surprising for 2010 to see California, Illinois, Louisiana, Ohio, and Pennsylvania in the lowest quartiles and Delaware, Florida, Georgia, Tennessee, and North Carolina in the top quartile.

The core PPD data and the research associated with collecting these data form the basis for the following description of benefits and the empirical analysis in subsequent chapters. But first, a comment is needed about Social Security coverage of state and local workers.

Social Security Coverage

Not all state and local workers are covered by Social Security. When Congress enacted the Social Security Act in 1935, it excluded employees of state and local governments from mandatory coverage owing to constitutional concerns about whether the federal government could impose taxes on state governments. As Congress expanded coverage to include virtually all private sector workers, it also

Figure 2-6. *Financial Status of State and Local Plans by State, 2010*

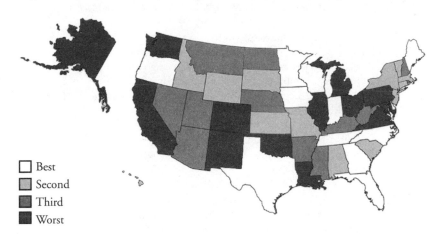

Best
Second
Third
Worst

Source: Author's calculations from *Public Plans Database* (2010).

passed legislation in the 1950s that allowed states to elect voluntary coverage for their employees (see box).

In the 1970s, the focus began to shift from voluntary to mandatory coverage for government workers. In response to increasing interest in such a change, the 1977 amendments to the Social Security Act required a study of the desirability and feasibility of covering all public employees.[20] In the wake of that study, Congress extended mandatory coverage to new federal employees in 1983 and to state and local workers who had no other pension plan in 1990.[21]

About 30 percent of the state and local workforce—roughly 6 million workers—still are not covered by Social Security. In most states only a portion of the workforce is uncovered, but in Ohio, Massachusetts, Nevada, and Louisiana the bulk of state and local wages are not covered by Social Security (see figure 2-7).

20. This effort culminated in U.S. Congress (1978).

21. The constitutional issues involved have not been fully resolved. The decision to extend mandatory coverage of Medicare to state and local workers has not been challenged, and, in a unanimous decision, the U.S. Supreme Court upheld a provision in the 1983 Social Security Amendments that prevented states from withdrawing from Social Security. On the other hand, in more recent decisions the Court has shifted more toward upholding states' rights. Thus, how the Court would rule regarding mandatory Social Security coverage seems less certain today than it did even a few years ago. If the Court ruled against direct taxation of state and local governments, the federal government could always tie some federal aid to coverage of all state and local workers. Thus, the real issues are costs versus equity—not the mechanics.

Key Dates in Social Security Coverage for State and Local Workers

1935:   Social Security Act is passed, prohibiting participation by states and localities.

1950:   Social Security Act is amended to permit coverage on an optional basis for state and local employees not already covered by a public employee retirement system. Legislation also permits state and local government groups to withdraw from Social Security two years after submitting notice of intent.[a]

1954:   Social Security becomes available to state and local employees already covered by a pension system when the majority of the group elects coverage and the state agrees.

1956:   Congress creates a divided option. If all new employees are to be covered by Social Security, current workers can choose to be covered by Social Security and the public plan or only by the public plan. Legislation also allows five states to cover police and firefighters, two groups that had been excluded from Social Security.

1977:   Social Security Act Amendments introduce a "Government Pension Offset" to reduce benefits to spouses and surviving spouses who worked in employment not covered by Social Security.[b]

1983:   Social Security Act is amended to eliminate the withdrawal provision and enact the Windfall Elimination Provision.[c]

1985:   Consolidated Omnibus Budget Reconciliation Act requires all state and local government new hires after March 1986 to participate in Medicare.

1990:   Omnibus Budget Reconciliation Act requires coverage of all state and local employees not covered by a state/local plan that provides benefits comparable to Social Security.

a. State and local organizations were required to participate for at least five years before submitting a notice of intent to withdraw. Any withdrawal was permanent.

b. The Government Pension Offset (GPO) and Windfall Elimination Provision (WEP) were introduced to address an equity problem created by the exclusion of some state and local workers from Social Security. These workers can easily gain Social Security coverage from a second career or moonlighting. Since a worker's monthly earnings for purposes of benefit calculation are averaged over a typical working lifetime rather than over the years actually spent in covered employment, a high earner with a short period of time in covered employment cannot be distinguished from an individual who worked a lifetime in covered employment at an exceptionally low wage. Thus, a worker who was entitled to a state and local pension and to Social Security could qualify for the subsidized benefits associated with the progressive benefit formula. Similarly, a spouse who had a full career in uncovered employment—and worked in covered employment for only a short time or not at all—would be eligible for the spouse's and survivor's benefits. The WEP instituted a modified benefit formula for people who qualify for Social Security based on a brief work history and who have earned a pension in noncovered employment. The GPO reduces spouses' benefits for those who have a government pension in noncovered employment. Although these provisions may not produce perfect adjustments for each individual, in the aggregate they have substantially solved the problem. See Shelton (2010a; 2010b).

c. By 1979, 674 jurisdictions had terminated coverage for 112,000 employees. An additional 222 notices were pending, affecting an additional 98,100 employees.

Figure 2-7. *Percentage of State and Local Government Wages Not Covered by Social Security, 2010*

Percent

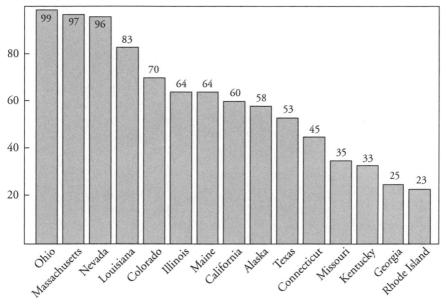

Source: U.S. Government Accountability Office (2010).

The majority of public safety employees—police and fire—are not covered by Social Security.

Benefit Provisions of State and Local Plans in 2010

The benefits provided by state and local plans differ because they cover several very different groups of workers—general government employees, teachers, and public safety personnel—each of which has a very different career path. Nevertheless, some unifying themes provide a helpful guide. In the wake of the financial collapse and ensuing recession, many sponsors have sharply curtailed benefits for new employees. The following discussion focuses on benefit provisions for current employees in 2009.

Most important, despite the introduction of some defined contribution plans, most state and local pensions are defined benefit plans that share the same basic structure.[22] They calculate the initial benefit at the normal retirement age

22. Nebraska is an exception to this generalization since it has a cash balance plan for general state employees. Nebraska still provides a traditional pension benefit for its public school teachers

Figure 2-8. *Distribution of State and Local Plans, by Years in Averaging Period, 2009*

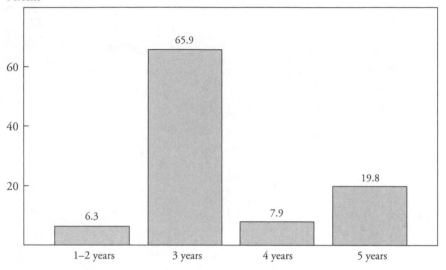

Percent

Source: *Public Plans Database* (2009).

as the product of three elements: the plan's benefit factor, the number of years of employee service, and the employee's average earnings. The calculation of average earnings is usually based on the three to five years of highest earnings (see figure 2-8). Such plans are referred to as final pay plans because the highest-earning years are typically the final years in a worker's career.

Benefit factors for state and local plans are clustered between 1.5 percent and 2.5 percent, with a typical rate of about 2 percent (see figure 2-9). That is, an employee who works for thirty years at a benefit rate of 2 percent would receive a benefit equal to 60 percent of final average pay upon retirement. Those plans where employees are not covered by Social Security tend to have slightly higher factors, those with coverage slightly lower. While most states use a single benefit factor, some increase the benefit factor modestly with tenure. Some plans impose a cap on the replacement rate (benefits relative to pre-retirement earnings), but 60 percent do not.

---

and state police. The Texas Municipal Retirement System, Texas County and District Retirement System, and California State Teachers' Retirement System (for part-time employees of community colleges) also provide a cash balance plan. For the implications of alternative plan design, see chapter 7.

Figure 2-9. *Distribution of State and Local Plans, by Benefit Factor, 2009*

Percent

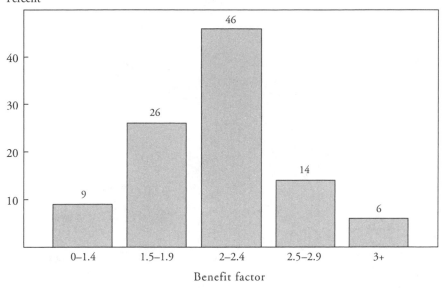

Benefit factor

Source: *Public Plans Database* (2009).

The age at which participants can claim full benefits varies with length of service. For example, age 65 with five years of service, age 60 with ten to twenty years of service, and any age with thirty years of service. Most plans allow early retirement with a *reduced* benefit. Most do not provide an *enhanced* benefit for work beyond the normal retirement age. However, employees usually can continue to accrue pension service credits if they continue working, as long as their replacement rate falls below the maximum.

In order to mitigate the effect of inflation on retirement income, many public plans provide retirees with a post-retirement COLA. The COLA varies substantially across plans in both form and generosity (see figure 2-10).[23] Only about 75 percent of plans provide automatic increases. Roughly half are linked to the consumer price index (CPI), and these increases are usually capped at 3 percent;

23. The COLA is an annual post-retirement increase in the pension benefit designed to help retain purchasing power over time. There are four main types of COLAs: (1) fixed rate: the increase is a constant percentage or dollar amount that is not tied to the consumer price index (CPI); (2) CPI-linked: the increase is tied to the CPI; (3) ad hoc: the increase is set by the legislature and revised on an ad hoc basis; and (4) investment-based: the increase is tied to some financial metric, generally the overall plan funded level or the level of assets in a special COLA fund.

Figure 2-10. *Distribution of State and Local Plans, by COLA Type, 2009*

Percent

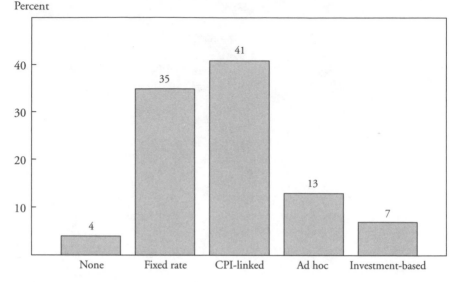

Source: *Public Plans Database* (2009).

the other half applies automatic adjustments at a fixed rate specified by the plan. The remaining plans provide increases either on an ad hoc basis or linked to investment returns.

Plans for police and firefighters tend to have higher annual benefit factors than other systems. This pattern probably reflects their shorter careers and the fact that only 43 percent of police and fire plans are covered by Social Security compared with 80 percent of plans for general employees and 58 percent for teachers.[24] Some police and firefighter plans require twenty years of service for vesting purposes, and these plans often provide a flat percentage of annual pay at retirement (usually 50 percent). Police and firefighters can usually retire at age 50 or 55 with twenty years of service, or sometimes at any age with twenty-five years.

In addition to retirement, most plans provide disability benefits in case of permanent and total service-related disability. Because disability benefits are based on age and salary, benefits can be quite low if disability occurs early in a worker's career, although many states establish a floor of 25 to 33 percent of salary. Some plans set a service requirement of either five or ten years before the worker is eligible for disability benefits. Plans for police and firefighters tend to

24. These data were obtained from the PPD and through an informal survey of local plan administrators to supplement the PPD.

be more generous; most pay 50 percent and some pay 75 percent for service-related disability.

State and local systems, with the exception of police and fire, offer only limited survivor benefits. Before retirement, the benefit is either a refund of employees' contributions or a lump sum, whichever is greater. After retirement, survivor benefits are available if employees select a joint-and-survivor option for their annuity. These annuities offer reduced benefits while workers are alive in exchange for providing benefits to their surviving spouse after their death. Systems without Social Security coverage do not appear to provide any more extensive survivor protection than those systems with coverage.

Public pension benefits are taxable under the federal personal income tax, to the extent that they exceed employee after-tax contributions. The taxability of public benefits at the state level was dramatically affected by the 1989 U.S. Supreme Court decision in *Davis* v. *Michigan*. This decision noted that federal law requires that federal and military retirees be treated at least as favorably as state and local retirees under state law. Facing a substantial loss of revenues, states became less willing to exempt state and local pensions from taxation. One survey shows that while forty-five of eighty-five plans were exempt from state income taxes in 1986, this number had dropped to twenty-one by 1996 and remained there in 2010.[25]

State and local pensions are financed by a combination of employee and government contributions plus earnings on pension assets. This approach differs markedly from the private sector, where employees rarely contribute to defined benefit plans.[26] In 2010, roughly 9 percent of annual receipts came from employees, 18 percent from government employers, and the bulk (73 percent) from investment earnings.[27] As a percentage of payroll, contributions vary by type of employee covered. In 2010, general government employee contributions were 5.6 percent of payroll and employer contributions were 11.0 percent; the comparable numbers for police and fire personnel were 4.9 and 18.5 percent, respectively.

In summary, state and local plans provide pensions that are relatively generous compared to those in the private sector. Although public sector workers bear a substantial portion of the cost, their employers still pay more than private sector

---

25. State of Wisconsin Retirement Research Committee (1996); Schmidt (2011).

26. Until the 1990s, employees made their contributions to state and local plans from after-tax dollars, so they did not enjoy the benefits of deferral most often associated with contributions to employer-sponsored pensions. A noticeable trend in the past fifteen years, however, has been the adoption of Internal Revenue Code 414(h) provisions. Under these provisions, employers may "pick up" employees' contributions, presumably in lieu of a salary increase, or employees can continue to make contributions but on a tax-sheltered basis. See State of Wisconsin Retirement Research Committee (1996); and Schmidt (2011).

27. See U.S. Census Bureau, *State and Local Public-Employee Retirement Systems* (2010).

employers. Plans not covered by Social Security appear to have slightly higher benefit accrual rates and more cost-of-living protection than the group as a whole, although virtually none provide the full inflation protection offered by Social Security. State and local plans, with the exception of police and fire, also provide little in the way of dependent and survivor benefits, except the option of joint-and-survivor annuities. Disability protection is available, but sometimes only after five or ten years of service, and benefits are not fully indexed for inflation.

The final section of this chapter offers a brief overview of retiree health insurance to remind the reader that pension payments are not the only expense associated with a growing retiree population.

Retiree Health Insurance

This book focuses on state and local pensions, but most state and local governments also provide other post-employment benefits (OPEBs), the largest of which is health insurance for retired workers. Employer contributions to retiree health insurance vary widely among states, from none to fairly generous. Retiree health plans have received increased attention in recent years because of rapidly rising health care costs and the issuance of GASB Statements Nos. 43 and 45.[28] These statements, which were released in 2004 and became effective in 2007, require states and localities to change the way they account for the cost of retiree health plans from a cash to an accrual basis.[29] Specifically, public sector employers must report for their retiree health plans, on a regular basis, the actuarial accrued liability, the actuarial value of assets, the unfunded liability, the funded ratio, and the annual required contribution (ARC)—the payment to cover the plan's normal cost and to amortize the unfunded liability.

As shown in appendix 2C, the unfunded liabilities of the seventy-five state-administered retiree health plans amounted to about $588 billon, according to the plans' latest valuations.[30] Although prudent public policy would require

28. GASB No. 43, "Financial Reporting for Postemployment Benefit Plans Other Than Pensions," was released in April 2004; GASB No. 45, "Accounting and Financial Reporting by Employers for Postemployment Benefits Other Than Pensions," was released in June 2004.

29. Implementation was phased in over a three-year period, with the largest governments—those with total annual revenues of $100 million or more—to report their liabilities in their fiscal year 2008 financial statements; see U.S. Government Accountability Office (2009).

30. Early studies had estimated the total unfunded OPEB liability for all state and local government plans to be between $600 billion and $1.6 trillion. See U.S. Government Accountability Office (2008). The 2009 U.S. Government Accountability Office study estimated a total of $530 billion for its sample of plans. Clark and Morrill (2011a; 2011b) put the total for state plans at $440 billion. The Pew Center on the States (2012) estimates the unfunded liability in 2010 for retiree health care at $627 billion. The total liabilities for retiree health plans are likely consider-

today's taxpayers to cover the cost of today's services, most plans in the public sector, as in the private sector, operate on a pay-as-you-go basis. That is, employer premiums come from the state's annual operating budget. Fewer than ten states have undertaken any significant degree of funding.[31] Although GASB 45 does not require sponsors to establish trust funds or move toward full funding, it provides an incentive to fund by allowing the use of a higher rate to discount obligations once the sponsor sets up a trust and commits to making payments at least equal to the ARC.[32] That is, the actuary can discount obligations by the expected long-term return on plan assets (roughly 8 percent) rather than the short-term rate (roughly 4.5 percent) used for plans without funding. Nevertheless, budget pressures, especially in the wake of the 2008 financial collapse, have made it difficult to find the additional revenues to fund these plans. As a result, most states have not yet adopted comprehensive strategies for addressing unfunded liabilities.

Instead of funding, states have focused on strategies to reduce their costs. The strategies take three forms: wellness programs, gatekeeping efforts, and shift of the cost from the employer to the employee. Wellness programs include annual physical exams, individual counseling, seminars, weight loss and exercise clinics, and smoking cessation efforts. Gatekeeping involves steps such as precertification or utilization reviews before receiving treatment and post hoc audits to recover money for unnecessary medical treatment. But with health care costs rising rapidly and the number of retirees growing substantially each year, wellness programs and gatekeeping alone cannot control employer costs.

To manage the rising cost of retiree health insurance, sponsors are also looking to shift costs to the employee. Most states had been amending their plans for active workers and retirees in response to rising health care costs even before GASB 45. They have more freedom to make changes in the case of health benefits than pensions; in most states, case law, constitutional provisions, or statutes prohibit plan sponsors, under the Contract Clause of the U.S. Constitution, from changing *future* pension benefits for current employees. Sponsors have more leeway with respect to health benefits, but many state laws limit unilateral actions. Moreover, most sponsors view retiree health insurance as a valuable tool for attracting talented employees and for workforce planning, where retiree health care can facilitate early retirement by bridging the gap to Medicare.[33] Most states see themselves as unlikely to take drastic actions. Thus the strategy

---

ably larger than the total reported for state plans, because a large number of retiree health plans are locally administered. See U.S. Government Accountability Office (2009).

31. According to higher assumed discount rates reported in appendix 2C, Alaska, Arizona, Colorado, Kentucky, North Dakota, Ohio, Oregon, and Virginia appear to have accumulated meaningful amounts of assets. But other researchers identify a slightly different set of funders.

32. It is not clear to what extent sponsors need to follow through with such a commitment.

33. Cogghurn (2010).

appears to be to incrementally reduce future retiree health care costs by boosting deductibles and co-payments and, most important, increasing the share of the premium paid by the employee.

In addition to raising employee payments, some sponsors have shifted the cost to employees by changing the age and service requirements for new employees. This change involves having different vesting rules for cash benefits and health insurance benefits. The rationale is that retiree health benefits, like pension benefits, should be based on how long the employee has worked. Once the vesting for retiree health insurance is delinked, sponsors pro-rate the retiree health contribution that they make based on years of service. For example, some states pay 25 percent of the subsidy for people with ten years of service and 100 percent of the subsidy for people with twenty-five years of service, with an increasing percentage between the two points.

It should be noted that the unfunded liabilities vary across the states even more on the health care side than on the pension side. The key to whether a state is in trouble hinges on the extent to which the government subsidizes the insurance premium. Historically, some states have required retirees to pay the full cost; others have offered health insurance that does not require any premium payment (see table 2-1).

The central question is how big a problem retiree health insurance is for state and local governments. One metric is to compare the unfunded liabilities of the state-administered health plans with those of state-administered pension plans. It is difficult to be precise because the health plans put out their data at uneven intervals. But dividing the $588 billion of unfunded liabilities of state retiree health plans from appendix 2C by the $2.9 trillion of unfunded liabilities in 2010 for state-administered pensions (assuming a 4.5 percent discount rate as used by most of the retiree health plans) shows that, in terms of unfunded liabilities, retiree health is about 20 percent of pensions.

Although retiree health insurance constitutes only one-fifth of the unfunded pension liability, it is a serious concern. The main issue is that the future burden depends crucially on the cost of health care, which has been rising inexorably. This phenomenon is a national problem that requires a national solution. The Affordable Care Act of 2010 is designed to rein in the cost of medical care, but identifying the levers that control national health care costs will take time. The other major concern is that the liabilities associated with retiree health insurance have not been pre-funded, so the commitments will have to be met on a pay-as-you-go basis. With the relentless rise in costs and growing number of retirees, the bill for retiree health care will put increasing pressure on state and local government budgets.

On the positive side for budgets, states and localities have some freedom to extricate themselves from the business of retiree health insurance, at least for new

Table 2-1. *Retiree Health Insurance Premium Paid by the State, 2006*

	Percent paid[a]		
0	1–49	50–99	100
Idaho	Arizona	Alabama	Alaska
Indiana	Florida	Arkansas	California
Iowa	North Dakota	Colorado	Hawaii
Kansas	Oklahoma	Connecticut	Illinois
Minnesota	Virginia	Delaware	Kentucky
Mississippi		Georgia	Maine
Montana		Louisiana	New Hampshire
Nebraska		Maryland	New Jersey
Oregon		Massachusetts	New Mexico
South Dakota		Michigan	North Carolina
Wisconsin		Missouri	Ohio
Wyoming		Nevada	Pennsylvania
		New York	Rhode Island
		South Carolina	Texas
		Tennessee	
		Utah	
		Vermont	
		Washington	
		West Virginia	
Total	12	5	19	14

Source: Clark and Morrill (2011b).

a. The percent paid is extremely difficult to classify because it frequently varies by date hired, years of service, and whether the retiree is under or over age 65.

employees. Certainly a significantly smaller share of employers in the private sector provides retiree health insurance than in the public sector (see figure 2-11). In addition, the really expensive component of retiree health insurance—coverage for those under 65—may decline as sponsors increase retirement ages as part of their pension reforms. For participants over the age of 65, retiree health insurance is not especially expensive; plan sponsors usually require participants to sign up for Medicare, so the public plans simply provide supplementary benefits.

Conclusion

The financial management of state and local pension plans has improved dramatically since the scathing assessment in the 1978 congressionally mandated study. Most plan sponsors are committed to funding but have been thrown off course

Figure 2-11. *Percentage of Employers Offering Retiree Health Insurance, by Sector, 1997–2010*

Percent

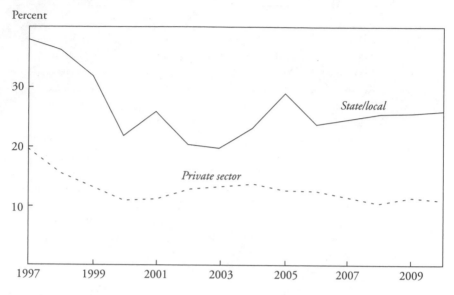

Source: Agency for Healthcare Research and Quality, Insurance Component National-Level Summary Tables from *Medical Expenditure Panel Survey* (MEPS) data (1997–2010).

by two financial crises since the turn of the century. Some observers are more critical, arguing that the failure to discount benefits by the riskless rate was inevitably going to lead to trouble. This issue is discussed at length in the next chapter.

Despite more attention to financial management, systematic analysis of public pensions has been difficult because the plans vary substantially and data are not collected in a central repository. The Census provides information about plan membership, assets, and financial flows, but nothing about the other side of the equation: benefit design and liabilities. That information must be collected from individual actuarial reports and comprehensive annual financial reports. The availability of consistent data for 126 plans for the period 2001–10 in the *Public Plans Database* allows the analysis in the subsequent chapters.

Finally, retiree health insurance is too complicated to include in an analysis of public pensions, but also too big to ignore. Therefore readers should keep this commitment in mind as they evaluate the pension issues.

Appendix 2A. The Constitutional Question

The most obvious jurisdictional basis for congressional regulation of public employee retirement systems is the Commerce Clause found in Article 1 of the Constitution. This clause gives Congress the power to regulate interstate commerce, and over the years the meaning of interstate commerce has expanded significantly. In 1964, the Supreme Court wrote: "In short, the determinative test of the exercise of power by the Congress under the Commerce Clause is simply whether the activity sought to be regulated is 'commerce which concerns more states than one' and has a real and substantial relation to the national interest." The lawyers argue that the impact of public retirement systems on the national securities market and the frequent movement of public employees between states indicates that public plans involve more than the state in which they are located and therefore could be regulated under the Commerce Clause.

Because the power of Congress under the Commerce Clause is not unlimited, determining the degree to which it can support federal legislation regulating the compensation of state and local employees has been a real challenge. In *National League of Cities* v. *Usery*, decided in 1976, the U.S. Supreme Court ruled that the extension of the minimum wage and maximum hour provisions of the Fair Labor Standards Act to employees of state and local governments was unconstitutional as a violation of state sovereignty. This ruling was the result of a 5-to-4 decision. The court maintained that because these provisions would have a significant impact on the costs of running state governments, they would thereby intrude on a basic state function that is protected under the Tenth Amendment. In 1985, less than ten years later, the Supreme Court faced the same issue in *Garcia* v. *San Antonio Metropolitan Transit Authority*. Again by a 5-to-4 decision, the court expressly reversed *National League of Cities* v. *Usery* and held that a municipal transit authority was not immune from the provisions of the Fair Labor Standards Act. Since the mid-1980s, the membership of the Supreme Court has gradually shifted once again toward being more supportive of arguments based on states' rights. It remains to be seen, however, how these issues will be resolved the next time they reach the Supreme Court.

With regard to the full extension of ERISA to public plans, probably the only provision that might affect the fiscal operations of state and local governments in a manner that could threaten their sovereignty would be the imposition of full funding standards. Most lawyers think that federal vesting requirements would probably not be considered an unconstitutional intrusion in basic state functions. Opinion is nearly unanimous that legislation limited to reporting, disclosure, and fiduciary standards would have only a very slight cost impact on compliance by state and local governments and would not be a problem, even under the *National League of Cities* standard. Therefore, federal reporting, disclosure, and fiduciary standards are likely to be found within the power of Congress granted by the Constitution. The imposition of federal funding standards, however, would probably raise more difficult constitutional issues.

Appendix 2B. Characteristics of State and Local Pension Plans in the Public Plans Database, 2010

Plan name	Funded ratio (percent)	Percent ARC paid 2005–10	Normal cost (percent)			Percent in risky assets[a]
			Total	Employee	Employer	
Total	76.4	85.0	13.6	5.5	8.1	71.2
Alabama ERS	68.2	100.0	8.4	5.2	3.2	72.0
Alabama Teachers	71.1	100.0	11.4	7.5	3.9	73.0
Alaska PERS	62.4	83.3	10.2	5.5	4.8	79.9
Alaska Teachers	54.3	80.9	12.5	7.2	5.4	80.3
Arizona Public Safety Personnel	67.7	103.1	19.3	7.7	11.6	80.0
Arizona SRS	76.4	100.0	12.7	10.5	2.2	76.3
Arkansas PERS	74.1	100.0	11.7	5.0	6.7	76.4
Arkansas Teachers	73.8	108.8	12.9	4.7	8.2	73.5
California PERF	83.4	100.0	18.2	7.5	10.7	69.1
California Teachers	71.0	64.2	17.7	6.0	11.7	77.3
Chicago Teachers	66.9	52.2	14.3	8.4	5.9	72.8
City of Austin ERS	69.6	65.3	16.3	8.0	8.3	73.3
Colorado Municipal	73.0	88.0	10.1	8.0	2.1	76.5
Colorado School	64.8	62.2	11.4	8.0	3.4	76.5
Colorado State	62.8	58.0	9.9	8.0	1.9	76.5
Connecticut SERS	44.4	95.5	10.9	1.9	9.0	68.8
Connecticut Teachers	61.4	158.1	10.1	6.0	4.1	67.5
Contra Costa County	80.3	100.0	28.6	11.0	17.6	71.4
Delaware State Employees	96.0	100.0	9.6	2.7	6.9	70.2
Denver Employees	85.0	92.9	9.7	5.5	4.2	73.9
Denver Schools	88.9	190.8	13.6	8.0	5.6	76.5
District of Columbia Police & Fire	100.7	100.0	39.8	7.5	32.3	73.5
District of Columbia Teachers	118.3	100.0	12.9	8.9	4.0	73.5
Duluth Teachers	81.7	69.8	5.9	5.5	0.4	62.0
Fairfax County Schools	76.5	102.5	5.9	4.0	1.9	73.2
Florida RS	86.6	106.3	11.9	0.1	11.8	71.1
Georgia ERS	80.1	100.0	7.9	1.9	6.0	64.2
Georgia Teachers	85.7	100.0	12.4	6.0	6.4	61.9
Hawaii ERS	61.4	100.5	12.6	6.7	5.9	63.2
Houston Firefighters	93.4	100.0	27.0	9.0	18.0	62.0
Idaho PERS	78.9	109.3	13.9	6.5	7.5	66.7
Illinois Municipal	83.3	98.5	12.1	4.5	7.6	67.5
Illinois SERS	37.4	60.6	17.5	5.8	11.7	81.5
Illinois Teachers	48.4	60.1	18.2	9.8	8.4	81.6

Plan name	Funded ratio (percent)	Percent ARC paid 2005–10	Normal cost (percent)			Percent in risky assets[a]
			Total	Employee	Employer	
Illinois Universities	46.4	46.9	20.9	7.5	13.4	77.5
Indiana PERF	85.2	97.7	9.8	3.2	6.6	64.2
Indiana Teachers	44.3	96.9	8.9	3.0	5.9	57.2
Iowa PERS	81.4	86.2	9.9	5.4	4.5	59.1
Kansas PERS	62.0	66.9	7.9	4.2	3.8	65.5
Kentucky County	65.5	109.5	10.1	5.5	4.6	74.8
Kentucky ERS	40.3	49.4	9.2	5.2	4.0	74.8
Kentucky Teachers	61.0	83.5	13.3	7.6	5.7	67.2
LA County ERS	83.3	100.0	15.6	5.8	9.8	71.8
Louisiana SERS	57.7	99.1	15.5	8.5	7.0	75.0
Louisiana Teachers	54.4	104.6	14.4	8.5	6.0	83.9
Maine Local	96.3	100.6	14.6	6.7	7.9	69.0
Maine State and Teacher	66.0	102.4	13.2	7.7	5.5	69.0
Maryland PERS	62.8	67.1	11.5	5.0	6.5	75.4
Maryland Teachers	65.4	91.3	12.3	5.1	7.2	75.4
Massachusetts SERS	81.0	91.5	12.0	8.3	3.7	75.2
Massachusetts Teachers	66.3	89.7	11.5	9.7	1.9	75.2
Michigan Municipal	74.5	105.3	13.0	5.0	8.1	64.3
Michigan Public Schools	71.1	91.4	9.2	5.4	3.8	82.4
Michigan SERS	72.6	84.4	6.9	0.0	6.9	82.1
Minneapolis ERF	65.6	127.4	5.9	9.8	0.0	100.0
Minnesota PERF	76.4	80.6	6.5	6.1	0.4	73.1
Minnesota State Employees	87.3	64.0	7.8	5.0	2.8	73.2
Minnesota Teachers	78.5	100.3	8.4	5.5	2.9	73.2
Mississippi PERS	64.2	97.8	10.4	8.2	2.2	73.9
Missouri DOT and Highway Patrol	42.2	100.0	11.9	0.0	11.9	64.6
Missouri Local	81.0	100.0	10.1	0.8	9.3	72.2
Missouri PEERS	79.1	82.8	11.0	6.6	4.4	65.8
Missouri State Employees	80.4	100.0	8.4	0.4	7.9	72.4
Missouri Teachers	77.7	75.6	22.0	14.0	8.0	65.8
Montana PERS	74.2	89.0	12.6	6.9	5.7	71.6
Montana Teachers	65.4	125.2	9.7	7.2	2.6	72.0
Nebraska Schools	82.4	98.3	11.1	8.3	2.9	85.4
Nevada Police Officer and Firefighter	67.8	88.5	29.8	2.6	27.1	61.1
Nevada Regular Employees	71.2	96.0	16.2	2.8	13.5	61.1
New Hampshire Retirement System	58.5	91.7	10.7	5.8	5.0	69.2
New Jersey PERS	69.5	50.7	8.9	5.2	3.8	61.2
New Jersey Police & Fire	77.1	61.3	18.7	7.6	11.1	64.1

Plan name	Funded ratio (percent)	Percent ARC paid 2005–10	Normal cost			Percent in risky assets[a]
			Total	Employee	Employer	
New Jersey Teachers	67.1	18.3	10.5	5.3	5.3	63.1
New Mexico PERF	78.5	98.6	20.7	11.1	9.5	88.7
New Mexico Teachers	65.7	80.0	12.5	9.4	3.1	64.0
New York City ERS	77.2	96.8	24.1	3.3	20.8	73.0
New York City Police	71.2	98.7	70.6	6.6	64.1	66.2
New York City Teachers	62.9	99.0	32.8	1.7	31.1	71.2
New York State Teachers	100.3	100.0	12.6	0.4	12.2	80.9
New York State & Local ERS	93.9	100.0	15.8	0.5	15.3	72.3
New York State & Local Police & Fire	96.7	100.0	21.2	0.0	21.1	72.3
North Carolina Local Government	99.6	100.0	12.8	6.0	6.8	59.9
North Carolina Teachers and State Employees	95.4	99.8	11.1	6.0	5.1	59.9
North Dakota PERS	73.4	65.0	9.2	4.0	5.2	58.9
North Dakota Teachers	69.8	72.9	10.6	7.8	2.8	71.0
Ohio PERS	76.1	100.0	15.5	10.1	5.4	72.9
Ohio Police & Fire	69.4	70.2	22.3	10.0	12.3	78.9
Ohio School Employees	72.6	96.2	13.8	10.0	3.8	73.4
Ohio Teachers	59.1	84.7	14.3	10.0	4.3	77.7
Oklahoma PERS	66.0	61.5	12.6	4.1	8.5	61.1
Oklahoma Teachers	47.9	84.4	11.8	7.0	4.8	70.7
Oregon PERS	86.9	89.7	7.9	0.0	7.9	69.5
Pennsylvania School Employees	75.1	36.0	15.5	7.4	8.1	72.8
Pennsylvania State ERS	75.2	38.6	10.3	6.3	4.1	82.1
Phoenix ERS	69.3	100.0	13.9	5.0	8.9	72.7
Rhode Island ERS	48.4	100.0	11.7	9.2	2.4	70.3
Rhode Island Municipal	73.6	100.0	17.7	7.4	10.3	70.3
San Diego County	84.3	106.8	25.7	10.9	14.8	56.3
San Francisco City & County	91.1	100.0	17.9	7.5	10.4	67.4
South Carolina Police	74.5	100.0	13.7	6.5	7.2	53.2
South Carolina RS	65.5	100.0	10.0	6.5	3.5	53.0
South Dakota PERS	96.3	100.0	11.5	6.2	5.3	77.7
St. Louis School Employees	88.6	127.8	9.9	5.0	4.9	75.6
St. Paul Teachers	68.1	68.6	8.3	5.6	2.7	76.9
Tennessee Political Subdivisions[b]	87.9	100.0	9.7	2.8	6.9	49.0
Tennessee State and Teachers[b]	91.4	100.0	10.1	3.1	6.9	49.0
Texas County & District	89.4	102.7	13.7	6.7	7.0	70.7
Texas ERS	85.4	80.7	12.3	6.5	5.8	63.2
Texas LECOS	86.3	74.7	2.1	0.5	1.6	63.2

Plan name	Funded ratio (percent)	Percent ARC paid 2005–10	Normal cost			Percent in risky assets[a]
			Total	Employee	Employer	
Texas Municipal	82.9	95.5	15.6	6.6	9.1	33.1
Texas Teachers	82.9	91.0	10.4	6.4	4.0	75.1
University of California	86.7	84.8	19.0	2.0	16.9	75.0
Utah Noncontributory	82.2	100.0	14.1	0.9	13.2	74.0
Vermont State Employees	81.2	93.1	10.1	5.2	4.8	69.0
Vermont Teachers	66.5	81.5	6.8	5.0	1.8	69.0
Virginia Retirement System	72.4	83.5	10.2	5.0	5.2	77.0
Washington LEOFF Plan 1	127.0	100.0	0.0	0.0	0.0	76.7
Washington LEOFF Plan 2	117.0	100.0	14.7	7.4	7.4	76.7
Washington PERS 1	74.0	28.3	11.0	6.0	5.0	76.7
Washington PERS 2/3	97.2	74.5	9.9	4.9	5.0	76.7
Washington School Employees Plan 2/3	98.5	58.3	9.7	4.4	5.4	76.7
Washington Teachers Plan 1	85.0	24.2	11.6	6.0	5.6	76.7
Washington Teachers Plan 2/3	100.5	58.0	10.4	4.8	5.6	76.7
West Virginia PERS	74.6	99.8	10.0	4.5	5.5	75.3
West Virginia Teachers	46.5	173.8	9.4	6.0	3.4	80.8
Wisconsin Retirement System	99.8	101.3	12.2	5.1	7.1	64.3
Wyoming Public Employees	84.6	92.5	11.1	7.0	4.1	67.6

Source: *Public Plans Database* (2005–10).

a. Risky assets equal all assets that are not held in bonds or cash.

b. The Tennessee Retirement Systems perform an actuarial valuation only in odd numbered years. For this reason, the 2010 funded ratios are estimates.

Appendix 2C. Normal Cost and Liabilities of Largest State-Administered Public Employee Retiree Health Plans

Plan name	FY	Discount rate (percent)	Normal cost (percent)[a]	UAAL	
				Billions of dollars	Percent of payroll
Total		4.8	7.1	588.3	170.8
Alaska PERS Postemployment Healthcare Plan	2010	8.0	6.1	3.1	145.2
Alaska Teachers Postemployment Healthcare Plan	2010	8.0	4.3	1.4	222.3
Alabama State Employees' Health Insurance Plan	2009	5.0	8.3	4.1	252.2
Alabama Public Education Employees' Health Insurance Plan	2009	5.0	7.4	11.2	180.3
Arkansas State Employees Postretirement Health Plan	2010	4.5	5.6	1.7	125.1
Arizona State Retirement System Health Benefit Supplement Plan	2009	8.0	0.4	0.2	1.9
California State OPEB	2010	4.5	11.7	59.9	341.5
California Teachers Medicare Premium Payment Program	2010	4.0	0.0	0.9	18.0
Colorado PERA Retiree Health Care Trust Fund	2009	8.0	0.2	1.5	20.1
Connecticut State OPEB Program	2008	4.5	761.0[b]	26.6	
Connecticut TRS Retiree Health Insurance Plan	2010	4.5	2.8	3.0	82.2
Delaware OPEB Plan	2009	5.0	14.3	5.6	306.6
Florida State Employees' Health Insurance Program	2009	4.0	3.5	4.8	104.1
Georgia Schools Personnel Post-Employment Health Benefit Fund	2009	4.5	5.3	11.9	102.0
Georgia State Employees Post-Employment Health Benefit Fund	2009	4.5	5.7	4.4	160.6
Hawaii State Employees OPEB (Employee-Union Trust Fund)	2007	5.0	11.8	7.2	403.6

Plan name	FY	Discount rate (percent)	Normal cost (percent)[a]	UAAL	
				Billions of dollars	Percent of payroll
Hawaii State Teachers Association Voluntary Employees' Beneficiary Association OPEB	2007	5.0	10.4	1.6	234.8
Iowa Postretirement Medical Plan	2008	4.5	0.7	0.3	18.8
Idaho Retiree Healthcare and Long-Term Disability Plan	2008	4.0	2.5[b]	0.0	
Illinois Comm. College Insurance Program	2009	4.5	15.3	1.9	209.6
Illinois State Employees Group Insurance Program	2009	4.5	14.1	27.1	382.5
Illinois Teachers' Retirement Insurance Program	2009	4.5	9.2	14.9	176.5
Indiana State Personnel Healthcare Plan	2009	4.5	23.1[b]	0.5	
Kansas Health Policy Authority Post-Retirement Medical Plan	2009	3.9	0.8	0.2	11.6
Kentucky ERS Retiree Health	2010	4.6	8.5	4.2	213.1
Kentucky CERS Retiree Health	2010	7.8	6.3	2.8	105.3
Kentucky TRS Employee Health Plan and Medicare Eligible Health Plan	2010	4.5	5.6	3.0	89.3
Louisiana State Post-Retirement Benefit Plan	2009	4.0	407.1[b]	10.9	
Massachusetts Postemployment Benefit Plan	2009	4.5	16.4	14.9	403.3
Maryland State Retiree Health Plan	2009	4.3	12.1	15.3	322.3
Maine State Employee Retiree Healthcare Plan	2008	4.5	4.9	1.1	192.3
Maine Teachers Retiree Healthcare Plan	2008	4.5	2.0	1.0	85.9
Michigan Public Schools Retirement System's Retiree Health Plan	2009	4.0	12.7	27.6	279.1

Plan name	FY	Discount rate (percent)	Normal cost (percent)[a]	UAAL	
				Billions of dollars	Percent of payroll
Michigan SERS Retiree Health Plan	2009	4.0	12.2	12.6	424.6
Minnesota State Postretirement Medical Plan	2008	4.8	2.0	0.7	35.1
Missouri DOT and Highway Patrol Medical Plan	2009	4.5	43.2[b]	1.1	
Missouri Consolidated Healthcare Plan	2008	7.5	2.0	1.6	98.5
Mississippi State and School Employees' Health Insurance Plan	2010	4.5	0.6	0.7	16.3
Montana State Employee Group Benefits Plan	2009	4.3	3.9	0.4	67.9
North Carolina State Health Plan	2009	4.3	11.9	32.8	216.2
North Dakota PERS Retiree Health Insurance Credit Fund	2010	8.0	0.4	0.1	6.8
New Hampshire State Postemployment Welfare Benefit Plan	2008	4.5	18.3	2.5	420.9
New Jersey Local Employees' Health Benefits Program	2009	4.5	16.4	10.0	384.0
New Jersey State & School Employees Health Benefits Program	2009	4.5	12.3	56.8	273.1
New Mexico Retiree Health Care Authority OPEB Program	2010	5.0	4.6	3.3	83.6
Nevada Public Employees' Benefits Program's Retiree Health Insurance Plan	2009	4.0	7.3	1.9	118.9
New York State Health Insurance Program	2008	4.2	16.4	55.9	477.7
Ohio PERS Retiree Health Care Plan	2008	6.5	6.4	18.9	147.5
Ohio Police & Fire RS Retiree Health Care Plan	2009	6.0	6.7	2.7	140.3
Ohio SERS Retiree Health Care Plan	2010	5.3	3.1	2.0	71.9

Plan name	FY	Discount rate (percent)	Normal cost (percent)[a]	UAAL Billions of dollars	UAAL Percent of payroll
Ohio TRS Retiree Health Care Plan	2008	4.9	3.6	10.7	106.6
Oklahoma State and Education Employees Group Insurance Board	2007	3.5	2.0	1.3	3.1
Oregon Retiree Health Insurance Account and Health Insurance Premium Account	2009	8.0	0.1	0.3	2.9
Pennsylvania Retired Employee Health Program	2009	5.0	6.6	13.2	322.7
Pennsylvania Retired State Police Program	2009	5.0	18.0	2.1	612.4
Rhode Island State Employees' and Electing Teachers OPEB	2009	3.6	4.1	0.9	144.9
South Carolina State Employee Insurance Program	2009	5.5	4.9	9.2	119.0
South Dakota Postemployment Benefit Plan	2008	3.0	0.7	0.1	10.9
Tennessee Local Education Employee Group Plan	2009	4.5	63.8[b]	1.0	
Tennessee Local Gov. Group Plan	2009	4.5	8.7[b]	0.1	
Tennessee State Employee Group Plan	2009	4.5	4.1	1.7	81.5
Texas Employees Group Benefits Program	2010	5.5	10.0	22.3	213.9
Texas TRS-Care	2010	5.3	3.6	25.0	81.3
Utah Postretirement Medical & Life Plan	2008	4.5	1.8	0.5	50.5
Virginia State Health Insurance Credit Program	2009	7.5	0.3	0.7	12.3
Virginia Teachers Health Insurance Credit Program	2009	7.5	0.2	1.0	13.9
Vermont SERS Postretirement Benefit Plan	2010	4.0	10.1	1.0	230.1
Vermont TRS Postretirement Benefit Plan	2010	4.0	3.8	0.7	125.5

Plan name	FY	Discount rate (percent)	Normal cost (percent)[a]	UAAL	
				Billions of dollars	Percent of payroll
Washington K-12 School Districts OPEB Program	2008	4.5	3.7	3.5	69.3
Washington LEOFF Plan 1 OPEB Plan	2007	4.5	10.0	1.7	3632.1
Washington Political Sub-divisions OPEB Program	2008	4.5	4.1	0.3	58.1
Washington State OPEB Program	2008	4.5	3.7	4.0	77.6
Wisconsin State Postretire-ment Medical Plan	2008	4.0	2.7	1.3	43.5
West Virginia Public Employees Insurance Agency OPEB Benefits	2009	3.6	13.7	7.0	201.3
Wyoming State Employee Group Insurance Retiree Benefit Plan	2009	5.0	1.3	0.2	28.4

Sources: Various other post-employment benefits (OPEB) actuarial valuation reports. Nebraska's plan is excluded because state officials believe that their plan is so minimal that it is not necessary to prepare a report.

a. Unlike pensions, normal costs and annual required contributions (ARC) for retiree health benefits are generally reported in dollar amounts and not as a percent of payroll. However, payroll numbers are often provided separately from the normal costs and ARC. These payroll numbers were used to estimate the normal costs as a percent of payroll. For example, in the January 2010 actuarial valuation for the Massachusetts Postemployment Benefit Plan, the normal costs for FY 2010 are reported on page 9 as $604.4 million. Separately, on page 11, the total covered payroll as of January 2010 is reported as $3.684 billion in the plan's schedule of funding. The two were used to estimate normal costs as a percent of payroll equal to 16.41 percent.

b. Payroll information was not readily available. Normal costs are reported in millions of dollars.

3

The Discount Rate and Other Accounting and Funding Issues

It is widely agreed that each generation of taxpayers should pay the full cost of the public services it elects to receive. And taxpayers need to know the total compensation paid to public employees in order to evaluate whether the government has been a good steward of their resources. If a worker's compensation includes a defined benefit pension, the cost of the benefit earned each year should be recognized at the time the worker performs his or her job, not when the pension is paid in retirement. The benefits earned in a year, however, involve a stream of promises far out into the future. To measure the promises to employees and the liability to the government requires discounting that stream to the present. An important question is the appropriate discount rate.

The discount rate may sound like a technical and dry topic, but the issue can get people engaged in the debate red-faced and shaking with rage. State and local plans usually follow an actuarial model and discount their obligations by the expected long-term yield on the assets held in the pension fund, roughly 8 percent. The economics profession, which can barely agree on the day of the week, is united in the conviction that the discount rate, for any stream of obligations, should reflect the risk associated with those obligations and, given that benefits are guaranteed under most state laws, that the appropriate discount factor is a riskless rate. Thus, today the economists' model would produce much higher liabilities than those currently reported on the books of states and localities.

In order to put the discount rate debate in perspective, this chapter explores pension accounting and funding more broadly. The discussion begins with the standards established in the 1990s by the Governmental Accounting Standards Board (GASB) for state and local plans. Accounting and funding are closely linked in the public sector, because sponsors, if they satisfy certain parameters, can use the numbers that emerge from the actuary's funding exercise for reporting purposes. This outcome differs noticeably from procedures in the private sector. Since the selection of the discount rate is central to the valuation process, the second section explores how changing the discount rate would affect both the funded ratio and the normal cost. Moving from the current 8 percent to the riskless rate has an enormous impact. The aggregate funded ratio for public plans drops from 76 percent to 51 percent; the required amortization payment more than doubles; and the normal cost increases nearly threefold. But what are the real-world ramifications? The third section discusses how using the riskless rate might have affected the level of benefits, the amount of funding, and investment allocation in the past and how it might affect these dimensions of public plans going forward.

The message that emerges is that adopting a riskless rate for reporting purposes has clear advantages: it reflects the guaranteed nature of public sector benefits, would increase the credibility of public sector accounting with private sector analysts, and could well forestall unwise benefit increases when the stock market soars. Interestingly, in the early 1980s, the riskless rate exceeded the expected return on assets, so pension liabilities would actually have been smaller than reported. And if inflation should take off, the liabilities of states and localities would once again appear to be minuscule. Thus, the issue is not whether liabilities should be larger or smaller, but whether they are measured correctly. Finally, although some argue that the rationale behind discounting by a riskless rate has implications for both how much should be set aside for funding and whether public plans should invest in equities, this chapter contends that those questions need to be resolved independently.

Pension Accounting and Funding

Taxpayers need to know the amount of benefits earned each year so that they can evaluate whether they are getting good value for their dollar and in order to determine how much needs to be put aside to fund them.[1] Calculating the value of benefits earned each year requires answering three questions: (1) what benefits are earned in a given year? (2) how should those costs be allocated over time? and (3) how should those streams of promised benefits be discounted to the present? In the public sector, the answers to these questions define both accounting values and funding targets.

---

1. The public discussion is based on the assumption that benefit promises should be pre-funded. Academics, however, have argued that funding is not always optimal. See Bohn (2011).

Figure 3-1. *Present Value of Future Benefits for a Hypothetical Plan*

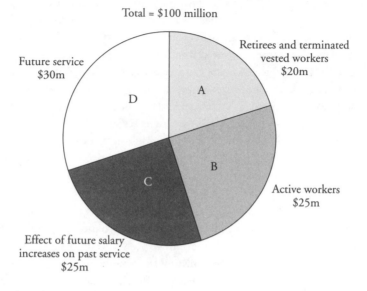

Source: Author's illustration.

What Benefits Are Earned Each Year?

In thinking about the appropriate definition of the liability, it is useful to start with the broadest concept—namely, the present value of future benefits. That is, it is possible to project a stream of benefits for current workers and retirees based on salary, age, sex, length of service, and assumptions about wage growth and inflation and about the probability of separating, retiring, and dying. This stream can then be discounted to the present and separated into the four components shown in figure 3-1. The two main liability concepts are the projected benefit obligation (PBO) and the accumulated benefit obligation (ABO). The PBO includes pension benefits paid to retired employees, benefits earned to date by active employees based on their current salaries and years of service, *and* the effect of future salary increases on the value of pension rights already earned by active workers (A+B+C in figure 3-1). The ABO (A+B in figure 3-1) includes retirees' benefits and benefits earned to date by active employees, but it does not include the effect of future salary increases on the benefits of active workers. Neither concept includes the impact of future service (D in figure 3-1).

GASB defines liabilities in terms of the PBO. One could argue that the PBO is appropriate for pension plans in the public sector. Benefits promised under a public plan historically have been accorded a higher degree of protection than those in the private sector because, under the laws of most states, the sponsor cannot close down the plan for current participants.[2] Although this presumption is under challenge in various jurisdictions, protections in the public sector exceed those in the private sector. Whereas in the private sector the Employee Retirement Income Security Act of 1974 (ERISA) protects benefits earned to date, the consensus legal view has been that employees hired under a public plan have the right to earn benefits as long as their employment continues.[3] Unlike private sector sponsors, public plan sponsors cannot halt accruals under most state laws, so the PBO, which includes the effect of future salary increases on the value of pension rights already earned by active workers, seems a reasonable measure of liability.

Economists, in contrast, contend that the ABO is the appropriate liability.[4] The ABO puts pension benefits on the same basis as salaries. In financial reports, employers are required to disclose the salaries that their employees have earned by the end of the reporting period, and the change in the ABO is what employees have earned in future pension benefits over that period. The anticipation of future salary increases appears to be conservative because the PBO is always equal to or greater than the ABO, but, they contend, the ABO accrual pattern properly recognizes higher cost for older employees. Thus, while PBO accruals are higher than ABO accruals for a young workforce, ABO accruals are higher for an older workforce. Inaccurate reporting of accruals could lead to bad decisions. To the extent that the PBO makes pension plans appear more expensive for young workers, employers may offer less than competitive total compensation and vice versa for older workers.[5] Thus, most economists maintain that the ABO is the preferred measure of liability. But few view the liability concept as a hot-button issue.

How Should Costs Be Allocated over Time?

For both accounting and funding purposes, it is necessary to assign, in a systematic fashion, the pension costs to the year when benefits are earned. The technique used to assign that cost is the actuarial cost method. The portion of the actuarial present value of benefits assigned to a particular year is designated as the normal cost. The two main cost methods are the unit credit and the entry-age normal. The unit credit approach can be based on earnings to date (the traditional unit credit) or on earnings projected at retirement (the projected unit credit). Whereas in the private sector the Pension Protection Act of 2006

2. National Conference on Public Employee Retirement Systems (2010).

3. Steffen (2001). Assuming that employers are constitutionally barred from changing all benefit provisions slightly overstates the riskless nature of public liabilities, since some states and localities have been able to alter the cost-of-living adjustment that they grant beneficiaries from year to year.

4. See Brown and Wilcox (2009); Novy-Marx and Rauh (2011b); and Bulow (1982). Gold, who is both an actuary and an economist, also supports the ABO (see Gold 2005).

5. Gold (2005 and 2009).

requires the traditional unit credit method, in the public sector actuaries use primarily the projected unit credit (PUC) or the entry-age normal (EAN). The subject of actuarial cost methods is even less controversial among economists than the question of liability concept.

Under the projected unit credit approach, the employer's cost in a given year is the value of additional pension benefits that each employee earned in that year based on his projected salary. If the benefit formula and salary projections remain unchanged, the additional pension benefits each employee earns in subsequent years will also remain unchanged. The cost of that benefit, however, will still rise as workers approach retirement since the investment horizon shortens. So employers that use this cost method will see their annual pension expense rise over time.

The entry-age normal cost method smooths the employer's pension expense over time.[6] Under this cost method, the actuary projects the future pension benefits earned by the entity's active workforce. This projection includes credits that current workers will earn through future service as well as the effect of future salary increases on credits already earned. The actuary then sets the employer's annual normal cost equal to a level payment (typically a level percentage of payroll) needed to fund that benefit obligation. Compared to the projected unit credit method, entry-age normal "frontloads" the employer's pension expense by pre-paying a portion of pension benefits earned in the future.

A numerical example may help clarify the difference between the projected unit credit and the entry-age normal methods. Suppose that a plan sponsor needs to contribute $15,000 for a particular employee who will retire in five years, and that the sponsor fully funds the cost specified by either method. Under projected unit credit, the sponsor recognizes and funds, say, $1,000 in the first year, $2,000 in the second year, $3,000 in the third year, $4,000 in the fourth year, and $5,000 in the fifth year. Under entry-age normal, the actuary would level the contributions over the five-year period so that the sponsor would recognize and pay a normal cost of $3,000 a year.

The two approaches thus have different patterns of liability recognition and asset accumulation over time. Up to the point of retirement, the entry-age method would recognize a larger accumulated pension obligation for active

6. The other major cost method used by public plans is aggregate cost. This approach allocates the value of future benefits in excess of assets over the earnings or service of the entire group between the valuation date and the exit date. The normal cost in any particular year is the result of this cost allocation. Thus, unfunded liabilities are allocated as future normal costs instead of being separately identified, amortized, and added to normal cost. As a result, a plan using the aggregate cost method shows no unfunded liabilities and a 100 percent funded ratio. GASB 50 now requires governments that use this funding method to report the funded ratio using the entry-age normal method as well.

Figure 3-2. *Accrued Liability by Method, by Year*

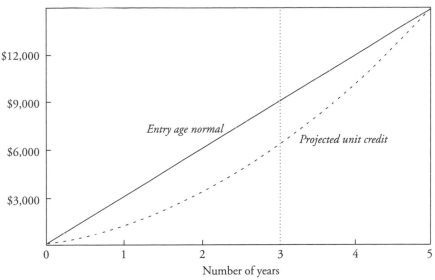

Source: Author's illustration.

employees. For example, after three years using the entry-age normal cost method, the plan would have an actuarial accumulated liability of $9,000 compared to $6,000 for the plan using the projected unit credit method (see figure 3-2). If both plans were fully funded, the plan using the entry-age normal method would have put aside more assets.

The dominant cost method among state and local plans is entry-age normal; 13 percent use the projected unit credit and 14 percent the aggregate cost or other method (see table 3-1). In contrast, most private sector sponsors shifted to the projected unit credit after 1985, when the Financial Accounting Standards Board (FASB), the body that sets accounting standards in the private sector, issued rules requiring this method for reporting purposes.[7] Some suggest that sponsors interpreted the FASB standard as an endorsement of the projected unit credit for funding as well as reporting or simply found it more convenient to use the same method for funding and reporting.[8] Others say that the shift to the projected unit credit was an effort to lower cash contributions when the

7. Financial Accounting Standards Board (1985).

8. The shift in actuarial methods in the private sector had a significant impact on funding because it reduced funding when the baby-boom generation (those born between 1946 and 1964) were young workers (age 20 to 40). As the baby boomers aged, funding contributions grew more than they would have under the entry-age normal cost method.

Table 3-1. *Percentage of Large Private Sector and State/Local Plans Using Alternative Actuarial Methods*

Actuarial cost method	Private sector, 2006 (percent)	State/local, 2010 (percent)
Projected unit credit	74	13
Entry-age normal	19	73
Aggregate cost and other	7	14

Sources: Watson Wyatt Worldwide (2006); and *Public Plans Database* (2010).

enactment of an excise tax in the mid-1980s made the retrieval of excess funds prohibitively expensive.[9] In the wake of the Pension Protection Act of 2006, all single employer plans in the private sector now are required to use the traditional unit credit method, which does not take into account future salary increases, for both funding and reporting.

As noted, in the public sector the selection of an actuarial cost method from the list of permissible options is not very controversial among economists. Those who think that future salary increases should not be taken into account argue for the traditional, as opposed to the projected, unit credit approach, because it recognizes the accumulation of benefits exactly as they accrue.[10] But since the PBO is the liability concept currently used in the public sector, such a method is not currently applicable.

How Should Streams of Promised Benefits Be Discounted to the Present?

In sharp contrast to the actuarial method, the appropriate discount rate to transform a stream of promised benefits into a present value is extremely controversial. This discussion first examines the history and then turns to the economics.

HISTORY. GASB's current standards for public plans rely heavily on actuarial methods that were developed decades ago for different purposes. Actuaries are in the business of determining funding rates. They need to figure out how much cash needs to be put aside today to pay benefits tomorrow. In this process, they make their "best guess" regarding all the factors that will affect future costs, such as mortality rates, termination rates, real wage growth, inflation, and asset returns. Since a portfolio of stocks and bonds has a higher "best guess" expected return than a bonds-only portfolio, most actuaries discount obligations by the higher rate. Although all the factors in the cost calculation involve a significant degree of uncertainty, actuaries do not explicitly account for risk. The goal is to develop

9. At the same time, declining interest rates were increasing pension costs.
10. Gold (2009); and Gold and Latter (2008).

a schedule of smooth contributions that may be expected, on average, to pay for benefits at much later dates. If the cost estimate proves too low, they revise their calculations, and the sponsor has to increase its contributions to the plan.

Since both actuaries and accountants must identify resources today that will be delivered in the future, it might seem, at first blush, that the actuarial approach could be applied to the accounting world. But accountants are not in the business of maintaining stable contribution rates; their job is keeping score. In pursuit of that goal, they are interested in the value of promises made today. The value of the promises and the payment by the employer would be the same only under the rarest circumstances. For example, decades ago, pension plans were sold and managed by insurance companies, who offered deferred annuity contracts to employers.[11] These annuities were commitments made to pay employees future amounts determined and paid for today by the employer. The employee's compensation each year included his wage and his interest in the deferred annuity. The employer paid the salary and the premium for the deferred annuity. In this rare case, the actuarial and accounting approach provided the same answer.

Once pensions were separated from insurance companies, actuarial and financial accounting values began to diverge. Actuaries adopted methods for employers that were conservative and produced stable required contributions. Their methods overcharged for benefits earned early in an employee's career and undercharged for those earned later, by using the entry-age normal actuarial cost method. And in the face of increasing investment in equities in the 1960s, they used expected rates of return. No one complained because, whatever happened, employers were responsible for making good on the promised benefits. But it meant that actuarial and financial reporting were being driven further and further apart. The standards set down by GASB are much closer to the actuarial approach than to financial accounting based on market transactions.

THE ECONOMICS. Standard financial theory suggests that future streams of payment should be discounted at a rate that reflects their risk.[12] In the case of state and local pension plans, the risk with the stream of future payments is the uncertainty about the extent to which benefit commitments will be honored. Since not only accrued benefits but also future accruals traditionally have been protected under most state laws, observers have argued that the payments are,

11. This example comes from Gold (2009).

12. The analysis of choice under uncertainty in economics and finance identifies the discount rate for riskless payoffs with the riskless rate of interest. See Gollier (2001); and Luenberger (1997). This correspondence underlies much of the current theory and practice for the pricing of risky assets and the setting of risk premiums. See Sharpe, Alexander, and Bailey (2003); Bodie, Merton, and Cheeton (2008); and Benninga (2008).

as a practical matter, guaranteed. To the extent that they are guaranteed, future benefits should be discounted by a riskless—that is, default-free—interest rate.[13] For simplicity, the following discussion assumes that a riskless rate is appropriate, even though the reduction or suspension of cost-of-living-adjustment (COLA) payments in Colorado, Minnesota, New Jersey, South Dakota, and several other states suggests that some public pension promises may not be met in the future.[14]

Just what rate best represents the riskless rate is a subject of debate. Researchers have laid out some general characteristics.[15] The rate should reflect as little risk as the obligations themselves, be based on fully taxable securities (because pension fund returns are not subject to tax), and not have a penalty for liquidity (because most pension fund obligations are long term and do not require liquidity).[16] Among the interest rates quoted in financial markets, those on Treasury securities come the closest to reflecting the yield that investors require for getting a specific sum of money in the future free of risk. Although the prices of Treasury bonds fluctuate in line with movements in interest rates, they are risk-free assets to pension plans because the plan sponsor can assemble a portfolio of Treasuries with interest receipts and returns of principal that exactly match its obligation to pay pension benefits.[17]

Ideally, one would want to use the entire Treasury yield curve so that obligations of different duration are discounted by the appropriate rate.[18] But for expositional purposes, it is necessary to use a single rate. That rate should be the yield on a security that roughly matches the average duration of pension obligations. Earlier studies have shown that the average duration of state and local pension obligations was around fifteen years, and since duration is sensitive to interest rates, in a low-rate environment the duration could be slightly longer.[19] The twenty-year Treasury bond, which has a duration of about sixteen years, is the best match. Over the past few years (since the financial crisis of the late 2000s),

13. Such an approach has been adopted by other public or semi-public plans. The Ontario Teachers' Pension Plan 2011 Report used a discount rate in the financial valuation of 3.4 percent, which was based on the market rate of long-term Canadian government bonds plus 0.9 percent to reflect the credit risk of the province of Ontario (Ontario Teachers' Pension Plan 2011). In the Netherlands, fair value accounting for defined benefit plans replaced the actuarial approach several years ago (Ponds and van Riel 2007).

14. See Reinke (2011); and Williams Walsh (2011).

15. Brown and Wilcox (2009).

16. Novy-Marx and Rauh (2011c) employ a state-specific taxable municipal bond rate based on the zero coupon municipal bond curve. Their rationale is that states are equally likely to default on their pension obligations as on their other debt.

17. Campbell and Viceira (2001).

18. Gold (2009).

19. Gold (2000); Barclays Global Investors (2004); and Waring (2004a and 2004b).

the yield on twenty-year Treasury bonds has been about 4 percent.[20] This yield is artificially low because of the valuable liquidity these securities offered investors in the wake of the financial crisis, so the recent rate is increased by about one percentage point to produce a pre-financial-crisis riskless rate of 5 percent for the ensuing analysis.[21]

Funding in the Public Sector

Sponsors need to put money aside for two types of obligations. The first is to cover the cost of accruing benefits—that is, the normal cost. The second is to amortize the plan's unfunded pension liabilities, which arise because either the sponsor did not put away money at the time the benefits were recorded or provided benefits retroactively, or because the value of plans' assets dropped unexpectedly. GASB in essence set standards for how much should be set aside each year with its 1994 Statement No. 25. The statement specified that if sponsors satisfy certain "parameters," they could use the same actuarial cost method for both reporting and funding. The GASB parameters established an acceptable amortization period, originally up to forty years but reduced to thirty years effective in 2006, and the notion of the annual required contribution (the normal cost plus a payment to amortize the plan's unfunded actuarial liability) as the acceptable annual required contribution (ARC).[22] Whereas the ARC technically was a component of pension expense that appeared in the sponsor's income statement, it has been used as a metric for funding. Thus, judging the adequacy of funding in the public sector requires looking at two numbers: the funded ratio, which presents a snapshot of the ratio of assets to liabilities, and the percentage of ARC paid, which indicates whether the sponsor has a funding plan and is sticking to it. Unfortunately, as discussed later in this chapter, GASB's 2012 changes will reduce funding discipline in future years.

Comparison with the Private Sector

Behind much of the criticism of the public sector is the implicit assumption that the private sector has got it right. But the array of calculations that have been used in the private sector suggests that there is not a single correct liability

---

20. Treasury discontinued the twenty-year constant maturity series at the end of calendar year 1986 and reinstated that series on October 1, 1993.

21. A 5 percent rate is also consistent, for example, with a riskless real rate of 2.5 percent and an inflation rate of 2.5 percent. Gold (2009) argues for a lower discount rate than Treasuries because untradeable pension liabilities are greater than bond liabilities of comparable value.

22. In 1996, when GASB reduced the maximum amortization period from forty years to thirty years, it gave plans ten years to comply. Most took advantage of the phase-in option, so the effective date became 2006.

measure and discount rate; rather, the appropriate concept depends on the question being asked.

When ERISA established funding standards, it followed the actuaries' approach. As discussed, actuaries recognized the liabilities associated with an ongoing plan and used expected returns to assess the ability of the assets on hand to cover future liabilities. If their estimates of obligations proved too low, they revised their calculations and the sponsor increased its contributions.

In the 1980s, a rash of bankruptcies and plan failures showed policymakers that many sponsors did not have the wherewithal to increase contributions when the return on equities fell short of expectations. These failures placed enormous pressure on the Pension Benefit Guaranty Corporation (PBGC), the agency established to insure benefits of insolvent plans. To protect the PBGC and the community of pension sponsors that funds the agency, the government in 1987 introduced an alternative minimum funding requirement. That minimum was based on a concept of benefits close to that of the accumulated benefit obligation, a proxy for the benefits the PBGC insures, with benefits discounted by modified corporate bond rates to reflect the contractual nature of the guarantee.[23] In 2006, the Pension Protection Act established more stringent minimum funding requirements, based on the ABO and the traditional unit credit approach with prescribed discount rates and mortality assumptions, whereby any unfunded liability has to be amortized over seven years (see table 3-2).[24]

For their financial statements, private plan sponsors must follow guidelines established by the accounting profession. These accounting rules require that plans use the PBO to value their obligations and use a low-risk rate to reflect the plans' contractual bond-like obligations.[25] When reporting their current year's pension expense, sponsors use the PBO and separate interest rates for different components of the expense. The expected return on pension fund assets is used to estimate the dollar return on the actuarial value of plan assets, and the corporate rate, discussed above, is used to determine the current year's interest on the PBO. Thus, in the private sector the liability concept and discount rate depend on how the numbers are being used.

23. The concept used by the PBGC is "current liabilities," which differs from the ABO in two ways. First, it requires a specific mortality table, and second, it mandates that the discount rate be a four-year weighted average of the thirty-year Treasury rate (McGill and others 2010).

24. Specifically, the Pension Protection Act requires plans to use a twenty-four-month average of a yield curve, which in turn is segmented into three periods: zero to five years, five to twenty years, and more than twenty years. The Moving Ahead for Progress in the 21st Century Act of 2012 (the highway reauthorization measure) changed the averaging period from twenty-four months to twenty-five years.

25. See FASB (2006).

Table 3-2. *Approaches to Valuing Liabilities, 2011*

Plan type/purpose	Governing entity	Liability concept	Discount rate
Private plans			
Funded status[a]	ERISA/IRC	ABO	Corporate bond rate[b] (5.0)
Financial reporting			
Expense	SEC/FASB	PBO	Return on assets (4.0)
Funded status	SEC/FASB	PBO	Corporate bond rate[c] (5.0)
State and local plans			
Funded status	GASB	PBO	Return on assets (8.0)
Financial reporting	GASB	PBO	Return on assets (8.0)

Abbreviations: ABO = accumulated benefit obligation; ERISA = Employee Retirement Income Security Act; FASB = Financial Accounting Standards Board; GASB = Governmental Accounting Standards Board; IRC = Internal Revenue Code; PBO = projected benefit obligation; SEC = Securities and Exchange Commission.

a. ERISA and the IRC require plan sponsors to report funding information to the Department of Labor, the Pension Benefit Guaranty Corporation (PBGC), and the Internal Revenue Service (IRS); the agencies develop a joint report, Form 5500.

b. The IRS publishes interest rates, which in the wake of the Pension Protection Act of 2006 consist of segment rates to reflect the timing of the plan's liabilities. The numbers reported in the table are the weighted average for these segments. In addition, the Pension Protection Act requires that plan liabilities be calculated using a standard mortality table published by the IRS.

c. FASB 158 allows plans to choose a discount rate from among several corporate bond measures

Source: Author's update of Center for Retirement Research at Boston College (2010a).

What Difference Does the Discount Rate Make? The Numbers

The discount rate has a large impact on the value of a plan's liabilities. These liabilities, in turn, determine both the funded ratio and the ARC. Changing the value of liabilities directly affects the funded ratio—assets divided by liabilities—by increasing the denominator. It affects the ARC both through the amortization amount (the bigger the unfunded liability the larger the annual payment) and through the normal cost (the bigger the present discounted value of future benefits the more cost allocated to each period). The following discussion looks first at funded ratios and then at the ARC.

Funded Ratios for Public Plans

Figure 3-3 shows the aggregate funded ratio for the period 2001–10 from the *Public Plans Database* (PPD) sample of 126 plans, based on an interest rate of 5 percent and on GASB's recommended discount rate—the expected long-run rate of return on fund assets.[26] In the wake of the financial crisis, some plans

26. *Public Plans Database* (2001–10).

Figure 3-3. *State and Local Funded Ratios under Different Discount Rates, 2001–10*

Percent

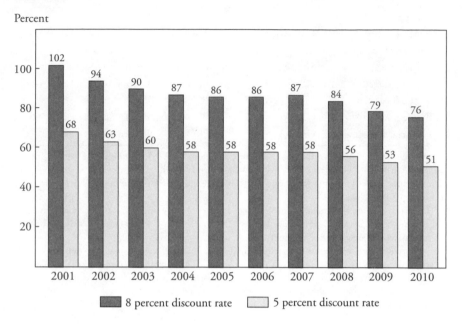

Source: Center for Retirement Research at Boston College (2012a).

have started to reduce their assumed return from the standard 8 percent of the past twenty years, but the changes have been modest; only a few plans have assumed less than 7.5 percent.[27]

In 2001, under GASB accounting, assets amounted to 102 percent of liabilities. With the bursting of the tech bubble, funded levels began to drop as market losses replaced the gains from earlier years. Funding then stabilized with the run-up of stock prices, which peaked in 2007. But the collapse of asset values in 2008 has once again led to declining funded ratios. In 2010, assets covered only 76 percent of promised benefits (see figure 3-3).

The reason for the decline in funded levels from 2009 to 2010 is that liabilities grew at their historical rate while assets increased more slowly. This outcome may seem strange given that the stock market rose 50 percent between the trough in 2009 and December 2010. The explanation is that actuaries tend to smooth the fluctuations in market values by averaging, typically over a five-year period. So while market asset values in 2010 were significantly higher than

27. For example, Maine used 7.25 percent in 2011.

Figure 3-4. *Annual Required Contribution as a Percentage of Payroll, 2001–10*

Percent

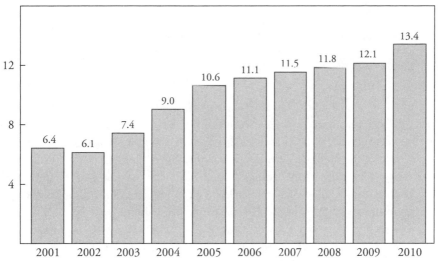

Sources: Various 2010 actuarial valuations; and *Public Plans Database* (2001–10).

in 2009, they were only slightly higher than in 2005, the year replaced in the five-year moving average.

The picture looks very different if funded ratios are calculated assuming an interest rate of 5 percent rather than 8 percent. The lower discount rate causes the funded ratio in 2010 to drop from 76 percent to 51 percent. Perhaps more important, plans never came close to full funding, and therefore overfunding could never have been an excuse for raising benefits.

The ARC

As noted above, GASB established the ARC, an accounting concept that has been construed as the appropriate annual contribution. As shown in figure 3-4, the ARC increased steadily between 2001 and 2010. The bursting of the dot.com bubble led to higher unfunded liabilities and thereby increased the amortization component of the ARC. When the financial crisis in 2008 dealt another blow to funded ratios, the ARC increased further. In 2010, the ARC was 13.4 percent of payroll.

How would a reduction in the discount rate have affected the ARC? First, decreasing the discount rate increases the present discounted value of future benefits and thereby the unfunded liability. The increase in the unfunded liability

Table 3-3. *Annual Required Contribution as a Percentage of Payroll, 2010*

Discount rate	Normal cost	Amortization	Total
8 percent	8.1	5.3	13.4
5 percent	21.5[a]	10.9	32.4

Source: Author's estimates from *Public Plans Database* (2010).

a. The increase in the employer's normal cost as a result of reducing the discount rate from 8 percent to 5 percent is based on the assumption that the employee's contribution rate remains at 5.5 percent.

raises the required amortization payment. In 2010, the aggregate liability was $3.4 trillion, calculated under a discount rate of 8 percent. A riskless discount rate of 5 percent raises that liability to $5.2 trillion. Since actuarial assets in 2010 were $2.6 trillion, the unfunded liability rises from $0.8 trillion ($3.4 trillion less $2.6 trillion) to $2.6 trillion ($5.2 trillion less $2.6 trillion). A tripling of the unfunded liability leads to a somewhat smaller increase in amortization payments because the sponsor is paying less interest on the unfunded liability (see table 3-3).

The second way that a lower interest rate affects the ARC is through the normal cost. Here the effect is much larger because the increase in liability is allocated only to the years before retirement. In fact, the normal cost increases nearly threefold. Combining the increase in the amortization payment with the increase in the normal cost means that the ARC would rise from 13.4 percent to 32.4 percent of payrolls.

Thus, shifting the discount rate from the expected long-run rate of return to the riskless rate increases liabilities and reduces funded levels. But what are the larger effects? While the riskless rate is undeniably the conceptually correct discount factor, would it have changed history? And going forward, how would the world proceed differently with liabilities discounted by one rate rather than the other? Finally, how does the discount rate debate relate to discussions of asset allocation and funding?

What Difference Does the Discount Rate Make? The Policies

Given that the discount rate is such a hot topic of debate, it is worth considering whether people are spending their time arguing about the right issue. It is conceptually interesting, and it has a profound effect on the numbers. But is it important?

The Past

The data suggest that liabilities—and therefore funded ratios and, if it had existed, the ARC—would have looked very different using a riskless rate (the

Figure 3-5. *Investment Return Assumption Compared to Twenty-Year Treasury Rate, 1977–2010*

Percent

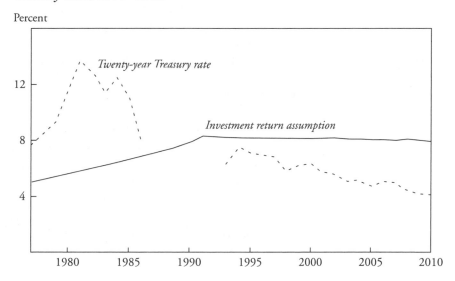

Sources: Author's calculations from Treasury; Gold (2009); Zorn (1990–2000); and *Public Plans Database* (2001–10).

a. The break in the line for the twenty-year Treasury rate is due to a temporary halt in issuing new twenty-year Treasury bonds.

twenty-year Treasury rate) instead of the long-run expected return on assets. Interestingly, though, they would not have always looked higher. As shown in figure 3-5, Treasury rates far exceeded the actuarial rates during the 1980s, so actuaries were in fact overpricing the value of benefits. In more recent years, they have been underpricing them.

Revisiting history requires speculation about what might have happened. But it is at least possible that liabilities in the early 1980s may have looked so small that the burgeoning movement toward funding would have lost steam. If so, fewer assets would have been put aside, and states and localities would not have shared to the same extent in the stock market boom that ended with the bursting of the dot.com bubble—that is, states and localities would have accumulated significantly less than $2.3 trillion by 2000.[28] On the other hand, the undervaluation of liabilities in the 1990s and the 2000s has almost certainly led to less funding than would have occurred otherwise. The net effect of the offsetting forces is an empirical question. But it is not obvious that, on the funding side, the failure to use a riskless rate has produced less asset accumulation.

28. U.S. Board of Governors of the Federal Reserve System, *Flow of Funds Accounts* (2011).

On the benefit side, recognizing the riskless nature of state and local pension obligations could avoid the type of benefit liberalizations that took place in the late 1990s when many state and local plans appeared to be overfunded. For example, in 1999, CalPERS reported that assets equaled 128 percent of liabilities, and the California legislature enhanced the benefits of both current and future employees. It reduced the retirement age, increased benefit accrual rates, and shortened the salary base for benefits to the final year's salary.[29] If CalPERS liabilities had been valued at the riskless rate (5 percent), the plan would have been only 96 percent funded.[30] An accurate reporting of the ratio of assets to liabilities would avoid this type of expansion for current employees. Similarly, an accurate accounting of liabilities today would increase the incentive for policymakers to make necessary changes in retirement ages and other provisions for new employees to reflect the fact that Americans are living longer and healthier lives. But again, what about the 1980s? Would the sense that benefits were extremely cheap have led to much greater expansion in benefits than actually occurred during that period? In theory, sponsors could have avoided cost increases by matching enhanced benefit commitments with high-yield bonds, but would they have?

The Future

How would the public pension world change if GASB announced that it had decided that using the riskless rate were the way to go? Certainly liabilities would increase, funded ratios would drop, and the ARC would soar. The question is how plan sponsors would respond to such a change in numbers in terms of plan benefits, investments, and contributions.

BENEFITS. The key point to remember when contemplating benefit changes in state and local plans is that traditionally the protections in the public sector have far exceeded those in the private sector. Several states, such as Illinois and New York, have specific constitutional clauses stating that public retirement plans cannot reduce benefits for currently active employees below the level set at the date of hire. Many other states, including California, Massachusetts, and Nevada, view both current and future accruals as protected under the contract clause of the U.S. Constitution. Amendments to plan provisions must be vetted by the courts, and a reduction in one provision usually needs to be offset by an increase in another.

Because, in many plans, benefits for current employees are protected, any change in benefit provisions applies only to new employees. A number of states and localities—shocked by the impact of the financial crisis and the ensuing

---

29. CalPERS (2009).
30. Author's calculations from CalPERS (2009).

recession—are already in the process of increasing retirement ages and reducing benefit factors for future hires. Some states, such as New Jersey and Rhode Island, have made changes that affect existing plan participants as well. These changes are being challenged in court.[31]

It would be wonderful if adopting the riskless rate and showing large unfunded liabilities provoked states to amend their constitutions or to more aggressively retest the benefit protections in the courts. Public sector workers should have the same protection as their private sector counterparts. Core benefits earned to date should be protected. Current workers accepted public employment with the understanding that they were accruing pension benefits at a certain rate, and remained employed with that understanding. But future benefits in the public sector, like those in the private sector, should be allowed to vary based on economic conditions. Unfortunately, reducing the discount rate from 8 percent to 5 percent for reporting purposes is likely to have little impact on reforming the legal framework within which public plans operate.

INVESTMENTS. Pension funding involves two issues: how pension assets should be invested and how the annual contribution should be determined. It is easiest to start with the investment question. Specifically, should pension funds invest in equities? Among academics, opinions on whether public plans should hold any equities range from agnostic to affirmative.

Purists who deal with perfect models are agnostic on the question of equity investment.[32] In theory, equity investment in the pension fund can be offset by adjustments in individuals' own portfolios, so it makes little difference. However, they argue that since dividends and capital gains are taxed at lower personal income tax rates than those applicable to interest, the pension fund should invest in high-taxed bonds and individuals should hold equities in their personal portfolio when possible.[33]

Other researchers approach the topic with the assumption that the goal of public plan investing is to match assets and liabilities.[34] One important moti-

---

31. The one exception to the prohibition against cuts for current employees appears to be cost-of-living adjustments. Nine states—Colorado, Maine, Minnesota, New Jersey, Oklahoma, Rhode Island, South Dakota, Washington, and Wyoming—have already reduced or suspended their COLAs for current retirees. Sponsors were sued, but in Colorado, Minnesota, New Jersey, and South Dakota the courts ruled in the states' favor. See Reinke (2011). The Colorado ruling is under appeal to the state court of appeals. Lawsuits are outstanding in Maine, Rhode Island, and Washington. It seems that sponsors are interpreting the legal protections as applying to "core benefits" and not to the inflation adjustments. The legal status of public pension benefits is discussed in more detail in chapter 8.

32. Gold (2000).

33. Bader and Gold (2003).

34. Peskin (2001); and Pennacchi and Rastad (2011).

vation for matching is the asymmetry, where surpluses are appropriated by politicians or employees and lost to the pension funding effort. If assets and liabilities were matched perfectly, the pension plan would not experience surpluses or deficits. The issue becomes how to immunize—that is, what types of investments have returns that best match the stream of promised benefits. For retirees, the answer is straightforward; future benefit payments are known with some degree of certainty, and bonds are the logical investment. For plans with a high proportion of young workers, future benefits are less certain; benefits will depend on the rate of wage growth, quit rates, and a number of other factors. Wage-indexed bonds might be a good immunization investment option, but they do not exist. Under these circumstances, equities can play a useful role to the extent that their returns are correlated with wage growth.[35]

Still others contend that, under a number of restrictive assumptions, the exercise can be boiled down to minimizing the expected cost of distortionary taxes that discourage work effort and reduce output.[36] Assuming that the cost of the distortion is a quadratic function of the tax rate—that is, if the tax rate goes up 5 percent, costs increase 25 percent—creates a strong incentive to smooth taxes over time. A simple model shows that equity investment involves a trade-off. On the one hand, the higher average return on equities lowers average taxes; on the other hand, the greater risk associated with equities leads to high taxes to make up for underfunding when the market collapses. Thus, equities have a role, but since very high tax rates create expensive distortions, equities should be used with moderation.

Another argument for investing pension fund assets in equities is that it can improve risk sharing.[37] In general, efficient risk sharing requires individuals to bear more risk when they are young and less when they are old.[38] However, the young often hold no risky, high-yielding assets. Investing pension fund assets in

---

35. Black (1989). Under this rationale for equity investment, immature plans should hold more equities than mature plans.

36. Lucas and Zeldes (2009). Families are assumed to maximize expected discounted utility of consumption and leisure, subject to the constraint that initial wealth and lifetime earnings pay for lifetime consumption and taxes. Consumption and leisure are additively separable. Capital markets are complete, so pension plan asset allocation does not affect individual consumption risk because people can take offsetting positions in their personal portfolios.

37. See Bohn (1997); and Diamond (1997).

38. The reason is that it is easier for the young to work more if they suffer a capital loss. They can also average returns over time and take advantage of the fact that declines in stock prices are typically associated with higher returns in the next period. Because the old are in the process of liquidating their equity holdings, they cannot take full advantage of this property. It is also reasonable to assume that the young are less risk-averse and more inclined to carry stock market risk.

equities has the potential to shift risk from the old to the young and to make all generations better off.[39]

In short, a number of arguments suggest that public pension plans should invest at least some of their assets in equities and other risky investments. Note that the arguments for and against investing in equities have nothing to do with the appropriate rate used to discount obligations for reporting purposes. They simply pertain to the composition of the assets in the trust funds.[40]

CONTRIBUTIONS. Assuming that the pension fund should hold some equities, how much should the plan sponsor contribute each year? Should the amount be based on the riskless rate, or should it be based on the long-run expected rate of return? Here the lines are sharply drawn. It is a highly controversial issue, and either approach creates problems.

Financial economists argue strongly that the contribution should be based on the riskless rate and that contributing anything less simply shifts risks forward to the next generation.[41] Consider three states of the world. In the first, the sponsor calculates contributions based on the risk-free rate and invests only in bonds. In this scenario, plan assets will always be adequate to cover future benefit obligations, and each generation contributes the same amount. In the second state, the sponsor calculates contributions based on the expected return of a portfolio that includes equities. The first generation pays less than in the first scenario and does not have to worry about the risks associated with equity investment. (The assumption is that equity values do not fluctuate in the first period.) Subsequent generations also get to contribute less than the amount based on the riskless rate but bear the risk that equities might not perform as the first generation anticipated. To hedge this risk, the second and all subsequent generations are compelled to, in essence, buy insurance; the cost of the insurance raises their total pension expense. In the third state, the sponsor calculates contributions based on the riskless rate and invests in equities. In this case, the pension fund becomes increasingly well funded over time (because the return on equities exceeds the assumed riskless return) and, as a result, required contributions decline. On the other hand, exposure to equity risk increases over time and the cost of insurance

39. Arrow and Lind (1970).

40. But one could argue that the discount assumption does impact the share of the portfolio invested in equities. The reason is that GASB permits public plans to use the expected long-term return to discount their liabilities. Higher risk/return portfolios justify a higher discount rate, which produces lower liability values and improves the funded status of the plan. A shift to the riskless rate for reporting purposes would reduce the incentive for aggressive investing.

41. Bader and Gold (2007).

rises. The combination of increasing insurance costs and declining contributions once again leads to an equal burden across generations.

This last scenario is the most relevant given the strong case for some equity investment. While calculating contributions based on the riskless rate ensures intergenerational equity by keeping risk-adjusted costs level across generations, it has some peculiar implications. First, making contributions at the riskless rate and earning a higher rate will lead to higher and higher levels of funding. Over-funded plans raise the real world specter of sparking benefit increases both going forward and perhaps retroactively. Second, the required pension contribution for each generation will be lower than for the previous generation, which taxpayers may view as unfair. In theory, the declining contribution is offset by increasing insurance costs, but that concept may not resonate with taxpayers who are not actually taking steps to hedge the equity risk in the pension fund.

Calculating contributions based on the riskless rate raises not only theoretical concerns but also very practical considerations. As discussed above, reducing the discount rate from about 8 percent to 5 percent would raise the present value of benefits, leading to a large increase in the ARC. What would a 250 percent increase in the ARC mean? States and localities have already seen the ARC double since 2000. As a result, the share of ARC paid dropped to 80 percent in 2010 (see figure 3-6). The current struggle is to get back to paying the full ARC calculated using the 8 percent rate. It is hard to imagine how state and local plan sponsors would respond if told to contribute 32 percent of payroll.

Calculating contributions based on expected returns is not ideal; such an arrangement does involve risk. The financial crisis and ensuing recession have provided a natural experiment for determining who bears the burden of really bad market outcomes. What allowed the current arrangement to work is that liabilities turned out not to be fixed. In a number of states, retirees experienced a benefit cut through a suspension or reduction of the COLA, in addition to employees and taxpayers paying higher contributions. That is, some flexibility on the benefit side has enabled the existing system to respond to an extreme outcome. Using a long-run expected return for funding purposes appears to be the least bad option. Advocating expected returns for calculating contributions does not conflict with advocating the use of the riskless rate for valuing liabilities.

GASB's 2012 Standards

In 2006, GASB embarked on a project to review its accounting standards for pensions and propose changes as needed. The resulting proposals, outlined in two exposure drafts released for public comment in 2011 and adopted in 2012, encompassed a host of reforms pertaining to virtually every aspect of pension

Figure 3-6. *Percentage of Annual Required Contribution Paid, 2001–10*

Percent

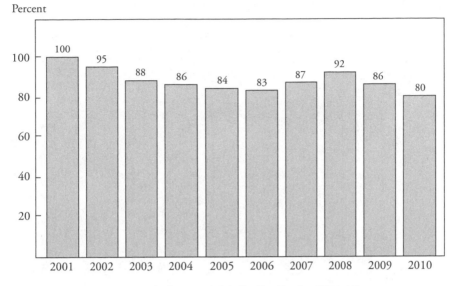

Sources: Various 2010 actuarial valuations; and *Public Plans Database* (2001–10).

accounting.[42] Three of the main changes, however, pertain to the valuation of plan assets and employer liabilities. First, plan assets that are netted against the total pension liability are no longer smoothed but rather valued at market. Second, obligations are discounted by a blended rate, which combines the expected return for the portion of obligations that is projected to be covered by existing and projected assets with the return on high-grade municipal bonds for the portion that is projected to be covered by other resources. Third, the entry-age normal/level percentage of payroll is the sole method used for reporting purposes.[43]

Using the market value of assets (net position), which immediately recognizes gains and losses, demonstrates clearly the degree to which plan funding is tied to the fate of the stock market. Figure 3-7 presents aggregate funded ratios for the 126 plans in the PPD calculated using the actuarial value of assets

42. Governmental Accounting Standards Board (2011a and 2011b).

43. Experts say that, in almost every case, actuaries and accountants will be able to use the long-run expected return (not the blended rate) to value liabilities, since they can project for any plan funding responsibly that assets will be adequate to meet all liability cash flows. Exceptions might occur in cases such as Illinois, which only aims to be 90 percent funded, or New Jersey, where the state has shown that it cannot be counted on to pay the ARC.

Figure 3-7. *Aggregate Funded Ratios for State and Local Pension Plans
Using Actuarial and Market Assets, 2001–10*

Percent

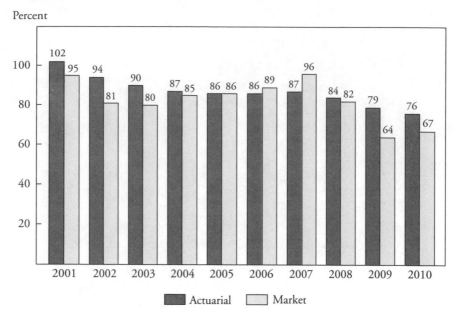

Source: Munnell and others (2012 forthcoming).

and the market value. Predictably, actuarial funded ratios lag market ratios. The 2008 financial crisis caused an enormous decline in market assets and an 18 percentage point drop in funding, whereas the funded ratio calculated on the basis of actuarial assets declined by only 5 percentage points. In contrast, 2010 funded ratios using market assets increased by 3 percentage points, while funded ratios using actuarial assets were still dropping. But the bottom line is that the aggregate funded ratio using market assets was only 67 percent in 2010, so policymakers may see a sharp decline in reported funding as the GASB changes are implemented.

The next step is to estimate how funded ratios will change when obligations are discounted using a blended rate of return. To calculate the impact requires knowing for each of the plans in the PPD sample the underlying stream of benefit payments owed by the plan in future years. Public pensions typically do not disclose this information, so the benefit stream must be re-engineered based on demographic assumptions about the age, salary, and tenure of the workforce, as well as actuarial assumptions regarding retirement, separation, and mortality. These assumptions are available in most actuarial valuations. With flows of

Figure 3-8. *Aggregate Funded Ratios for State and Local Plans, before and after GASB Changes to Valuing Assets and Liabilities, 2009–10*

Percent

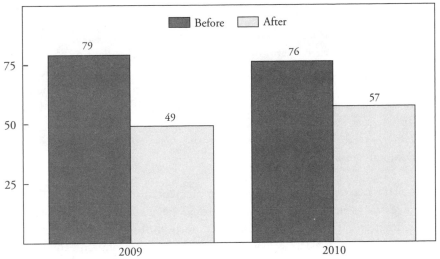

Source: Munnell and others (2012).

projected government and employee contributions, benefits, and investment returns, it is possible to calculate the date when assets will be exhausted.[44] All benefits payable in years before the exhaustion date are discounted using each plan's assumption regarding the expected return on assets. Benefits payable after the run-out date are discounted by 3.7 percent, which is the current yield on high-grade municipal bonds.[45]

Figure 3-8 compares the funded ratios currently reported with estimates of what these ratios would have looked like for 2009 and 2010 under GASB's new standards. The bottom line is that the headline number would have declined

44. The methodology for first re-engineering the benefit stream and then re-discounting this stream is an adaptation of the framework used to estimate trust fund run-out dates under the termination framework described in Center for Retirement Research at Boston College (2011a). The key changes pertain to contributions and assumed returns. In the termination analysis, the assumption was that employees and the government contributed nothing to the current unfunded liability. In the current analysis, the employee and government are both assumed to maintain their current contributions measured as a percentage of payroll. In the termination analysis, run-out dates were estimated under a range of alternative investment returns. In the current analysis, investment returns are assumed to be the plan's long-run expected return as proposed by GASB.

45. Bloomberg (2011).

in 2010—the latest year for which data are available—from 76 percent to 57 percent.

Implications of GASB's Changes

GASB's rationale for its blended rate in the exposure drafts was that while the expected rate of return is appropriate for discounting obligations backed by assets, obligations not covered by assets fall to the sponsoring government and therefore should be discounted by the sponsor's borrowing cost.[46] The argument remains at odds with economists' view that the discount rate should reflect the riskiness of the obligations, irrespective of how the obligations are funded. Moreover, the GASB changes raise additional issues with regard to implementation, interpretation, and the ARC.

IMPLEMENTATION ISSUES. The main implementation problem with GASB's blended rate is that it requires a complicated calculation based on a number of assumptions. The determination of the portion of benefits funded requires a projection of plan assets available each year to cover promised benefits. The asset projection includes assumptions not only about plan returns but also about future contributions from the government and from employees.[47] These contributions may or may not come to pass. One can imagine extended disputes about the validity of the underlying assumptions.

INTERPRETATION CHALLENGES. Economists use pension data generated under GASB's standards to address three main economic issues: (1) basic comparisons of pension finances across states and over time; (2) the impact of pensions and other post-employment benefits (OPEBs) on government budgets and borrowing capacity; and (3) the relative compensation of public sector workers. In order to produce useful analysis, the data need to provide meaningful measures of government obligations and be consistent across states and localities and over time. The new GASB discounting procedure fails on a number of counts.

—It creates a liability number with no theoretical underpinnings. It makes no theoretical sense for two identical streams of benefits to have different values based on the intended funded status of the plan. Having the present discounted value of obligations depend on both the long-run expected rate of return and

---

46. Governmental Accounting Standards Board (2011a and 2011b).

47. Interestingly, FASB considered and rejected such an approach not only because the contribution assumptions are so uncertain but, importantly, because it would "unnecessarily complicate the recognition and disclosure requirements"; see Financial Accounting Standards Board (1985).

on the funded status makes the numbers even more difficult to interpret and difficult to adjust for alternative returns than the current liability numbers.

—It makes comparisons across states and localities impossible because the denominator of the funded ratio (that is, liabilities) will reflect the value of the assets. Moreover, a change in the funded status of a given plan will be attributable to both the change in assets and the impact of that change on the value of liabilities. This feedback complicates a systematic analysis of why funding has improved or deteriorated.

—It creates a new "projected" funded ratio that will compete with the traditional funded ratio—assets divided by liabilities—and create unnecessary confusion.

IMPLICATIONS FOR THE ARC. GASB's changes eliminate the reported ARC. In its place, plan sponsors report either an "actuarially calculated employer contribution" or a statutory contribution. Those that report an actuarially determined contribution provide information on the underlying actuarial assumptions and methods used. However, GASB no longer offers guidance regarding acceptable parameters, which raises the possibility that assumptions and amortization periods might vary among plans more than they have in the past. To the extent that the underlying parameters vary, comparisons among plans will become difficult. Plans that have a statutory contribution rate are not required to report an actuarially calculated employer contribution.[48] This change not only represents a loss in analysts' ability to assess how close plan contributions are to those required to keep the system on track but also creates a tempting escape valve: introduce a statutory rate and dispense with reporting actuarial calculations.

Conclusion

The argument is compelling that the liabilities of public pension plans, most of which are guaranteed under state law, should be discounted by a rate that reflects their riskless nature. Such a change would increase liabilities from $3.4 trillion to $5.2 trillion in 2010. With $2.6 trillion of assets on hand, unfunded liabilities would rise from $0.8 trillion to $2.6 trillion.

What difference would such a change make? First, a more realistic measure of the funded status of the plans would deter plans from offering more generous benefits in response to supposed "excess" assets. Second, lowering the return

48. Governmental Accounting Standards Board (2011a and 2011b). Relying on statutory rates raises potential concerns: they may not be set to adequately reflect a plan's funding needs, and their static nature makes it more difficult for a plan's funding strategy to respond to changing conditions.

target would reduce the incentive for plans to increase their expected rate of return through aggressive investment in equities. Third, using a riskless rate would inspire the confidence of private sector observers in the reports of state and local pension funds.

The argument about the discount rate pertains to *reporting*; investing and calculating contributions are separate issues. Discounting the stream of future benefits by a riskless rate does not imply that plans should hold only riskless assets. A number of considerations suggest that state and local plans should continue to invest in equities. If the returns on these equities resemble their long-run historical performance, then, for any given level of contributions, plans' unfunded liabilities would be paid off more quickly than if funds were invested in bonds.

Determining contributions is a trickier issue. Academic models suggest that the calculation should use the riskless rate. But contributing based on the riskless rate and investing in equities produces ever growing funding levels and declining contributions for each successive generation. These outcomes have political ramifications in the real world. Calculating contributions based on the expected rate of return is probably the least bad option and does not conflict with using the riskless rate for reporting purposes. The risk is that public sector sponsors using one liability measure for determining contributions and another one for reporting purposes may create confusion and reduce transparency.

The riskless rate debate is going to be muddied by GASB's new blended rate that is based on the degree to which assets are projected to be available to cover benefit promises. The change will lower rates in a number of cases where plans are projected to be underfunded for the foreseeable future. GASB's changes cannot be viewed as a step in the right direction, because they not only maintain the tie to how plans are funded but also create a system in which well-funded plans use a higher discount rate than poorly funded ones.

In the end, the choice of the discount rate is neither the source of the problem nor a quick solution. While the discount rate affects the present value of plans' promised benefits, it does not affect the promised benefits themselves. When teachers or firefighters retire, they will get the amount calculated under the plan provisions, and how that future amount is reported today has no impact on the ultimate payment.

4

Why Are Some Plans in Trouble and Others Not?

The discussion in chapter 3 progressed as if state and local plans were one homogeneous whole. As discussed earlier, nothing could be further from the truth. Plans vary within states; plans for teachers and general employees are very different from plans for police and fire personnel. Plans administered at the state level have different financing structures than those administered by localities. And plans of similar types vary enormously from state to state. That is, the plan for general employees in California costs more than twice as much as a percentage of payroll as that in Georgia. Also, participants in some plans are covered by Social Security, and in other plans not. States and localities also have different commitments to funding their plans.

This chapter looks at differences among plans with an emphasis on why some plans are in trouble and others are not. The material is, by necessity, empirical. It is impossible to follow the traditional model, whereby authors reframe or reinterpret work of earlier researchers—and perhaps add some new bits of information—in order to support a particular thesis, because our knowledge about the specifics of state and local pensions is too embryonic. Indeed, in many ways the data are the news. Thus this chapter reports on the status of plans and uses regression analysis to link that status with particular institutional or behavioral factors.

This chapter is also limited in its focus. It is a funding story. The broader question of the burden of plans on state and local revenues is addressed in chapter 5.

The discussion proceeds as follows. The first section explores the variation in funding by identifying the factors that lead sponsors to make their full annual required contribution (ARC) and the factors that, given the ARC payment, result in more or less funding. The second section looks at the difference in funding between state-administered and locally administered plans. The third section turns the focus to unions, which are viewed by governors in many states as a source of pension problems, and explores whether unions affect funding indirectly through pushing up benefit levels.

Three major conclusions emerge from this analysis. First, it is not true that all public plans are in trouble. Second, states with seriously underfunded plans, such as Illinois, Kentucky, Louisiana, New Jersey, and Pennsylvania, have behaved badly. They have either not made the required contributions or used inaccurate assumptions so that their contribution requirements are not meaningful. An equally large number of states—Delaware, Florida, Georgia, Tennessee, and North Carolina—have done a good job of providing reasonable benefits, paying their required contribution, and accumulating plan assets. Third, it is impossible to identify a link between the poorly funded plans and the two factors highlighted in the introduction as the source of the problem: (1) discounting liabilities by the long-run expected rate of return instead of the riskless rate or (2) the collective bargaining activities of unions. The poorly funded plans did not come close to surmounting the lower hurdle associated with a high discount rate; raising the hurdle is unlikely to have improved their funding behavior (although it might have curtailed benefit expansions). And union strength simply did not show up as a statistically significant factor in any of the empirical analysis. Pension funding is simply a story of fiscal discipline.

Explaining the Variation in Funding among State and Local Plans

As discussed in chapter 3, most experts agree that each generation of taxpayers should pay the full cost of the public services it receives. If a worker's compensation includes a defined benefit pension, the cost of the benefit earned in a given year should be recognized and funded at the time the worker performs that service, not when the worker receives benefits in retirement. In addition, many states also have some unfunded pension obligations from the past, either because they did not put away money at the time the benefits were earned, because returns fell short of expectations, or because they provided benefits retroactively.[1] The cost of these unfunded liabilities also needs to be paid off over time.

In order to put some structure to the goal of recognizing defined benefit plan costs when they occur and financing unfunded liabilities, the Governmental

1. For example, Massachusetts, the last state to defend pay-as-you-go financing, did not adopt a formal funding structure until 1987. The Massachusetts Retirement Law Commission recommended in 1976 funding all the state's pension plans on an actuarial basis, and the Massachusetts legislature passed the first bill allowing systems to put aside reserves in 1978. However, it took until 1987 for the state to adopt a formal funding schedule that moved the ad hoc reserves into the structure of the retirement system.

Accounting Standards Board (GASB) established funding standards in the 1990s. As noted in chapter 3, GASB allowed sponsors that satisfy certain "parameters" the convenience of using the numbers that emerged from the actuary's funding exercise for reporting purposes. Among other things, these parameters defined an acceptable amortization period, which was originally up to forty years and reduced to thirty years in 2006, and an annual required contribution, which would cover the cost of benefits accruing in the current year and a payment to amortize the plan's unfunded actuarial liability.[2] Thus standards were established that plans should pay off their existing liabilities and cover the full cost of accruing benefits. If plan sponsors followed these standards, their plans should have been on the path toward full funding.

Two caveats are important before looking at the variation in funding behavior. First, the liabilities to be funded were calculated using GASB's recommended expected long-run rate of return, which has been roughly 8 percent. While state and local plans achieved this return over the period 1989–2009, it is probably not an appropriate rate for the future, as is discussed in chapter 8. Second, while GASB specified amortization of the unfunded liability over a thirty-year span, sponsors were allowed to use a rolling method whereby each year they amortized their unfunded liabilities over the next thirty years. Most plans adopted the open-ended option, which slowed the path toward full funding.[3]

Observed Variation in Funding Status

In 2010, for state and local plans in the aggregate—based on a discount rate of 8 percent—assets amounted to 76 percent of liabilities. However, funded levels among the 126 plans in the *Public Plans Database* (PPD) varied substantially (see figure 4-1).[4] Only about 5 percent were fully funded, and 12 percent had assets between 35 and 59 percent of liabilities. The question is why some plans were in relatively good shape and others were not.[5]

---

2. This amortization period applied to both the plan's "initial" underfunding and any subsequent underfunding created by benefit increases attributed to "past service" or experience losses.

3. In addition, most plans amortize their unfunded liability as a constant percentage of the projected payroll for both current members and new hires. Since payroll is growing, this method backloads contributions and can result in initial contributions that in some instances do not even cover the annual interest on the unfunded liability.

4. These ratios are not quite comparable across plans in that actuarial cost methods differ. For example, plans using the EAN cost approach will report a larger accrued liability and a lower funded ratio for any level of assets than plans using the PUC approach. Of particular concern in an earlier survey was the use of the aggregate cost method, which always shows a funded ratio of 100 percent. However, in recent years, many plans using the aggregate cost method have also begun to report liabilities using the EAN or PUC method.

5. For an earlier analysis of this issue, see Munnell, Aubry, and Quinby (2011).

Figure 4-1. *Distribution of Funded Ratios for State and Local Pension Plans, 2010*

Percent

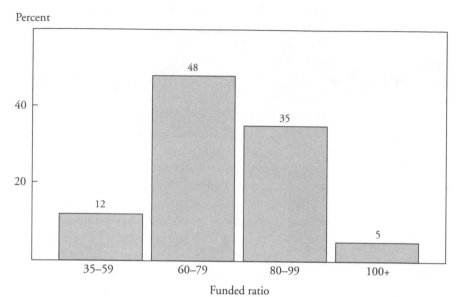

Funded ratio

Sources: Author's calculations from *Public Plans Database* (2010); and various financial and actuarial reports.

A useful place to start is a list of the most expensive plans—that is, plans with high normal cost (see table 4-1). They fall into two categories: police and fire plans not covered by Social Security and plans primarily in New York, New Jersey, and California that are covered. In both cases, however, the ARC paid is usually close to 100 percent and the plans tend to be about 80 percent funded. Thus factors other than the cost of the plan appear to determine the level of funding.

Some insights emerge from looking at the ten worst-funded plans, all of which had funded ratios under 50 percent (see table 4-2). First, five of the ten plans are for teachers, and one plan (Rhode Island ERS) covers teachers as well as general employees. Second, the plans are not particularly expensive on average. Normal cost—the cost of accruing benefits—averaged about 13 percent of payroll. Compare this figure with the 20 percent to 30 percent of payroll for the most expensive plans. Third, more than half did not pay the full ARC over the period 2005–10. Fourth, the proportion with Social Security coverage roughly mirrors the pattern for the nation as a whole. Finally, not shown, four of the ten plans have adopted the projected unit credit cost method, which is used by only 14 percent of plans in the sample and is a less stringent funding program than entry-age normal, the method used by most public sector plans.

Table 4-1. *Most Expensive State and Local Plans, 2010*[a]

Plan[b]	Funded ratio	Normal cost	Percent of ARC paid 2005–10	Social Security
New York City Teachers[c]	62.9	32.8	99.0	Yes
Contra Costa County	80.3	28.6	100.0	Yes
San Diego County	84.3	25.7	106.8	Yes
NYCERS[c]	77.2	24.1	96.8	Yes
New York State & Local Police & Fire[c]	96.7	21.2	100.0	Yes
University of California	86.7	19.0	84.8	Yes
New Jersey Police & Fire	77.1	18.7	61.3	Yes
California PERF	83.4	18.2	100.0	Mostly
District of Columbia Police & Fire	100.7	39.8	100.0	No
Nevada Police Officer and Firefighter	67.8	29.8	88.5	No
Houston Firefighters	93.4	27.0	100.0	No
Ohio Police & Fire	69.4	22.3	70.2	No
Missouri Teachers	77.7	22.0	75.6	No

Source: *Public Plans Database* (2010).

a. Two plans with Social Security coverage—New Mexico Public Employees Retirement Fund (normal cost of 20.7 percent) and Arizona Public Safety Personnel (normal cost of 19.3 percent), both of which pay virtually 100 percent of their ARC—are not shown because they are quite small.

b. NYCERS = New York City Employee Retirement System; California PERF = California Public Employees' Retirement Fund.

c. Aggregate cost and frozen initial liability plans are presented with their entry-age normal funded ratio. However, normal cost and percent ARC paid are calculated according to the plan's own actuarial method.

Perusal of tables can only take one so far. In order to identify the characteristics of well-funded plans relative to their poorly funded counterparts, the following section reports regression analysis to identify factors that lead sponsors to pay the ARC and then, given the ARC payment, result in higher or lower levels of funding.

Making the ARC Payment

GASB standards, until the adoption of the recent proposals described in chapter 3, involved an annual payment to cover the normal cost and to pay off the unfunded liability over thirty years—albeit, to date, a rolling thirty-year period over open-group rising payroll. Figure 4-2 shows that over the period 2005–09, fewer than half of plan sponsors paid 100 percent of the ARC. Employers that contribute less than the full ARC are generally setting aside enough money to cover currently accruing benefits. And they could even be reducing the plan's unfunded liability from previous years, albeit at a slower pace than if they paid the full ARC. Not making the full ARC payment, nevertheless, indicates a failure

Table 4-2. *Ten Worst-Funded State and Local Plans, 2010*

Plan[a]	Funded ratio	Normal cost	Percent of ARC paid 2005–10	Social Security
Illinois SERS	37.4	17.5	60.6	Yes
Kentucky ERS	40.3	9.2	49.4	Yes
Missouri DOT and Highway Patrol	42.2	11.9	100.0	Yes
Indiana Teachers	44.3	8.9	96.9	Yes
Connecticut SERS	44.4	10.9	95.5	Yes
Illinois Universities	46.4	20.9	46.9	No
West Virginia Teachers	46.5	9.4	173.8	Yes
Oklahoma Teachers	47.9	11.8	84.4	Yes
Illinois Teachers	48.4	18.2	60.1	No
Rhode Island ERS	48.4	11.7	100.0	Mostly

Source: *Public Plans Database* (2010).

a. Illinois SERS = Illinois State Employees' Retirement System; Kentucky ERS = Kentucky Employees Retirement System; Missouri DOT and Highway Patrol = Missouri Department of Transportation and Highway Patrol; Connecticut SERS = Connecticut State Employees Retirement System; Rhode Island ERS = Rhode Island Employees' Retirement System.

to follow GASB's suggested funding plan. The question is why such a large percentage of plan sponsors are not making the full ARC.

One explanation is that some plan sponsors face statutory contribution rates. A review of the annual reports found that thirty-two plans in the sample were legally constrained.[6] The degree of constraint varied significantly. For example, the statutory rates in Texas roughly equaled the actuarially determined ARC, so the contribution level fell only slightly short of the required amount.[7] In contrast, the rate in Kansas was well below the required amount, so the sponsors contributed only about 65 percent of the ARC.[8] In the case of Kansas, the state legislature is aware of the inadequacy of the statutory contribution rate and has

6. Other entities also faced legal limitations, but they were not binding at this time. One could argue that legal constraints are not really binding in the sense that future legislatures can change the contribution rate. If so, fiscally disciplined states would have rules that allowed plan sponsors to make their ARC payment; irresponsible states would not.

7. Before the 2008 financial crisis, all four Texas plans were contributing at least 90 percent of the ARC. As ARCs increased in the wake of the crisis, the legislature has been simultaneously increasing statutory rates, although none of the plans are currently contributing at the 90 percent level. See actuarial valuation reports for Employees Retirement System of Texas, Teacher Retirement System of Texas, Texas Municipal Retirement System, and Law Enforcement and Custodial Officer Supplemental Retirement Fund of the Employees Retirement System of Texas (2007–10).

8. *Public Plans Database* (2010).

Figure 4-2. *Distribution of State and Local Pension Plans, by Percentage of Annual Required Contribution (ARC) Paid, 2005–09*[a]

Percent

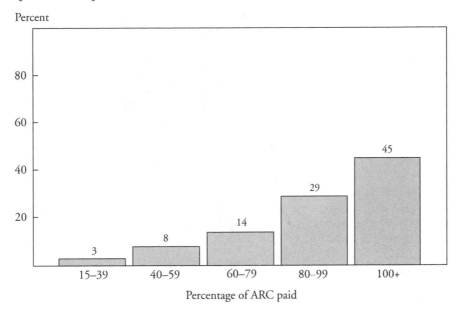

Percentage of ARC paid

Source: Author's calculations from *Public Plans Database* (2005–09).
a. Plans that used the aggregate cost method were coded with 100 percent of ARC paid.

been steadily increasing the legislated rate in an attempt to catch up to the actu-arially required contribution level.[9] In fact, most states where funding is legally constrained appear aware of this problem and have been gradually increasing their contribution rates.

While legal constraints may be part of the reason that sponsors did not make their ARC, a number of unconstrained sponsors also fell short over the past few years (see figure 4-3). A probit regression was used to estimate the relationship between various factors and the probability that the sponsor made 100 percent of the ARC between 2005 and 2009. Plans that were constrained by legal fund-ing limitations were excluded from the analysis, which reduced the sample size from 126 to 94. The equation included four types of factors: the discipline of the sponsor; the presence of other plans; the characteristics of the plan; and the priorities of those involved in governance of the plan.[10]

9. See actuarial valuation reports for Kansas PERS (2008–10).
10. One reviewer suggested that the diversion of employer contributions to cover health care costs may explain why some states have failed to pay 100 percent of their ARC.

Figure 4-3. *Distribution of Pension Plans by Annual Required Contribution (ARC) Payment and Legal Constraint, 2005–09*

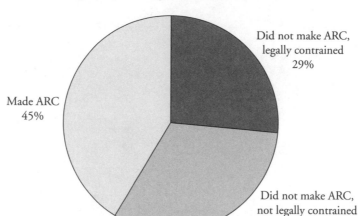

Did not make ARC, legally contrained 29%

Made ARC 45%

Did not make ARC, not legally contrained 25%

Source: Author's calculations from *Public Plans Database* (2005–09).

LACK OF FISCAL DISCIPLINE. Two characteristics would signal that a plan sponsor is not disciplined in its fiscal effort. The first is the actuarial cost method used; the second is the state's ratio of debt to gross state product (GSP).

—*Actuarial cost method*. Up to the point of retirement, the entry-age normal (EAN) method recognizes a larger accumulated pension obligation for active employees than the projected unit credit (PUC) method. Therefore, the EAN method is a more stringent funding program. The hypothesis is that sponsors that opted for the currently cheaper funding regime—namely, the projected unit credit—may be less committed to funding their plans and therefore will have lower reported funded ratios.

—*Ratio of debt to GSP*. If a state is having fiscal problems, it may meet current non-pension obligations by not making the annual contribution to the pension plan.[11]

11.The U.S. General Accounting Office (1993, 1985) provides examples of states that closed budget gaps by reducing the pension contribution, while Chaney, Copley, and Stone (2002) and Bohn and Inman (1996) consider the general effects of balanced budget requirements in states. Since almost all states have some type of balanced budget requirement, this variable was not included in our analysis. The concept of the debt to GSP is similar to the leverage variable used in Davis, Grob, and de Haan (2007) for private employers.

OTHER RETIREMENT PLAN. Plans where other sources of retirement income are available to participants may be less likely to pay the ARC.

—*Social Security coverage.* Government employers might feel less responsibility to fund the plan if participants are also covered by Social Security.

—*Defined contribution plan.* Sponsors that also offer a primary defined contribution plan may view paying the full ARC as less essential.

PLAN CHARACTERISTICS. The likelihood of paying the ARC might depend on the cost of the plan and the type of employees covered.

—*ARC as a percentage of payroll.* The notion is that the higher the ARC as a percentage of payroll, the more costly it is to make the full payment and therefore the less likely the sponsor will contribute 100 percent of the ARC.

—*Police and fire plan.* Evidence suggests that plans for police and fire personnel tend to be well funded.

—*Teachers' plan.* Teachers' plans accounted for a disproportionate share of the worst-funded plans.[12]

GOVERNANCE. The governance structure could affect the likelihood of paying the ARC. The analysis incorporates two measures:

—*Employees/retirees on the board.* One view is that boards with a lot of workers and retirees could be more interested in benefit expansion or greater cost-of-living adjustments than in funding benefit promises. An alternative view is that because workers and retirees have a greater stake in the plan's success than outside board members their presence on a board would tend to have a positive impact. Earlier studies have shown mixed results.[13]

—*Union.* Governors' attempts to eliminate collective bargaining suggest they view unions as having contributed to the funding problem. Union strength is measured by the participants' legal right to collectively bargain.

The results of the regression equation are reported in appendix 4A (table 4A-1 and summary statistics in table 4A-2). The coefficients show the relationship between the explanatory variables and the probability of making 100 percent of the ARC. The relationship may not necessarily be causal because an omitted variable, such as a commitment to fiscal responsibility, could affect both making the ARC and, say, the choice of an actuarial cost method. Most variables

---

12. Teachers have longer tenure than general government employees, higher earnings (due to higher education levels), and longer life expectancy, and these factors translate into larger pension liabilities; see Weller, Price, and Margolis (2006).

13. See Carmichael and Palacios (2003); Mitchell and Hsin (1997); Schneider and Damanpour (2002); and Yang and Mitchell (2005).

Figure 4-4. *Factors Associated with Probability of Paying the Full ARC, 2005–09*[a]

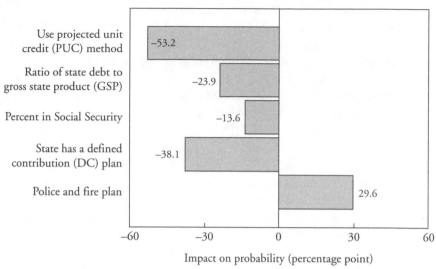

Impact on probability (percentage point)

Sources: Author's calculations from *Public Plans Database* (2005–09); and U.S. Census Bureau, *State and Local Government Finances* (2005–09).

a. Marginal effects reflect a one unit change for dichotomous variables and a one standard deviation change for continuous variables. Standard errors have been adjusted for state-level clustering. All coefficients are significant at the 10 percent level or better. Additional controls not depicted include: ARC as a percentage of payroll, teachers' plan, employees/retirees on the board, and permission to collectively bargain.

have their expected signs and statistically significant coefficients. A few had no significant effect. The lack of significance of ARC/payroll is not surprising given that the expensive plans examined earlier tended to have large ARC payments and were fairly well funded. Similarly, given earlier inconclusive work on the governance variables, it is not surprising that board composition and union strength did not have a significant effect. The variables with a statistically significant coefficient appear to be strongly correlated with the probability of a sponsor to pay the full ARC (see figure 4-4). For example, using the PUC cost method reduces the probability by 53 percentage points. Having a defined contribution plan reduces it by 38 percentage points. Being a police and fire plan increases the probability by about 30 percentage points.

Funding the Plan

Making the ARC payment is an important step in the funding process. But the correlation between having made 100 percent of the ARC and the funded ratio is only 20 percent. Clearly other factors are at play. These factors fall into three categories: history, sophistication, and assumptions.

HISTORY. Today's funded status depends very much on what has happened in the past. Here two factors appear important.

—*Actuarial cost method*. The choice of actuarial cost method in this case reflects the extent to which the funding has been deferred. For any given level of contribution, the use of the PUC method is likely to be associated with less funding.

—*Age of system*. Older plans are likely to have promised benefits over a longer period of time without putting aside funds to cover the promises, thereby creating a large unfunded liability. Therefore the older the plan, the lower the expected funded ratio.

SOPHISTICATION AND SIZE. These two characteristics of the plan could also affect its funded status.

—*Investment council*. If a plan has a dedicated investment board or hires financial advisers in making its investment decisions, the plan should have greater returns, more assets, and a higher funded ratio.[14] The variable included is a dummy variable indicating if the plan has a separate investment council that directly makes investment decisions.

—*Plan size*. Other studies have shown that plan size and funded levels are closely related.[15] Possible reasons for this pattern may be better discipline, because not funding could have a huge impact on taxpayers in the future, or the effect of being more in the national political spotlight than smaller plans. In any event, plan size and funding are expected to be positively related.

ASSUMPTIONS. The meaningfulness of the ARC as a mechanism for prefunding benefits depends crucially on the realism of the underlying assumptions. For example, Rhode Island ERS, which had a funded ratio of 48 percent in 2010, had historically paid 100 percent of the ARC. With a severely outdated mortality table that underestimates how long retirees will receive benefits, the ARC will significantly understate how much money needs to be put aside for accruing benefits.[16]

14. Previous studies have directly included a measure of the rate of return on investments. See Yang and Mitchell (2005).

15. See, for example, Center for Retirement Research at Boston College (2008a) and Munnell, Aubry, and Quinby (2011).

16. From 2001 to 2009, Rhode Island ERS used the 1994 Group Annuity Mortality (GAM) tables, set forward one year for males. In 2010, it switched to the RP-2000 table, with various offsets and projections.

Figure 4-5. *Factors Associated with State and Local Pension Funded Ratios, 2010*[a]

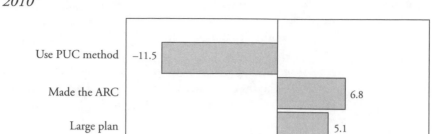

Impact on funded ratio (percentage point)

Sources: Author's calculations from Freeman and Valletta (1988); and *Public Plans Database* (2005–10).

a. Values for percentage of ARC paid are averaged over the 2005–09 period. The results shown are for a one unit change for dichotomous variables and one standard deviation change for continuous variables. Standard errors have been adjusted for state-level clustering. All coefficients are significant at the 10 percent level or better. Not depicted is a control variable for having a separate investment council.

—*Outdated mortality assumptions.* Even though actuaries make ad hoc adjustments to seemingly outdated mortality rates, the use of a 1983 table would probably lead to an understatement of the ARC.

The full results of the regression can be found in appendix 4A (table 4A-3 and summary statistics in table 4A-4). As shown in figure 4-5, all of the variables have the expected relationship with the funded status of the pension plan, and all relationships except the investment council were statistically significant. The most interesting fact is that paying the full ARC is associated with only a 6.8 percentage point higher funded ratio, roughly the same magnitude as for a large plan. Using a PUC method or a very old mortality table, both mechanisms to delay funding, is associated with an 11.5 percentage point lower funded ratio.

The Story

The story that emerges from the ARC and funding equations is as follows. First, paying the ARC reflects a commitment to fiscal discipline. States that borrow freely and have high levels of debt relative to GDP are less likely to pay the ARC. And as it turns out, the choice of an actuarial method—in the context of state and local plans—also appears to be a signal that politicians in the state want to postpone pension payments. Although only 14 percent of state and local plans use the PUC, four of the ten worst-funded plans have adopted that cost method. Other factors, such as the availability of other sources of retirement income, have an effect, but being fiscally responsible is the key.

Second, on the funding side, it matters not only how much money is put aside through the ARC payment but also how that money is invested. Large plans can hire more sophisticated financial managers and have an independent investment council. History is also important. Plans that have promised benefits for seventy-five years but funded them for only twenty-five years cannot be close to fully funded even if they have paid 100 percent of the ARC for ten or fifteen years. Similarly, plans that have back-ended their contributions through their choice of actuarial cost method also fall short.

In the end, a relatively small group of states—Illinois, Kentucky, Louisiana, New Jersey, and Pennsylvania—could be considered bad actors as pension funders. Interestingly, their funding behavior would most likely have been unaffected by adopting a riskless rate to discount their liabilities, since they consistently failed to meet even the lower hurdle associated with the higher discount rate.[17] These states have led many observers to conclude that public pension plans have been widely mismanaged. But an equal number of states—Delaware, Florida, Georgia, North Carolina, and Tennessee—have done a good job of providing reasonable benefits, paying the ARC, and funding. They, like all entities, have been battered by the financial collapse and ensuing recession, but their funding status should improve as the economy recovers. California and New York raise a different funding issue. Their pension funds are reasonably well funded, but their benefits are so expensive that they may be crowding out other priorities at both the state and local levels. This latter issue is explored in the next chapter.

State- versus Locally Administered Plans

The discussion so far has focused mostly on state-administered plans. This section reports on findings from a 2010 survey of locally administered plans and compares how these plans have fared relative to state-administered plans between 2006 and 2010. The sample covers ninety-seven locally administered plans in forty states. The data for nineteen of these plans come from the PPD; the variables for the other seventy-eight were newly collected for the analysis.[18]

17. Reviewers have noted that a lower rate might have curtailed benefit expansions.

18. For the specifics of the sample plans, see Center for Retirement Research at Boston College (2011d).

Figure 4-6. *Aggregate Funded Ratios for State- and Locally Administered Pension Plans, 2006 and 2010*

Percent

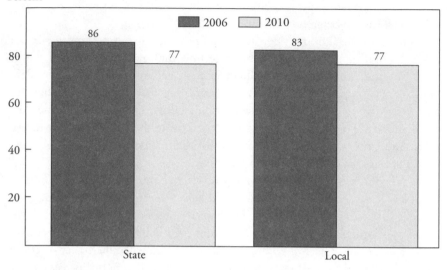

Although locally administered plans tend to be small on average, they range enormously in size. Three plans—the New York City Employee Retirement System, the New York City Teachers plan, and the Los Angeles County Employee Retirement System—had assets in excess of $30 billion. The three smallest plans—Dover (Del.) General Employee Pension Plan, Greenville City (S.C.) Fire Department's Pension Plan, and Bismarck City (N.D.) Employees' Pension Plan—each hold less than $50 million.

Funded Ratios

Figure 4-6 presents the aggregate funding information for state- and locally administered plans for 2006 and 2010. For both state and local plans, funded levels dropped from the mid-80 percent range in 2006 to 77 percent in 2010, when liabilities are discounted by the expected long-term rate of return. Of course, the magnitude of the liabilities would be larger and the funded ratios lower if liabilities were discounted by the riskless rate. But the major message from the exercise is that the experience of local plans on average has been very similar to that of state plans.

The pattern does vary among the three main types of locally administered plans: general employees, teachers, and police/fire employees. Of the three, general

Figure 4-7. *Funded Ratios for Locally Administered Plans by Type of Pension Plan, 2006 and 2010*

Percent

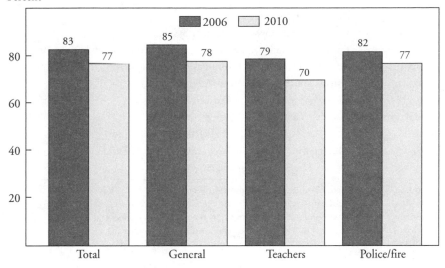

Source: Center for Retirement Research at Boston College (2011d).

employees are the best funded, while teachers' plans have the lowest funded ratio and suffered the greatest decline between 2006 and 2010 (see figure 4-7).

Finally, states and localities have nearly the same percentage of fully funded plans; localities have more plans with mid-level funding and a greater percentage of plans with very low levels of funding. The plans with the lowest-funded ratios are listed in table 4-3.[19]

The ARC

While the funded ratio provides a snapshot, the question remains about the extent to which the plan sponsor has a funding strategy and is sticking to it. As discussed, the key measure of funding discipline is whether the sponsor makes the ARC. Because of the deterioration in the funded status of plans, the ARC increased over the four-year period at both the state and local levels. In addition to change over time, it is important to note that the ARC at the local level is substantially larger than at the state level (see figure 4-8). A part of the explanation is

19. The Portland (Ore.) Fire and Police Disability Retirement Fund has a funded ratio of less than 1 percent because the sponsor purposely finances the plan on a pay-as-you-go basis. For this reason, it is not included in the table.

Table 4-3. *Locally Administered Plans with the Lowest Funded Ratios, 2010*

State	Plan	Funded ratio
Georgia	Atlanta Board of Education Fund[a]	17.4
Rhode Island	Providence Employees Retirement System	34.0
Pennsylvania	Pittsburgh Municipal, Police, and Firemen Pension Funds	34.3
Arkansas	Little Rock City Police Pension and Relief Fund[b]	39.0
Nebraska	Omaha Police and Fire Pension Fund	39.5
Delaware	Dover General Employee Pension Plan	43.7
Pennsylvania	Philadelphia Municipal Retirement System	47.0
Arkansas	Little Rock City Firemen's Relief and Pension Fund[b]	48.0
Illinois	Chicago Municipal Employees Annuity Benefit Fund	50.8
Nebraska	Omaha Employees Retirement System	52.9

Source: Center for Retirement Research at Boston College (2011d).

a. Most Atlanta school employees are covered by the Georgia Teachers Retirement System (TRS). The Atlanta Board of Education Fund is administered by the City of Atlanta General Employees' Pension Fund for the minority of school district employees who are not covered under the TRS.

b. Closed to new hires in 1983.

that police and fire plans, which are more common at the local level, are expensive because participants retire at a younger age and receive benefits for a longer time. But the ARC for general employees and teachers is also more expensive at the local level. This pattern may reflect lack of Social Security coverage at the local level.[20]

Figure 4-9 shows the percentage of the ARC paid by state- and locally administered plans. While sponsors at the state level significantly reduced the share of ARC paid, locally administered plans appeared to do a better job in covering the ARC. Therefore, while local plans in general have a higher ARC per dollar of payroll, they also contribute a higher percentage of total ARC each year. These offsetting factors explain why the funded ratios for local plans declined less between 2006 and 2010 than state plans.

In short, while press accounts would suggest that locally administered plans would be significantly less well funded than those administered by the state, the sample of ninety-seven plans from forty states indicates that, in 2010, locally administered plans were as well funded as state plans. A number of city plans

20. An inquiry was sent out to the seventy-two localities in the sample, and fourteen responded. Among the plans in these localities, half were not covered by Social Security. Interestingly, this lack of coverage does not necessarily coincide with the situation for state-administered plans. For example, Atlanta general employees and police and fire personnel are not covered by Social Security, while employees of the State of Georgia are covered. Similarly, in Florida, employees of the city of Jacksonville are not covered while their counterparts who work for the state are covered.

Figure 4-8. *Annual Required Contribution as a Percentage of Payroll for State- and Locally Administered Pension Plans, 2006 and 2010*

Percent

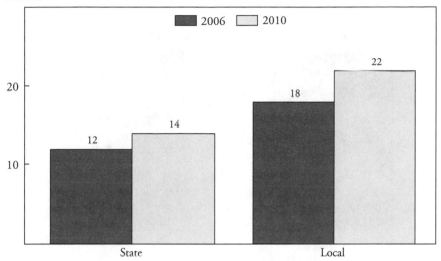

Source: Center for Retirement Research at Boston College (2011d).

are significantly underfunded, however, and will require substantial increases in their contribution rates to eliminate the unfunded liability.

The Role of Unions

Although, in the regression results reported earlier, union strength did not appear to have a statistically significant effect on the percentage of ARC paid and thereby on the funded status of state and local plans across the country, governors in several states launched initiatives to curb collective bargaining as part of their response to the sharp decline in pension funding.[21] The implication is that unions have contributed to the problem—if not through their impact on the ARC or funding then by pushing up state and local pension benefits. The question is whether any evidence supports this concern.

Two facts about the public sector relative to the private sector are undeniable. First, pensions in the public sector are more generous. They are more generous in the sense that a greater share of public sector workers have an

21. Wisconsin, Michigan, and Oklahoma passed laws in 2011 eliminating or curtailing collective bargaining of wages and/or benefits. See National Conference of State Legislatures (2011).

Figure 4-9. *Percentage of Annual Required Contribution Paid by State- and Locally Administered Pension Plans, 2006 and 2010*

Percent

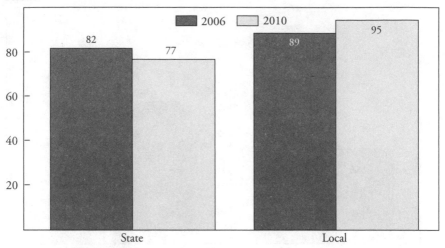

Source: Center for Retirement Research at Boston College (2011d).

employer-sponsored plan and, despite significant employee contributions, employer costs are higher in the public sector than the private. Second, the level of unionization in the public sector is much higher. While union membership in the private sector fell from 35 percent of the workforce in the 1950s to 7 percent in 2010, the rate in the public sector increased from about 10 percent in the 1950s to 38 percent today (see figure 4-10). Union membership varies by region and type of job; for example, public safety employees tend to be more unionized than general employees. The question is whether the second factor—union strength—explains the first—generous pensions. The following discussion attempts to sort out the role of unions in influencing pension benefits, wages, and the size of the workforce.

Pension Benefits

Figure 4-11 shows the average pension benefit over the period 1993–2010. Two interesting facts emerge. First, the average annual benefit in 2010 was $24,000, a figure substantially lower than most press reports would suggest. Second, the trend suggests a period of slower growth (1993–98), a period of rapid growth (1999–2003), and then a period of stability (2004–08). To figure out what was going on, an equation was estimated to explain the average annual rate of growth in each state over each of these three periods. Focusing on states, as opposed to

Figure 4-10. *Wage and Salary Workers in Unions, 1940–2010*[a]

Percent

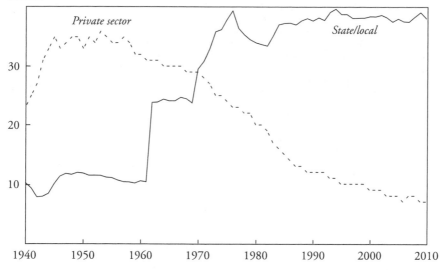

Sources: Troy and Sheflin (1985); U.S. Department of Labor, *Current Employment Statistics* (1939–83); and Hirsch and Macpherson (1983–2010).

a. The percent in unions shown for state and local workers before 1962 includes federal workers. The jump in union membership between 1961 and 1962 is due to the inclusion of associations, such as the National Education Association, which were previously excluded.

plans, was necessary because consistent plan data are not available going back to the 1990s. Five variables were thought to be important.

UNIONIZATION. The recent actions by governors would suggest that union power led to increases in pension benefits. But pension benefits are usually set by statute, which means that nonunion public employees, as well as union members, can lobby for benefit increases, so union strength may not be a factor.[22] Unionization is measured as the share of the public workforce that is a member of a union (see appendix 4B for alternative definitions of unionization).

CHANGE IN THE FUNDED RATIO. Stories abound about how overfunding can result in a push to liberalize benefits.[23] Indeed, much of the expansion in

22. Zorn (1990–2000).
23. For example, see the history of pension changes in Arizona State Retirement System (2011); Teacher Retirement System of Texas (1999); Tennessee Consolidated Retirement System (2010); and Wyoming Retirement System (2005).

Figure 4-11. *Average State and Local Pension Benefit, 1993–2010*

Thousands of 2010 dollars

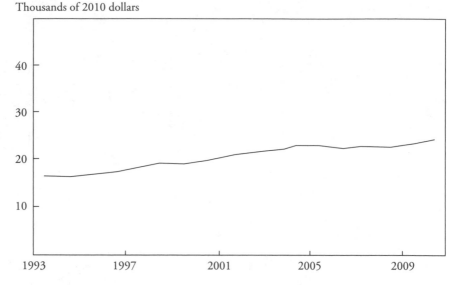

Source: Author's calculations from U.S. Census Bureau, *State and Local Government Public-Employee Retirement Systems* (1993–10).

California in the 1990s is attributed to the plans reporting funded ratios in excess of 100 percent.[24] However, the effect is not symmetric because most states cannot reduce benefits for current employees. Thus the variable is equal to 1 if the funded ratio increased, and zero otherwise. This change is calculated over the four years before the relevant benefit growth period. That is, for 2004–08, whether the funded ratio increased or not would be determined over the period 2000–03.

MEAN REVERSION. Some experts suggest that changes in states' pension policies are driven by what is going on around them. If neighboring states are raising benefits, then the lagging state will follow. To capture this phenomenon, this variable takes on a value of 1 if the state's pension benefit is lower than the average for the region in the four years before the relevant growth period. That is, for the 2004–08 period, the mean reversion variable reflects the situation over the period 2000–03. If a state starts behind, it is more likely to raise benefits.

RATIO OF DEBT TO REVENUE. For politicians to expand pension benefits, the state's financial accounts, as well as the pension fund, have to be in good order. One key to fiscal well-being is its debt burden. This variable is the average ratio of

24. Little Hoover Commission (2011).

Figure 4-12. *Impact of Selected Factors on the Average Annual Growth Rate of State and Local Pension Benefits, 1994–98, 1999–2003, and 2004–08*[a]

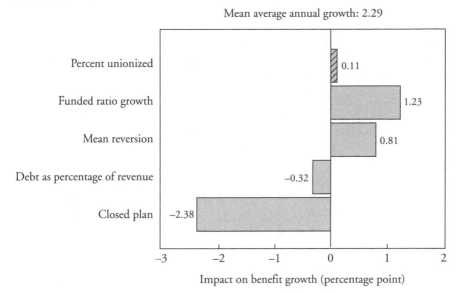

Mean average annual growth: 2.29

Impact on benefit growth (percentage point)

Source: Center for Retirement Research at Boston College (2011g).

a. Solid bars indicate that the coefficient is statistically significant at the 90 percent level or higher. Standard errors have been adjusted for state-level clustering.

debt to revenue for the four years before the relevant benefit growth period. If a larger debt burden does restrain benefit growth, the coefficient would be negative.

CLOSED PLAN. Some states have closed one or more of their defined benefit plans to new entrants. One would not expect benefits to increase under these circumstances. The variable is set equal to 1 if the state has a closed plan in the four years preceding the benefit growth period.

The results suggest that an increase in the funded ratio and catching up with the neighbors—that is, mean reversion—are important factors in explaining the growth in public sector benefits (see figure 4-12). In addition, states with a higher ratio of debt to revenue and with a closed plan experience less benefit growth. But union strength does not have a statistically significant effect. This finding is consistent with another recent study that was also unable to detect any impact of unions on pensions.[25]

25. See Schieber (2011).

Normal Cost

It could be possible that unions do not affect the *growth* in benefits because states with high levels of unionization always had a more generous benefit formula. In other words, unions pressed for high benefit factors early and therefore did not need to push for rapid growth. To test this hypothesis, another regression was estimated to identify the factors that affect the generosity of benefits. Generosity is measured as normal cost—the amount needed to be put aside in a given year to cover benefits earned that year—as a percentage of payrolls. By controlling for payrolls, the analysis focuses on the differences in benefits due to a more generous formula as opposed to the effect of higher wages feeding into the formula. The following variables are included in this equation:

UNIONIZATION. Unionization is measured slightly differently for this exercise. Because normal cost data are available only for those plans included in the PPD, the degree of unionization pertains only to plans included in the sample rather than the state's entire public sector workforce.[26] Again, if unions affect the level of benefits, the coefficient would be positive.

SOCIAL SECURITY COVERAGE. Roughly 30 percent of public sector workers are not covered by Social Security. The plans for these workers would be expected to be more generous since these public employees have no other source of retirement income. Social Security coverage is measured as the percentage of workers covered, so the coefficient would be negative: the more workers covered by Social Security, the less need for higher benefits.

POLICE/FIRE PLANS. Plans for police and fire personnel are considerably more expensive than those for teachers or general employees because public safety workers retire at a much younger age. Therefore states with more workers in police and fire plans would have a higher average normal cost, and the coefficient would be positive.

NUMBER OF SYSTEMS. The normal cost of plans at the local level tends to be higher than those administered by the state.[27] Part of the explanation is police

---

26. Because the PPD does not contain information on the unionization of plan members, it was necessary to rely on the NBER's Collective Bargaining Law Dataset, which can be merged with the PPD based on occupation (general employees, teachers, or police and fire personnel) and jurisdiction (state- or locally administered plan). Plans where members are allowed to collectively bargain are assumed to be fully unionized.

27. Center for Retirement Research at Boston College (2011d).

Figure 4-13. *Impact of Selected Factors on Normal Cost as a Percentage of Payroll, 2001–08*[a]

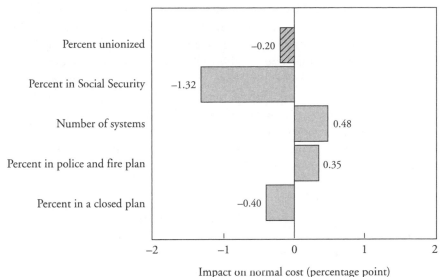

Mean normal cost as a percentage of payroll: 11.70

Impact on normal cost (percentage point)

Source: Center for Retirement Research at Boston College (2011g).

a. Solid bars indicate that the coefficient is statistically significant at the 90 percent level or higher. The results shown are for a one standard-deviation change. Standard errors have been adjusted for state-level clustering. Additional controls not depicted include a vector of year dummy variables. Percent unionized reflects the percentage of those state and local workers captured in the *Public Plans Database* who are allowed to collectively bargain under state law. West Virginia is omitted from 2001 through 2003 owing to data unavailability.

and fire plans as discussed above, but local plans for general employees and teachers also have higher normal cost. Therefore states with many local plans would tend to have higher normal cost, and the coefficient would be positive.

CLOSED PLAN. If the state has closed the plan to new entrants, it has probably not increased benefits over time. As a result, normal cost would be expected to be lower and the coefficient negative.

This simple equation explains more than a third of the variation in normal cost for the fifty states over the 2001–08 period. And Social Security coverage, number of systems, percentage in police and fire plans, and whether the plan is closed all have the expected effects and are statistically significant (see figure 4-13). But union strength does not appear to have a direct impact on the generosity of benefits.

Wages and Workforce

If union strength does not affect pension benefit growth or generosity, could it have an impact on wages, which are determined through bargaining rather than legislation? To test this hypothesis, an equation was estimated over the period 2001–08 to explain the ratio of public to private sector wages[28]—where private sector wages serve as a control for variations in the cost of living among states. The results suggest that after adjusting for differences in education, experience, percentage of the workforce that is female, and percentage of the total workforce in manufacturing—all of which have the expected and statistically significant effect—union strength has an important independent effect on the ratio of public sector to private sector wages. On average over the 2001–08 period, public sector wages were 93 percent of those in the private sector. Increasing the percentage of membership in a union by one standard deviation— that is bringing it from 33 percent to 50 percent—raises the ratio of public to private wages to about 96 percent.

One last thought. Some of the literature for the private sector, though not for the public sector, suggests that unions try to protect their existing workers by limiting the number of employees. The notion is that the smaller the workforce, the easier it is to preserve wages and benefits.[29] The results show some support for the hypothesis that unions hold down the number of public sector workers. On average, state and local workers accounted for 14 percent of the workforce. Increasing the share membership in a union by one standard deviation reduces the state and local share of the workforce by 0.82 percentage point.

A Possible Story

The empirical analysis presented above is by no means definitive; rather, it should be viewed as the beginning of a conversation. That said, what is the best way to explain what could be going on?

One known fact is that pensions in the public sector are more generous than those in the private sector. That outcome could be the result of pensions being the avenue of least resistance when public employees deal with state and local employers. It is simply easier to offer employees a dollar of future pension benefits than to pay a dollar of wages, given the flexibility that public sector employers have in terms of funding their pension obligations. Interestingly, within the public sector, the generosity of the pension formula does not appear to differ between states with high levels of unionization and those with low levels. This result is most likely explained by the fact that pensions are legislated, not

---

28. The wage ratio variable is for full-time workers only.
29. See Freeman and Medoff (1984); Freeman and Valletta (1988); and Zax (1985).

bargained, and the power to influence legislators is not simply related to membership figures. Particular groups can have disproportionate influence if they are articulate, politically active, locally well respected, and organized, even if their numbers are small when measured on a statewide basis.

In contrast to pensions, public sector wages are often bargained. And the known fact here is that the average wage in the public sector is below that in the private sector, taking into account that public sector workers have more education and experience. Public sector workers likely face substantial resistance to wage increases. Such an increase is very visible to taxpayers, and politicians may be unwilling to use their capital to argue the case for higher wages. Thus, the degree of success in the bargaining arena may well depend on the strength of union membership.

The last piece of the story is even more tentative—that is, an increase in union membership is associated with a decrease in the relative number of public sector workers. Such a finding would not be surprising in the private sector where, under a monopolistic model of price and quantity setting, unions hold down the number of workers in order to extract wage concessions from employers.[30] The results in the public sector, however, are less consistent.[31] And union representatives maintain that they never deliberately try to restrict hiring and often argue for more adequate staffing to meet program objectives. But given that unions appear to raise wages, reductions in employment would not be unexpected.

Conclusion

The funded status of state and local plans is often headline news. As of 2010, plan assets amount to 76 percent of liabilities, when liabilities are discounted by the plan's investment return assumption, typically around 8 percent. Funded ratios, however, ranged from 37 percent to 100 percent. This chapter explored the reasons for such sharply divergent outcomes. It turns out that the states with seriously underfunded plans, such as Illinois, Kentucky, Louisiana, New Jersey, and Pennsylvania, have behaved badly. They have either not made the required contributions or played with assumptions so that their contribution

30. See Freeman and Medoff (1984); and Freeman and Valetta (1988). A study by Zax (1985) finds that the more favorable the legal environment for unions, which the author defines as the adoption of a union contract, the higher the public sector wages and employment. Freeman and Valetta (1988) look at the legal environment and the presence of a union contract separately. Again, they find that municipalities with union contracts have higher public wages and a greater number of public employees. But among those municipalities with contracts, strong unions exercise monopoly power, trading lower employment for higher wages. Thus, some precedent exists for the finding of a negative impact of unions on employment, but the results still need more explaining.

31. Freeman and Valetta (1988).

requirements are not meaningful. Similarly they have run up large non-pension debt. Fiscal discipline simply appeared not to be part of the state's culture.

It would be a mistake to conclude that all state and local plans are in trouble. Several states—Delaware, Florida, Georgia, North Carolina, and Tennessee—have done a good job of providing reasonable benefits, paying their required contribution, and accumulating plan assets.

Finally, it is impossible to link poorly funded plans with the two popularly cited sources of the problem: (1) discounting liabilities by the long-run expected rate of return instead of the riskless rate; or (2) the collective bargaining activities of unions. The poorly funded plans did not come close to surmounting the lower hurdle associated with a high discount rate; raising the hurdle is unlikely to have improved their behavior.[32] And union strength simply did not show up as a statistically significant factor in any of the empirical analysis. This result, while consistent with findings of other researchers, was surprising; future work using different measures of union power or more complicated lag structures may come to different conclusions.

In short, the funded status of state and local plans today primarily reflects the sponsor's past and present attitude toward managing its pension and non-pension finances.

32. Some argue, however, that the public can tolerate only so much bad behavior, in which case raising the bar by using the riskless rate may have forced the bad states to "jump" a little higher.

Appendix 4A. Regression Results

Table 4A-1. *Factors Associated with Making the Annual Required Contribution, 2005–09*[a]

Variable	Marginal effect
Use projected unit credit (PUC) method	−0.532***
	(0.157)
State debt to gross state product (GSP)	−6.449**
	(2.799)
Percentage of employees covered by Social Security	−0.449**
	(0.229)
State has a defined contribution (DC) plan	−0.381**
	(0.158)
Annual required contribution (ARC) over payroll	−0.274
	(0.249)
Teachers plan	−0.113
	(0.096)
Police and fire plan	0.296***
	(0.076)
Employees/retirees on board	−0.223
	(0.317)
Allowed to collectively bargain	0.221
	(0.193)
Pseudo *R*-squared	0.225
Number of observations	94

Sources: Author's calculations from *Public Plans Database* (2005–09); and U.S. Census Bureau, *State and Local Government Finances* (2005–09).

a. Standard errors clustered at the state level are in parentheses. The marginal effects are significant at the 1 percent level (***) or 5 percent level (**). For continuous variables, the marginal effect is for a one-unit change from the mean. For dummy variables, the marginal effect is for a change from 0 to 1.

Table 4A-2. *Summary Statistics for Regression on Making the Annual Required Contribution (ARC), 2005–09*

Variable	Mean	Standard deviation	Minimum	Maximum
Made the ARC	0.606	0.491	0	1
Use PUC method	0.138	0.347	0	1
State debt to GSP	0.080	0.035	0.0175	0.1918
Percent of employees covered by Social Security	0.721	0.292	0	1
State has a DC plan	0.245	0.432	0	1
ARC over payroll	0.147	0.149	0.001	1.182
Teachers plan	0.309	0.464	0	1
Police and fire plan	0.096	0.296	0	1
Employees/retirees on board	0.561	0.237	0	1
Allowed to collectively bargain	0.851	0.358	0	1

Sources: Author's calculations from *Public Plans Database* (2005–09); and U.S. Census Bureau, *State and Local Government Finances* (2005–09).

Table 4A-3. *Factors Associated with the Funded Ratio, 2010*[a]

Variable	Coefficient
Use PUC method	−11.538***
	(3.422)
Made the ARC	6.809*
	(3.490)
Separate investment council	3.580
	(3.096)
Large plan	5.080*
	(2.540)
Age of system	−0.246**
	(0.098)
Use 1983 mortality table	−13.294**
	(5.645)
Constant	88.703***
	(6.649)
R-squared	0.315
Number of observations	126

Sources: Author's calculations from *Public Plans Database* (2005–10).

a. Standard errors clustered at the state level are in parentheses. The coefficients are significant at the 1 percent level (***), 5 percent level (**), or 10 percent level (*). For continuous variables, the coefficient is for a one unit change from the mean. For dummy variables, the coefficient is for a change from 0 to 1.

Table 4A-4. *Summary Statistics for Regression on the Funded Ratio, 2010*

Variable	Mean	Standard deviation	Minimum	Maximum
Funded ratio	75.681	15.623	37.399	121.171
Use PUC method	0.135	0.343	0	1
Made the ARC	0.270	0.446	0	1
Separate investment council	0.349	0.479	0	1
Large plan	0.333	0.473	0	1
Age of system	63.460	19.756	10	121
Use 1983 mortality table	0.048	0.214	0	1

Source: Author's calculations from *Public Plans Database* (2005–10).

Appendix 4B. Measuring Union Power

Studies looking at collective bargaining in the public sector have traditionally relied on two broad measures of union strength.[a]

The first is membership, which can be measured in two ways:

—percentage of the public workforce that has membership in a union, and

—percentage of the public workforce covered by a union contract.

The first variable includes only workers who pay union dues, while the second captures those who do not pay dues but still benefit from the union contract. Both of these variables come from tabulations of the *Current Population Survey*'s outgoing rotation files.[b]

The second broad measure of union strength is labor law. Recent studies have defined this measure by four variables listed in descending order of union strength:

—duty to collectively bargain;

—right to collectively bargain;

—right to work; and

—prohibited from collectively bargaining.

"Duty to collectively bargain" states are required by law to negotiate contracts with the union, while "Right to collectively bargain" states are allowed, but not required, to bargain. In both cases, the state can either allow or disallow strikes. Right-to-work states allow public employees to choose whether or not to join a union and preclude penalties for those who do not join. The most stringent law prohibits any collective bargaining whatsoever. These four variables are reported in the National Bureau of Economic Research's *Public Sector Collective Bargaining Law Data Set*.[c]

A recent study found a strong correlation between membership and labor law. Specifically, union membership is much higher in states where the legal environment is favorable toward unions.[d] In addition, data on union membership are available annually, while the legal variables have only been collected until 1996. For these reasons, the analysis uses the simple union membership variable instead of the more complicated legal variables.

---

a. See Ashenfelter (1971); Belman, Heywood, and Lund (1997); Farber (2005); Freeman (1986); Freeman and Valletta (1988); and Zax (1985).

b. Hirsch and Macpherson (1983–2010) perform these tabulations annually and make them available online.

c. The data set was originally collected by Freeman and Valletta (1988) for the years 1955 and 1984, and the data were updated through 1996 by Kim Rueben of the Urban Institute. The data contain nuanced information on the four basic variables described here.

d. Farber (2005) looks at averages across states from 1983 to 2004 and finds that union coverage is 17 percent in states that prohibit collective bargaining versus 50 to 75 percent in states that are required to bargain.

5

Are Public Plans Budget Busters?

While the previous chapter explored the state of funding among state and local plans, this chapter looks at current and future pension expense as a share of state and local budgets. The important question for policymakers is whether spending on pensions will squeeze out other priorities. Such a squeeze could result from the need to compensate for past shortfalls in the case of severely underfunded plans or from the demands of relatively expensive plans even if they are fairly well funded.

The chapter proceeds as follows. The first section provides an overview of state and local finances, highlighting the structural problem of slow-growing revenues and rapidly increasing expenditures. The second section turns to the specific issue of pensions and describes studies projecting the year when plan assets will be exhausted, as well as the limitations of those studies. Concluding that most plans are likely to muddle through and not run out of money, the third section investigates how burdensome these plans would be on state and local budgets if they began to fully fund their pensions once the economy recovers. This exercise covers current and future pension expense as a percentage of own-source revenue for all plans in the *Public Plans Database* in aggregate and for a sample of six states: Florida and Delaware (states with modest plans with a commitment to funding), Illinois and New Jersey (states with moderately expensive plans that have assiduously avoided funding), and California and New York (states with expensive plans that take funding seriously). Since one approach adopted by troubled states, such as Illinois and New Jersey, is to issue pension obligation bonds to alleviate their unfunded liability problem, the fourth section explores the issues associated with these instruments. The fifth section considers the possibility that pensions could squeeze operating budgets indirectly by raising the cost of non-pension-related debt.

Three major conclusions emerge from this chapter. First, pension contributions in 2009—the latest year for which budget data are available—accounted for only a small share (4.6 percent) of state and local revenue. They will account for more in the future. How much more depends crucially on how much sponsors earn on plan assets. If they earn the expected return of 8 percent, the share of the revenue required to fully fund their plans will be modest (5.1 percent). If they earn only 6 percent, the share will be greater (9.5 percent). If they earn only 4 percent, pension costs will rise to 14.5 percent of budgets.

Second, the picture varies enormously by state. Well-run plans will see little increase in the share of their revenue devoted to pensions. States that have systematically avoided funding, such as Illinois, will see pension costs soak up a huge share of future revenues. Illinois may indeed exhaust its pension assets and be forced to revert to pay-as-you-go. New Jersey would be in a similar position had it not in 2011 eliminated cost-of-living adjustments (COLAs), raised contribution rates for all employees, increased the retirement age for new hires, and adopted an ambitious funding schedule. If it adheres to the recent funding legislation, its pension costs as a percentage of budget will be about average. If, as in the past, it fails to make funding payments, the outlook will be much bleaker. California is unique; it has one of the most generous pension systems in the country, and the retroactive increase has left the state and many localities with huge unfunded liabilities. New York, in contrast, has expensive plans, and its commitment to funding is a significant burden on participating localities.

Third, as in the case of funding, the two factors highlighted in the introduction as the source of the problem—discounting obligations by the long-run expected rate of return instead of the riskless rate and the collective bargaining activities of unions—do not add much to the story. The shenanigans in Illinois and New Jersey, for example, have more to do with politicians behaving irresponsibly than with understating liabilities or with union power. Changing the discount rate or limiting union bargaining power does not provide a way forward. States where pensions are budget busters will have to make tough decisions that distribute the pain equitably among current retirees, current employees, future employees, and current and future taxpayers.

Background on State and Local Budgets

State and local governments are the main source of financing for K–12 education, public colleges and universities, health care, transportation, public safety,

Figure 5-1. *State and Local Tax Receipts, 2001–11*

Billions of 2011 dollars

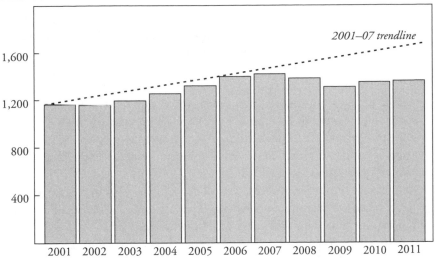

Source: U.S. Bureau of Economic Analysis (2011); and author's calculations.

and many other services.[1] They pay for these services mostly through fees and taxes, primarily income, sales, and property taxes, and revenues received from the federal government. Unlike the federal government, states must balance their budgets on an annual basis. States face two types of problems: a shortfall in revenues due to the Great Recession and a long-term mismatch between the growth in revenues and the growth in expenditures.

State and local revenue declined sharply as unemployment started to climb in the wake of the financial collapse (see figure 5-1). High unemployment and economic uncertainty, combined with households' drop in wealth due to the financial crisis and the collapse in housing prices, depressed consumption and reduced sales tax receipts. Income taxes also fell as workers lost their jobs. At the same time, the weak economy increased the demand for Medicaid and other services provided by the states. The American Recovery and Reinvestment Act initially cushioned the shortfalls, but many of its programs ended in 2011. To balance their budgets, states were forced to raise revenues, cut expenditures, and

1. The following discussion draws heavily on publications from the Center for Budget and Policy Priorities. See Williams (2012); McNichol, Oliff, and Johnson (2012); and Lav and McNichol (2011).

dip into rainy-day funds. States started to see stronger-than-expected revenue growth in late 2011, but their finances are still suffering from the most severe economic crisis since the Great Depression.

Even once the economy recovers, most states will face structural deficits because their annual revenue growth will lag behind the annual increase in the cost of services. To a significant extent, this problem reflects the rapid increase in health care costs, which states have limited ability to control. The Affordable Care Act of 2010 is intended to reduce the annual growth rate, but that is not going to happen in the next few years. In addition to health care, the costs to states and localities of K–12 education have grown faster than the economy over the past twenty years. Since education and health care expenditures account for more than half of state budgets and more than a third of local budgets, this growth creates a serious budget challenge.

At the same time that the cost of services is rising rapidly, states are relying on revenue systems that have remained largely static for the past fifty years. Yet during this time the world has changed dramatically. Services have increased relative to goods; Internet sales have become an important source of commerce; and income has become more concentrated among the wealthy. But state revenue systems have not responded. Few states tax the sales of services to the same extent that they tax tangible goods. Most Internet sales go untaxed. And most states have failed to tax the rapidly growing incomes of the top 5 percent or 1 percent of earners. In addition, states spend significant amounts through their tax code for purportedly public policy purposes; they offer big tax breaks for economic development, and they provide large tax exemptions for the elderly and for retirement income regardless of the income of the taxpayer.

In short, states and localities face both short-term cyclical and long-term structural budget pressures, aside from the issue of pensions. The question is how much pensions will add to these pressures. The first step toward answering this question is to look at studies that focus on the narrow issue of whether states and localities are going to exhaust their pension fund assets and be forced to provide benefits through operating budgets.

Will Some Plans Run Out of Money?

The simplest place to start investigating the exhaustion issue is to look at the ratio of plan assets to benefits for the 126 plans in the *Public Plans Database* (PPD). This ratio shows how long plans could—with no further investment returns, no additional contributions, and no growth in benefits—continue to pay benefits. In 2001, assets were nearly twenty-five times the annual benefit payments, suggesting that, with money on hand, state and local plans in the aggregate could continue to pay benefits for almost twenty-five years. In the

Figure 5-2. *Ratio of Market Assets of Public Pension Plans to Annual Benefit Payments, 2001–10*

Percent

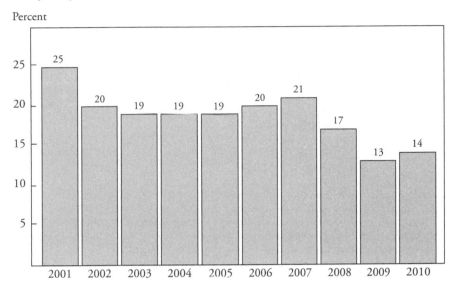

Source: Author's calculations from *Public Plans Database* (2001–10).

wake of the bursting of the dot.com bubble, this ratio dropped for the next few years to nineteen and was headed back up until the financial crisis of 2008. In 2010, the ratio was fourteen (see figure 5-2). As one would expect, plans are distributed around that average ratio. Kentucky ERS had a ratio of five, and twenty-seven plans—including large plans such as Illinois SERS and New Jersey PERS—had ratios between six and ten.

While the simple ratio is useful for describing trends over the last decade, in fact, plan sponsors will continue to make contributions, plans will earn returns on their assets, and benefit payments will grow as the baby-boom generation retires. Therefore, given realistic assumptions, how long before plans run out of money?

The answer to this question depends on how the exercise is structured. One approach is to adopt a "termination" framework, as suggested by Rauh (2009). This framework involves putting benefits earned to date and the existing assets in an "old" plan and creating a "new" plan in which all accruing benefits are covered by future normal cost contributions. The new plan will be fine, since it has no hangover liability and annual contributions will be set aside to cover accruing costs.[2] The old plan, however, is underfunded and, without additional

2. For the new plan to be fully funded, it must earn returns that correspond to its discount rate.

Table 5-1. *Exhaustion Date for State and Local Pension Plans under Ongoing and Termination Frameworks, by Rate of Return Earned on Pension Assets*[a]

| | Termination framework | | | Ongoing framework based on 2010 assets and contributions equal to | |
| Rate of return (percent) | Rauh | CRR | | | Historical percentage of ARC paid |
	2009 assets	2009 assets	2010 assets	Normal cost	
6	2021	2022	2026	2037	2043
8	2025	2024	2030	2046	2059
10	2030	2028	2043	Never	Never

Source: Center for Retirement Research at Boston College (2011a); and Rauh (2009).

a. "Termination" assumes that plans make future contributions exactly sufficient to cover the cost of future accruals. Benefit payments as calculated under an accumulated benefit obligation (ABO) concept are paid solely out of existing assets and returns on those assets. "Ongoing" assumes that future contributions are available to cover benefit payments for current and future employees.

contributions, will ultimately run out of money. The question is then, for how many years can the existing assets cover benefits promised to date in the old plan? The exercise involves calculating accrued benefits for current employees and estimating asset growth under a number of assumed rates of investment returns. (Note that this exercise has nothing to do with the debate about the appropriate rate for discounting liabilities but rather relates to how much income the plan's assets produce.) Rauh (2009) estimates that the exhaustion date for state and local plans as a group is 2021 with returns of 6 percent; 2025 with returns of 8 percent; and 2030 with returns of 10 percent. Estimates produced by the Center for Retirement Research at Boston College (CRR) under this same framework largely confirm those of Rauh (see table 5-1).

A critique of the termination framework is that it is an unrealistic approach for public plans. An alternative approach is to treat the plans as ongoing entities.[3] This approach to predicting exhaustion involves projecting benefit accruals for active current employees, adding new participants in the plan, and (to facilitate comparison with the Rauh study) assuming that the sponsor pays only the normal cost. Under the ongoing scenario, the exhaustion dates are 2037 with returns of 6 percent; 2046 with returns of 8 percent, and never with returns of 10 percent. Of course, using normal cost payments to cover current benefits

3. Center for Retirement Research at Boston College (2011a).

Figure 5-3. *Share of State and Local Pension Plans That Will Become Insolvent by Year under a Termination and an Ongoing Framework*[a]

Percent

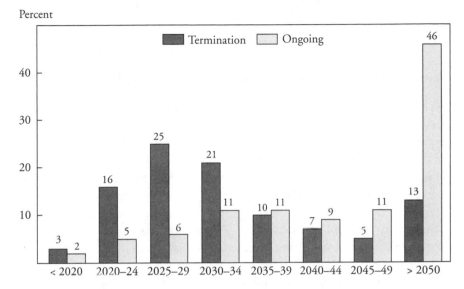

Source: Author's estimates based on *Public Plans Database* (2001–10); and Rauh (2009).

a. "Termination" assumes that plans make future contributions exactly sufficient to cover the cost of future accruals. Benefit payments under an ABO concept are paid solely out of existing assets and returns on those assets. "Ongoing" assumes that plans pay the normal cost in future years and that these monies are available to cover benefit payments for current and future employees.

rather than accumulating contributions in anticipation of future payments will worsen the funded status of plans. But the ongoing approach, even retaining the assumption that sponsors pay only the normal cost, shows that most plans will not be turning to current taxes to cover benefit payments.

Under either the termination approach or the ongoing approach, plans are distributed around the average exhaustion dates (see figure 5-3). As expected, the ongoing scenario shows far fewer plans exhausting their assets in the next ten years, suggesting that plans have more breathing room than the termination approach suggests. Even in the ongoing framework, however, a few plans—some large—may last for less than ten years. Remember, however, that this exercise assumes that sponsors pay only the normal cost and contribute nothing to amortize the unfunded liability. In fact, public plans as a group paid 80 percent of the annual required contribution (ARC) in 2010, about 80 percent of which constitutes the normal cost and the rest an amortization payment. In all likelihood, they will continue to pay more than the normal cost in the future. Thus the last column of table 5-1 shows exhaustion dates under the ongoing framework if plans were to contribute the historical percentage of ARC paid.[4] These dates are 2043 with returns of 6 percent; 2059 with returns of 8 percent, and never with returns of 10 percent. Overall, the numbers show that most state and local plans are likely to muddle through and not exhaust their assets.

Pension Expense as a Share of Total State/Local Budgets

Even if most plans are unlikely to run out of money, a decision to fully fund their commitments will mean that pension contributions will account for a larger share of state and local budgets in the future. First, as noted, states and localities have not been contributing their full ARC, so paying the full amount will require an increase in contributions. Second, the ARC has increased owing to the financial crisis and the poor performance of the stock market, which have increased the unfunded liability. Third, states have started to lower their assumed rate of return on assets. Lower assumed returns raise both the normal cost and the unfunded liabilities. The question is whether covering promised pension benefits will bust the budget.

Some of the rhetoric surrounding state and local pensions suggests that they already account for a major share of state and local budgets. In fact, in 2009 pensions accounted for 3.6 percent of state and local direct expenditures for the country as a whole (see figure 5-4). This share did not vary dramatically among states.[5] Of course, actual state and local expenditures do not reflect the full cost of pensions, because many plans do not pay 100 percent of the ARC. And if the ARC were calculated using a riskless rate instead of the long-run expected return on plan assets, the ARC would be substantially larger and the percentage of ARC paid even smaller, making the understatement more significant. But the actual expenditures are still a good grounding device.

Two studies—one by the Center for Retirement Research at Boston College and the other by Novy-Marx and Rauh[6]— have examined future pension expense

4. The contribution rate equals the 2010 ARC multiplied by the average percent of ARC paid over the past ten years.

5. It is also interesting to look at the pattern of contributions over time. For states and localities as a whole, contributions to pensions have ranged from 3 to 6 percent of their combined revenues. Contributions were about 4 percent from the mid-1950s to the mid-1970s, rose to 6 percent between the mid-1970s and mid-1980s when states and localities "got religion" about the importance of funding, then dropped back as the long bull market boosted asset prices. Long-run averages may not be meaningful, however, if the U.S. interest rates have been in a secular decline for thirty years. For those advocating the riskless rate for funding, actuaries have grossly overfunded in the 1980s and have underfunded in the past thirty years as interest rates have declined.

6. Center for Retirement Research at Boston College (2010b); Novy-Marx and Rauh (2011a).

Figure 5-4. *State and Local Government Direct Expenditure, by Type, 2009*[a]

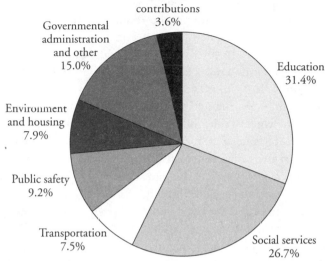

Source: Author's calculations from U.S. Census Bureau, *State and Local Government Finances* (2009); and U.S. Census Bureau, *State and Local Public-Employee Retirement Systems* (2009).
a. Total budget equals direct expenditures from the general fund, excluding capital outlays.

as a share of budgets.[7] The studies differ in four ways. First, they use different budget concepts: CRR focuses on the spending side—total noncapital expenditures—while Novy-Marx and Rauh use total own revenue, which excludes trust revenues (primarily the returns on pension fund assets) and intergovernmental revenues. (In 2009, the two amounts were quite close: $2.2 trillion for noncapital expenditures and $1.9 trillion for own revenues.) Second, they amortize different liability concepts: CRR uses the projected benefit obligation, the standard set by the Governmental Accounting Standards Board (GASB); Novy-Marx and Rauh use the accumulated benefit obligation, which does not include the effect of future salary increases and is preferred by many economists.[8] Third, CRR focuses solely on state and local pensions, while Novy-Marx and Rauh include the employer's share of payments into Social Security. As a result, Novy-Marx and Rauh start the exercise with retirement costs equal to 5.7 percent of state and local revenue. Finally, the two studies assume different rates for discounting

7. In both cases, projections made for sample plans are scaled to reflect the totals included in the Census.
8. See Brown and Wilcox (2009), Bulow (1982), and Gold and Latter (2008).

liabilities. Despite the differences, the calculations produce consistent numbers, with the difference in the reported values primarily reflecting the different interest rates used to discount the stream of benefit payments.

An update to the CRR study adopts the revenue approach advocated by Novy-Marx and Rauh. It assumes that pension contributions increase at historical rates between 2010 and 2014, after which states and localities start to pay the full ARC, amortizing their unfunded liabilities over a fixed thirty-year period.[9] Normal cost and unfunded liabilities are calculated under three rate of return assumptions: 8 percent, 6 percent, and 4 percent. Assuming an 8 percent return and discount rate, government contributions to pensions will rise from 4.6 percent of state and local revenue in 2009 to 5.1 percent in 2014. With a 6 percent return and discount rate, pension contributions would increase to 9.5 percent in 2014; and with a 4 percent return and discount rate to 14.5 percent. In all cases, the contribution rate remains constant thereafter for thirty years because contributions are set as a fixed percentage of payrolls, and payrolls are assumed to be a fixed percentage of state and local revenues.[10]

The Novy-Marx and Rauh study calculates benefits using a standardized 2 percent inflation assumption and then uses the Treasury inflation-linked securities (TIPS) yield curve to calculate the present value of future benefits. The TIPS curve corresponds to a 3.7 percent nominal rate for the average duration of liabilities. The results show contributions increasing from 5.7 percent of budgets to 14.2 percent, a rise of 8.5 percentage points. The results of the two studies appear relatively consistent. Assuming a 4 percent discount rate—very close to that used by Novy-Marx and Rauh—CRR shows contributions rising from 4.6 percent to 14.5 percent of state and local revenue, an increase of 9.9 percentage points.

In the end, policymakers will have to figure out whether the coming increased demand on state and local revenues will be big or small. That answer has little to do with how liabilities are discounted for valuation purposes but a lot to do with the return actually earned on pension assets. If plans end up earning nominal

---

9. Illinois and New Jersey do not follow the traditional thirty-year funding schedule described above. In Illinois, current legislation requires that the state plans become 90 percent funded by 2045 under GASB accounting standards. In 2003, Illinois issued $10 billion in pension obligation bonds, the proceeds of which reduced the unfunded liabilities of the state plans. Contribution rates in this state are therefore set as the minimum of either the statutory rate or the difference between the statutory rate and the amount required to service the debt. In New Jersey, 2010 legislation allowed the state to pay only one seventh of its full ARC in 2012. Each subsequent year's payment increases by an additional one seventh, until the full ARC is paid in 2018.

10. In reality, state and local payrolls as a percentage of operating budgets have steadily declined by a total of about 40 percent over the past fifty years. This decline is somewhat greater for states than for localities. If this trend continues, the assumption that payrolls remain a constant percentage of revenues in the future overstates the effect of pension contributions on future state and local budgets.

returns of 4 percent, their unfunded liabilities will increase and the ARC will rise. If low returns persist, sponsors may reduce their discount rate, thereby leading to an increase in the normal cost and a further increase in the ARC. With a low return, pension contributions will take up a large share of state and local revenues. On the other hand, if assets earn the assumed rate of return of 8 percent, pension costs will continue to account for a relatively modest share of revenues—rising from 4.6 percent of state and local revenues in 2009 to 5.1 percent in 2014, where it remains for the next thirty years.

Pension Expense as a Share of Budgets for Selected States

Aggregate data hide substantial variation. This section focuses on six states: Florida and Delaware (states with modest plans with a commitment to funding), Illinois and New Jersey (states with moderately expensive plans that have assiduously avoided funding), and California and New York (states with expensive plans where a commitment to funding is placing an enormous financial burden on localities). Table 5-2 summarizes the normal cost, percentage of ARC paid, and funded ratios for the plans included in the PPD in each state, as well as the contributions for those plans as a percentage of state and local revenue in 2009 and projected for the period 2014–44. The following section briefly summarizes how the plans in each state ended up where they are today.

Well-Run Systems

Florida is the poster child for a well-run pension system.[11] Interestingly, as recently as 1991, the Florida Retirement System (FRS) was only 60 percent funded. Part of the explanation for the system's improved funded status is the high returns experienced during the 1990s bull market. But constraints imposed by the legislature also played a major role. First, Florida made it difficult to expand benefits. Since 1976, the state has had a provision that requires any increase in pension benefits to be funded on a sound actuarial basis. Second, in 2000, Florida passed legislation that limited the extent to which surplus funding could be used to reduce contributions.[12] By keeping contributions and benefits steady in the period before 2008, Florida was in a good position to weather the financial collapse and ensuing recession. As a result, pension contributions

11. The Florida Retirement System (FRS) was established in 1970 when the legislature consolidated pensions for teachers, general employees, and police and fire personnel. One evaluation is provided for the plan, but contribution rates are set by statute for each class of employee. A potential flaw in the design of the Florida system is the opportunity to shift between the defined benefit plan and an optional defined contribution plan. In theory, the option could be quite expensive to the state (Lachance and Mitchell 2002), but so far few have taken advantage.

12. No offset was permitted for the first 5 percent of excess funding, and any offset on amounts above 5 percent had to be spread over a rolling ten-year period.

Table 5-2. *Plan Characteristics, 2010, and Contributions as a Percentage of State and Local Revenues, 2009 and 2014–44*[a]

| | Plan characteristics, 2010 (percent) | | | Contributions/revenue (percent) | | | |
| | | | | | Rate of return 2014–44 | | |
Government	Normal cost	Percentage of ARC paid 2005–10	Funded ratio	2009	8	6	4
U.S. total	13.6	85.0	76.1	4.6	5.1	9.5	14.5
Well run							
Florida	11.9	106.3	86.6	3.9	3.6[b]	6.7	10.3
Delaware	9.6	100.0	96.0	3.2	2.4[b]	5.5	9.3
Poorly run							
Illinois	16.6	62.5	53.5	7.7	9.6	14.2	20.4
New Jersey	11.0	40.2	70.4	3.5	6.1[c]	9.8	14.5
Expensive							
California	18.1	86.6	80.1	6.1	7.2	14.3	21.7
New York[d]	19.1	98.8	100.0	6.2	5.9	11.9	24.6

Sources: *Public Plans Database* (2010); U.S. Census Bureau, State and Local Government Finances (2009); and U.S. Census Bureau, State and Local Public-Employee Retirement Systems (2009).

a. Contribution rates are heavily dependent on funded ratios. The analysis estimates 2014 funded ratios following the methodology described in Center for Retirement Research (2012a). It assumes that, for each state, local plans follow the same funding trajectory as the weighted average of plans in the *Public Plans Database* (PPD). Similarly, the normal contribution rate is a weighted average of the rates reported by plans in the PPD. These rates reflect the most recent actuarial valuation report released by each plan.

b. The Florida Retirement System and the Delaware Public Employees' Retirement System are sufficiently well funded, so that, under an 8 percent discount rate, future required pension contributions decline as a share of revenue.

c. New Jersey contribution rates are for the fiscal years after 2018, when New Jersey legislation requires plans to fully pay the ARC.

d. New York uses the aggregate cost method, and therefore the numbers are not comparable to those of other states. However, funded ratios are available using entry-age normal for 2010, and they show a funded ratio of 91 percent. The projections are based on a weighted average contribution rate over the period, since contributions will trend over time.

in Florida are projected to actually decrease from 3.9 to 3.6 percent of state/local revenues, assuming liabilities are discounted by 8 percent; with a 6 percent assumption, pension costs rise to 6.7 percent.

Delaware is another system that professionals cite when queried about well-run plans. The Delaware state employees plan, which covers most of the public employees in the state, is one of the best-funded plans in the country. The funded ratio exceeded 100 percent for most of the 2000s and in 2010 was 96 percent. Funding is clearly a priority as the plan switched from a thirty-year to a

twenty-year amortization period in 2007. And when the plan was overfunded in the early 2000s and the required employer contribution was less than the normal cost rate, the plan set a minimum contribution rate of 2 percent.[13] Moreover, Delaware has reduced the assumed return on plan assets from 8.5 percent to 8 percent in 2004 and to 7.5 percent in 2011. The cost of the plan is modest, probably because the cost-of-living adjustment (COLA) is ad hoc. The plan paid no COLAs in 2002 or from 2007 to 2011. Observers attribute the good standing of the plan to the active participation of the business community on the board of trustees. The costs of the Delaware system will remain manageable even assuming low rates of return.

Poorly Run Systems

Illinois must take the prize for the worst-run state-administered pensions in the country. It has four major state-administered plans, three of which—Teachers' Retirement System (TRS), State Employees' Retirement System (SERS), and State Universities' Retirement System (SURS)—are among the ten worst-funded plans in the PPD sample, all with funded ratios under 50 percent.[14] The current situation reflects decades of inadequate funding and repeated expansions of pension benefits.

Part of the problem is that Illinois got a late start on funding. Until 1981, employer contributions covered current-year pension benefits, and only employee contributions were set aside for investments. This system remained in place (with employer contributions at their 1981 levels) until 1995 when the legislature established a funded ratio objective of 90 percent by 2045, with a fifteen-year phase-in to give the state time to adjust to the higher contribution. To reduce the ever-increasing unfunded pension liability, the legislature authorized a pension obligation bond of almost $10 billion in 2003. Part of the proceeds was used, however, to cover the state's required contributions in 2004 and 2005. In 2006, the governor signed legislation to reduce required payments in 2006 and 2007. Then came the financial collapse.

The shenanigans on the financing side were matched by repeated expansions of the benefit packages. For example, the benefit factor for TRS was increased in 1998, and an early retirement incentive program was introduced in 2002 for certain members of SERS and state employees covered by TRS. Moreover, the three major unfunded Illinois state-administered plans use the projected unit credit

13. Any contributions in excess of the normal cost go toward payment for health care benefits for retirees.

14. It appears to be a state-level problem, because a fourth state-administered plan (Municipalities), which is financed by local contributions, has a funded ratio of 83 percent.

(PUC) actuarial cost method, which backloads required contributions relative to the entry-age normal cost method and was shown in the previous chapter to be associated with poor funding practices in the state and local sector.[15]

Because Illinois has never seriously funded three of its four major state-administered plans, future contributions will put severe pressure on state and local revenues. Contributions are projected to rise from 7.7 percent to 9.6 percent of state and local revenues, assuming liabilities are discounted by 8 percent; with a 6 percent assumption, costs rise to 14.2 percent.

New Jersey is characterized as a poorly run system because of its performance over the past two decades. New Jersey did adopt significant pension legislation in 2011 that eliminated COLAs, raised contribution rates for all employees, increased the retirement age for new hires, and adopted a funding schedule that gradually raises the share of ARC paid to 100 percent over the next seven years.[16] The state issued revised 2010 numbers in August 2011 based on the legislated changes, and the revised numbers were used to forecast pension expense as a percentage of budgets. The real question is whether New Jersey will stick to its funding commitments (it hasn't done so for twenty years).

The funding history for New Jersey is just the opposite of that for Illinois; the New Jersey plans were well funded in the 1990s, after which their funding was systematically undermined by legislative actions. In 1992, the governor, facing a major budget deficit, increased the discount rate to 8.75 percent in order to reduce the pension contribution.[17] In 1994, legislation changed the actuarial method from the entry-age normal to the projected unit credit, which reduced the normal cost in the short term and set the stage for more rapid accruals in the future. In 1997, legislation did three things. First, it switched the valuation of plan assets from actuarial to market, which in a rapidly rising stock market produced much higher asset values. Second, it added $2.7 billion of pension obligation bond proceeds (issued at 7.5 percent) to the asset pile. (The problems associated with pension obligation bonds are discussed later in this chapter.) And third, it allowed any excess assets to offset government contributions. As a result of all the changes, New Jersey avoided paying anything into its largest plans

15. The use of the PUC method applies only to the normal cost. The open aggregate method is used to determine the amortization payment, which in Illinois represents the bulk of the contribution.

16. The reason for the phase-in is that New Jersey changed its actuarial cost method to a level dollar amortization method, which frontloads costs, unlike the more common percent-of-payroll approach. To fully fund under the new amortization schedule would have resulted in a substantial rise in employer contributions. As a result, the state plans to pay only one-seventh of the ARC in 2012 and to gradually increase to the full ARC in 2018. The target funded ratio for 2018 is 80 percent.

17. Benner (2009).

for almost ten years. On the employee side, successive legislation also reduced employee contributions.

While the state was avoiding pension contributions, the legislature repeatedly increased benefits. In 2001, the benefit factor was increased from 1.67 percent to 1.82 percent of final salary for current employees. The legislation also increased the retirement benefit for members with thirty-five or more years of service and reduced the age qualification from 60 to 55. The law also made a comparable percentage increase in the retirement allowances that existing retirees and beneficiaries received. In 2002, legislation provided early retirement incentives to employees who met certain age and service requirements.

With repeated benefit enhancements and virtually no employer contributions, the funded status declined sharply to below the national average when the financial crisis hit in 2008. Thus, in the case of New Jersey the financial crisis aggravated an already deteriorating situation. As noted above, the state passed significant pension legislation in 2011, and the projections for pension expense as a share of revenues are based on the revised numbers. If New Jersey sticks to its changes, pension expense will rise from 3.5 percent in 2009 to 6.1 percent in the period 2014–44, assuming an 8 percent discount rate; with a 6 percent assumption, costs rise to 9.8 percent.

Expensive Systems

California is in trouble because a retroactive expansion of benefits in the late 1990s made the state one of the most generous in the nation, but, unlike Illinois and New Jersey, it is not guilty of deliberately underfunding its plans. Nevertheless, pension commitments are putting enormous pressure on both state and local budgets in California.

California's public pensions are complex. Pension benefits differ from system to system, and sometimes within them. The two large state-administered systems are the California Public Employees' Retirement System (CalPERS) and California State Teachers Retirement System (CalSTRS). CalPERS not only covers state government workers but services the retirement programs of more than 2,000 local governments and school districts, which involve thirteen different benefit formulas with fifty-seven optional contract provisions.[18] Some counties and cities operate their own pension system, as does the University of California, but in all cases California benefits tend to be the highest in the country.[19]

18. Paul and Weinberg (2010).

19. State workers can retire at age 55 with a retirement payment of 2 percent of the highest final compensation for each year worked. Workers may retire at 50 with a reduced pension, and those who retire after 55 receive a higher percentage of pay (up to 2.5 percent at age 63 and above) for each year of service from the year they started their job until retirement. State employees are also covered by Social Security. Correctional officers, who are under the control of the governor and

Three factors—an enhanced incentive to promise pensions rather than pay wages from the Proposition 13 property tax limitation in 1978, a big retroactive pension benefit increase in 1999, and the financial collapse in 2008—have created the current situation in which pension costs are high, only partially funded, and set to consume an increasingly large share of state and local budgets.

Proposition 13 gave the legislature more responsibility over the financing of services and thereby shifted power from the locality to the state. At the same time, it made legislative action more difficult by requiring a two-thirds vote to raise tax revenues. The result was budget gridlock and fiscal gimmicks, such as handing out improved pensions in lieu of pay increases. Similarly, local governments, barred by Prop 13 from raising property taxes, often used promises of higher pensions to get through labor negotiations. In most—but not all—cases, however, the benefit promises were accompanied with funding commitments.

The break with prefunding occurred in 1999 when the governor and the legislature made up for a long freeze on state worker pay by approving a bill that raised pension benefits to their current high levels. The changes were made retroactive, thereby increasing the compensation for work done years or even decades earlier. Lawmakers accepted CalPERS's estimates that investment returns from the booming stock market would cover most of the costs of the higher benefits.

Thirteen years after the benefit expansion, the stock market has just reached its 1999 peak. Consequently, the required state pension contribution to CalPERS, measured as a percentage of payroll, has more than doubled. CalSTRS has suffered investment losses and will ask the legislature to sharply increase the state contribution to teacher retirement. And the University of California, which for twenty years has funded contributions out of investment earnings, is now seeking contributions from the state. The result is that contributions to California's plans, which amounted to 6.1 percent of California's state and local revenues in 2009, are scheduled to rise to 7.2 percent for the period 2014–44, assuming liabilities are discounted by 8 percent; with a 6 percent discount rate, costs will rise to 14.3 percent.

New York, like California, has expensive plans. These plans, however, are generally well funded, but the state's commitment to funding is placing an enormous pressure on the state and localities. The state-administered systems—New York State & Local Employees Retirement System, New York State & Local Police and Fire Retirement System, and New York State Teachers—are

---

legislature, may retire at age 50 with 3 percent for each year of service, the same as for many local police and fire personnel. The retirement plan for teachers is less generous. Educators can retire at 60 with 2 percent of highest pay credited for each year worked. They can receive up to an additional 0.4 percent for each year they work past age 60, or for having worked thirty years or more. Teachers do not participate in Social Security.

in particularly good shape. New York City plans are less well funded. But the overall picture is positive.

The New York State pensions have a unique governance structure. Instead of a board of trustees appointed by the executive and legislative branches, the New York State & Local Employees Retirement System and the New York State & Local Police and Fire Retirement System are governed by the state comptroller, an elected official who serves as the sole trustee. As an elected official, the comptroller has the independence to challenge attempts by the state government to skip or reduce contributions during economic downturns or stock market declines, such as in the early 1990s and at the end of 2003. On the other hand, the comptroller has acquiesced to reductions in contributions in the face of extraordinarily high returns during the stock market boom. Legislation passed in 2003 introduced a minimum contribution rate of 4.5 percent of payrolls to avoid such response to high returns in the future. The same legislation also contained some temporary relief.[20] But the commitment to funding is evident by the fact that in 2010 the three state plans were between 93 percent and 100 percent funded.[21] In contrast, the New York City plans, which amount to about 38 percent of the total city and state liabilities, were about 70 percent funded. But overall, New York, like California, has public pension plans that are very expensive yet fairly well funded. The burden that these plans impose on localities has received considerable publicity.[22] Projections show that contributions to New York plans, which amounted to 6.2 percent of New York's state and local revenues in 2009, are scheduled to dip slightly, to 5.9 percent, for the period 2014–44 assuming liabilities are discounted by 8 percent; with a 6 percent discount rate, costs will rise to 11.9 percent.

Exhausting Assets and Reverting to Pay-as-You-Go

The projections for the poorly managed, high-cost states suggest a very large increase in the share of the state and local budget that would need to be allocated to fund their pension promises. If policymakers were unable or unwilling to make such a commitment, what is the alternative? Promised benefits are legally protected and—perhaps with the exception of cost-of-living adjustments—will

20. To ease the pain of the high required rates in 2004–05, the 2003 legislation allowed local governments to bond any contributions in excess of 7 percent of payrolls, paying 8 percent interest on the amortized amount. Legislation passed in 2004 extended the ability to bond through 2007, but also raised the threshold to 10.5 percent of payrolls by 2007.

21. The New York State plans use an aggregate cost actuarial method, which does not separately identify an unfunded liability, so the funded ratio is always 100 percent. The numbers reported in the text, however, refer to the funded status of the state plans using the entry-age normal actuarial cost method.

22. Hakim (2012).

Figure 5-5. *Pay-as-You-Go (PAYGO) Contributions as a Share of State Revenue for the State of Illinois, by Rate of Return, 2009–44*[a]

Percent

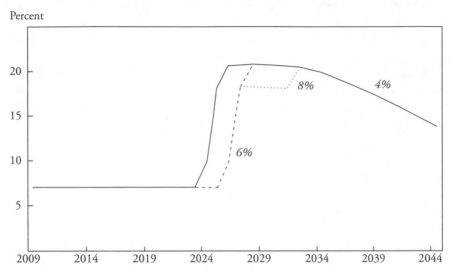

Source: Author's calculations from U.S. Census Bureau, *State and Local Government Finances* (2009) and U.S. Census Bureau, *State and Local Public-Employee Retirement Systems* (2009), Congressional Budget Office (2010), and *Public Plans Database* (2010).
    a. PAYGO costs for state-administered plans in Illinois.

be paid. One alternative is to contribute at current levels, run down assets, and then pay promised benefits on a pay-as-you-go basis. Take Illinois as an example. Figure 5-5 shows the pattern of expenditure as a percentage of the budget under a pay-as-you-go scenario. The pattern is complicated by the fact that Illinois has four main pension plans, and each of the three underfunded plans runs out of money at a different time.[23] Since the plan financed by localities is relatively well funded and the state government currently pays the majority of pension costs for the three poorly funded plans, the burden of covering benefits paid on a pay-as-you-go basis would fall primarily on the state. Pay-as-you-go contributions are projected to exceed 20 percent of the Illinois state budget by 2025.

The six examples of state public pension plans discussed above highlight the heterogeneity in the public sector. A large number of states are like Florida and Delaware, where pension promises are modest and the state has a commitment

23. Illinois Municipal Retirement Fund is entirely financed by localities. Illinois State Employees Retirement System and Illinois State University System are entirely financed by the state. Illinois Teachers Retirement System is financed jointly: 11.2 percent of contributions from localities and 88.8 percent from the state.

to funding. In those states, pensions will not significantly drain future budget resources. A few states, like Illinois and New Jersey, have deliberately avoided funding their pension commitments and have repeatedly enhanced pension benefits. Illinois is in serious trouble and faces enormous pressure on its budgets to meet its pension promises. New Jersey may have saved itself with the elimination of the COLAs, the increase in employee contributions, and an ambitious funding agenda. The question is whether all the provisions of the 2011 legislation hold. California is unique. It never deliberately underfunded its plans, but an enormous unpaid-for retroactive benefit increase at the end of the 1990s landed the state with very expensive plans and large unfunded liabilities. Add two financial crises and the state faces an unprecedented burden. New York also has very generous plans, but they are well funded. The funding requirements, however, are putting great pressure on the state and all participating localities. Thus, while the answer to the question of whether future pension commitments will bust budgets is most often "no," some notable exceptions exist.[24]

Pensions and Local Budgets

The discussion so far has treated state and local budgets as a single unit, whereas the relationship between state-administered plans and locally administered plans and state budgets and local budgets is complicated. In fact, many local governments make considerable contributions to state systems. That arrangement means that the financial commitment of local governments consists of two components: (1) required contributions to the locally administered plans (which constitute virtually all the contributions to these plans); and (2) contributions that localities are required to make to state-administered plans. In the aggregate, local payments to state systems account for 58 percent of total local contributions.[25] But these percentages vary enormously across states. They range from 15 percent in Massachusetts (where the state retirement system is almost entirely financed at the state level) to 100 percent in Alaska, Hawaii, Maine, Mississippi, Montana, Nevada, New Mexico, and Wyoming, where all localities are covered under the state plan.[26]

The CRR undertook a survey of local plans to figure out how much pension plans were costing localities in 2010.[27] The survey consisted of ninety-seven locally

24. In states where local governments are responsible for a large percentage of the total required contribution, such as Florida and California, these projections imply that rising pension costs could become a major burden on cities and towns.

25. Author's calculations from U.S. Census Bureau, *State and Local Public-Employee Retirement Systems* (2010).

26. Alaska has a separate Anchorage Police and Firemen Retirement Plan, but it is closed to new hires. The Census shows Utah as being entirely financed at the state level, but the State Comprehensive Annual Financial Report shows transfers from the localities to the state plan.

27. Center for Retirement Research at Boston College (2011b).

administered plans from forty states. The calculation of pension contributions for each plan requires two steps. The first step, which involves employer contributions to local plans, is straightforward. Each city in the sample publishes a Comprehensive Annual Financial Report (CAFR) that lists the payment the city made to all of its local plans. The second step, which involves local contributions to state plans, is more challenging. City CAFRs usually include contributions made directly by the city to the state for general employees and police and fire personnel, but typically not for teachers. For most teachers, pension contributions are made by independent school districts. Thus, to obtain data on the pension contributions made for teachers normally requires collecting the CAFR for each individual school district. Since these reports are not readily available, information was collected for about half the sample. For those localities without school district data, the best that could be done was to apply the statewide percentages from the Census, adjusted according to the school district data collected for half the sample.[28]

The results show that pensions on average accounted for 8.0 percent of local budgets in 2010, significantly higher than the 3.6 percent for states and localities together in 2009. As usual, aggregate data hide a lot of variation. Localities that have seriously underfunded plans and/or generous benefits or participate in state plans with these characteristics contribute significantly more. As shown in figure 5-6, pension contributions account for more than 16 percent of total own-source revenues in about 13 percent of the sample. Not surprisingly, three California plans and the City of Chicago appear among the most burdened localities (see table 5-3).

The important point is that localities are major contributors to state-administered plans. So their fate is as much tied to what happens to plans at the state level as it is to the plans they sponsor themselves.

Pension Obligation Bonds

As discussed above, both Illinois and New Jersey issued pension obligation bonds (POBs) in order to reduce their unfunded liability and the required contribution by the state. These instruments, which are general obligations of the government, alleviate pressure on the government's cash position and may offer cost savings if the bond proceeds are invested through the pension fund in risky assets that realize a high return. But the use of POBs is controversial. Are they

---

28. The sample focuses on localities that administer their own large pension plans and contribute less to state plans than most localities reported in the Census. In order to adjust for this difference between the sample and the Census totals, the analysis took the *aggregate* percentage of local contributions made to the state for the forty-nine localities with full data and divided it by the *aggregate* statewide percentage indicated by the Census. Then, for each locality for which full data were not available, the procedure was to adjust the statewide percentage from the Census by this aggregate ratio.

Figure 5-6. *Distribution of Localities by Annual Required Contribution (ARC) as a Share of Local Own-Source Revenues, 2010*[a]

Percent

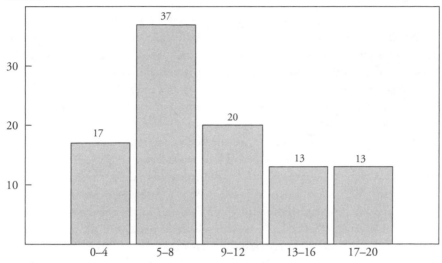

ARC as share of local own-source revenue (percent)

Source: Author's calculations from various financial and actuarial reports; and U.S. Census Bureau, *State and Local Government Finances* (2008).
a. Own-source revenue data are from 2008 and exclude transfers from other levels of government.

Table 5-3. *Top Ten Localities in Contributions as a Percentage of Own-Source Revenue, 2010*[a]

Locality	Percent
Marin County, Calif.	27.7
Portland City, Ore.	26.2
Chicago City, Ill.	24.8
Little Rock City, Ark.	22.4
Orange County, Calif.	22.3
Miami City, Fla.	20.5
Omaha City, Neb.	20.5
Contra Costa County, Calif.	19.2
Pensacola City, Fla.	17.8
Cincinnati City, Ohio	16.6

Source: Author's estimates from *Public Plans Database* (2010); and U.S. Census Bureau, *State and Local Government Finances* (2008).
a. Data on own-source revenue are from 2008.

a viable pension financing instrument or simply a device used by cash-strapped governments?

Background

In 1985, the city of Oakland, California, issued the first POB.[29] At the time, POBs offered city, municipal, and state governments a classic arbitrage opportunity. Issued on a tax-exempt basis, the government could immediately invest the proceeds through the pension fund in higher-yielding taxable securities, such as U.S. Treasury bonds, which would lock in a positive net return from the transaction.[30] However, because POBs (and all "arbitrage bonds") deprived the federal government of tax revenues,[31] Congress stopped state and local governments from issuing tax-exempt bonds for the sole purpose of reinvesting the proceeds in higher-yielding securities. Indeed, the Tax Reform Act of 1986 (TRA86), which did away with the tax exemption for POBs, appeared to mark an end for POBs.

Surprisingly, POBs re-emerged in the 1990s. The strong performance of the stock market led some governments (and bankers) to see a potential arbitrage opportunity for *taxable* POBs. Two factors were important. First, taxable interest rates had come down considerably, which meant that POB borrowing costs were lower as well. Second, pension funds had increased their equity holdings substantially over the decade,[32] which generated higher returns for the plans and thus led actuaries to assume higher future returns. The combination of these two factors was enough to convince some governments that POBs offered an attractive "actuarial arbitrage."[33]

Figure 5-7 shows the issuances of POBs from the early 1990s to July 2009.[34] The most notable characteristic is the spike in POB dollars issued in 2003, which is due to a single POB issuance worth almost $10 billion by Illinois. Even with the anomalous spike in 2003, the total amount of POBs issued in any given year has never been more than 1 percent of the total assets in public pensions. The bulk of activity in POBs has been centered in only about ten states, with California, Illinois, and New Jersey among the major players (see figure 5-8).[35]

29. Scanlan and Lyon (2006); Gold (2000; 2002).

30. The decrease in borrowing costs in issuing tax-exempt state and municipal POBs often exceeds the differential in the risk premium of state and local bonds over federal bonds of the same duration.

31. See Golembiewski, Bornholdt, and Jones (1999) for a discussion.

32. See Peng (2004).

33. Gold (2002).

34. Thad Calabrese generated the POB dataset from raw data on government bond issues from Bloomberg Online Service (1992–2009).

35. California and Illinois are, of course, large states. On a per capita basis, the biggest players are Oregon, Illinois, and Connecticut. California is number six.

Figure 5-7. *Pension Obligation Bonds Issued, 1992–2009*

Billions of 2009 dollars

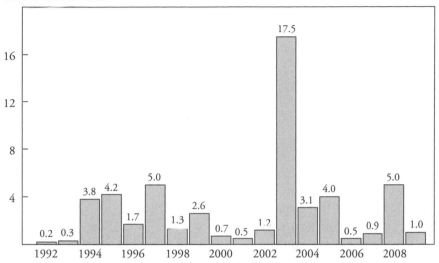

Source: Dataset compiled by Thad Calabrese using Bloomberg Online Service (1992–2009).

Market Drivers and Risks

The actuarial arbitrage highlighted above may be alluring, but the issuance of POBs poses serious risks.[36] First, the assumption that pension returns are on average more than the cost of financing the debt may not turn out to be correct, as the 2008 financial crisis has shown. Even over fifteen to twenty years, the duration of most POB debt, interest costs can exceed asset returns. Second, POBs involve considerable timing-risk, as the proceeds from the issuance are invested en masse into the pension plan. Third, while the issuance of a POB does not change the total indebtedness of the sponsor, it does change the nature of the indebtedness.[37] Requirements to amortize unfunded pension liabilities may be relatively flexible obligations that can be smoothed over time, while the POB is an inflexible debt with required annual payments. Finally, if the government uses the POB to fully fund the pension, it may end up with a pension system having more assets than liabilities. Such overfunding may create the political risk that unions and other interest groups will call for benefit increases, despite

36. Burnham (2003); R. Davis (2006); Calabrese (2009); Block and Prunty (2008); and Hitchcock and Prunty (2009).

37. Hitchcock and Prunty (2009).

Figure 5-8. *Pension Obligation Bonds Issued (1992–2009) as a Share of 2009 General State Revenue, in 2009 dollars*

Percent

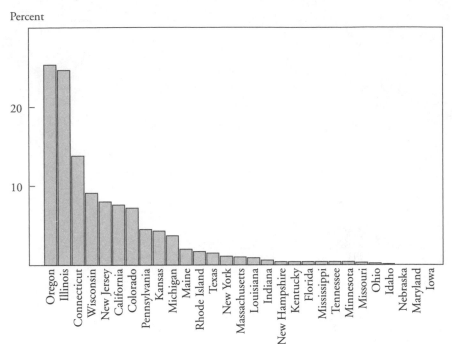

Source: Author's calculations from dataset compiled by Thad Calabrese using Bloomberg Online Service (1992–2009); and U.S. Census Bureau, *State and Local Government Finances* (2009).

the fact that the underfunding still exists; it was just moved from the pension plan's balance sheet to the sponsor's balance sheet.[38]

Even taking into account the risks, it is possible to conceive of situations where a POB would be useful. In theory, governments with well-funded pension plans and sound fiscal health might find POBs advantageous if issued when interest rates were particularly low. The questions are what type of government entity has issued POBs and how have the POBs fared over time?

The Issuers

The type of governments issuing POBs can be identified by estimating an equation that relates the probability of a government issuing a POB with variables describing the fiscal status of the issuer. The specific variables in the model included:

38. *GFOA Advisory* (2005).

—pension plan cash flow as measured by the ratio of employee and employer contributions plus investment returns to benefit payments and administrative expense;

—debt burden as measured by government debt as a percentage of government revenue;

—plan stress on government as measured by government contributions to the pension plan as a percentage of government revenue;

—government cash as measured by government cash and securities outside of trusts as a percentage of total revenues;

—transfers as measured by the percentage of government revenues received as intergovernmental transfers.[39]

The results show that governments are more likely to issue POBs if their pension revenues are low relative to benefits, they already have substantial debt outstanding, their pension contributions account for a large share of government expenditures, and the government is cash strapped (see figure 5-9). That is, the governments that issue POBs are those facing the greatest fiscal pressures and are thus least able to shoulder the additional risks from a POB.

How Have POBs Fared?

One way to assess the extent to which POBs have met issuers' expectations is to calculate the internal rate of return for all POBs issued in a given year. The analysis is based on the universe of taxable POBs issued since the passage of TRA86 through July 1, 2009.[40] The universe includes 2,931 serial POB bonds issued from 236 different governing entities, totaling approximately $53 billion in 2009 dollars.[41] The results demonstrate the risk associated with a POB

39. The equation also included a dummy variable for state plans. Since the *Census of Government Finances and Annual Survey of Government Finances* is more likely to have complete data for state plans, the expected coefficient could be positive. On the other hand, localities account for a disproportionately large share of POBs. It also included a variable for plan size. Again, the *Census of Government Finances and Annual Survey of Government Finances* is more likely to have complete data for large plans, so the expected coefficient is positive. In addition, larger plans would be more likely to issue a POB, because they could spread the transaction costs over a larger base. In addition to the variables described above, it would also be useful to include the funding status of the plan. Presumably, poorly funded plans would be more likely to issue a POB. Unfortunately, historical funding data are not available for most plans in the sample.

40. A dataset containing only nonfederal pension financing bonds issued from 1992 to 2009 was drawn from municipal bond data from Bloomberg Online Service.

41. For each bond, information is available on the date of issuance, the date of maturity, the coupon rate, the par value, and the purchase price as a percentage of par. The analysis begins by looking at each serial bond issued in a given year. Using the stated coupon rate for each bond, the next step is to calculate how much the issuing government has to pay to service the debt each year

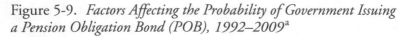

Figure 5-9. *Factors Affecting the Probability of Government Issuing a Pension Obligation Bond (POB), 1992–2009*[a]

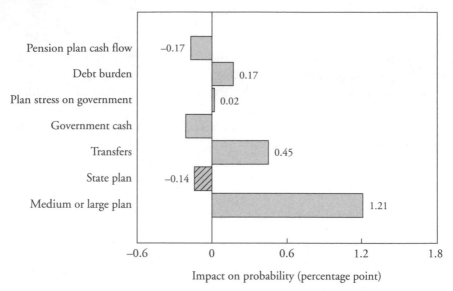

Impact on probability (percentage point)

Source: Center for Retirement Research at Boston College (2010c).

a. Solid bars indicate the coefficient is statistically significant at the 90 percent level or higher. For dummy variables, the effects illustrated reflect a shift from 0 to 1. In the case of continuous variables, the effects illustrated reflect a shift from the 20th to the 80th percentile value of the variable.

strategy. If the assessment date is the end of 2007, the peak of the stock market, the picture looks fairly positive (see figure 5-10A). On the other hand, by mid-2009 most POBs had been a net drain on government revenues (see figure 5-10B). Only those bonds issued a very long time ago and those issued during dramatic stock market downturns have produced a positive return; all others

---

and how much money the bond proceeds produce each year. The assumption is that the proceeds are invested in accordance with the allocation of the aggregate assets of state and local pensions from the Federal Reserve's *Flow of Funds*—approximately 65 percent in equities and 35 percent in bonds. Accordingly, the S&P 500 total return index and the Barclays ten-year bond total return index are used to approximate how the POB proceeds have grown over time. For each bond, beginning in year one, the analysis calculates the growth of the invested bond proceeds for that year, then subtracts the interest payment to get a new beginning balance for the following year; this process is repeated until the bond matures. For bonds that have not yet matured, the process is repeated until the date of the assessment. At maturity or date of assessment, the ending balance is compared with the initial proceeds to calculate an internal rate of return (IRR). These IRRs are then weighted by the size of the bond in order to calculate an aggregate IRR for each annual cohort of POBs.

Figure 5-10A. *Internal Rate of Return on Pension Obligation Bonds at the Peak of the Market, by Year Issued, 1992–2007*

Percent

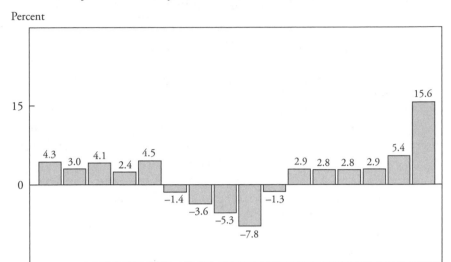

Source: Center for Retirement Research at Boston College (2010c).

Figure 5-10B. *Internal Rate of Return on Pension Obligation Bonds after Financial Crisis, by Year Issued, 1992–Mid-2009*

Percent

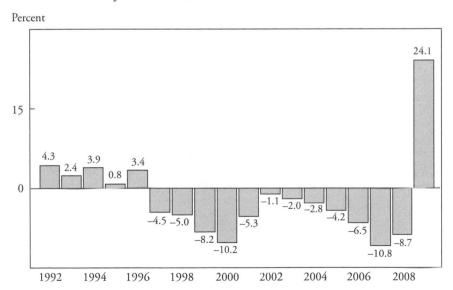

Source: Center for Retirement Research at Boston College (2010c).

are in the red. While the story is not yet over, since 2010 about 80 percent of the bonds issued since 1992 were still outstanding, some may end up being extremely costly for the governments that issued them.

The Impact of Pensions on State Borrowing Costs

The discussion so far has focused on the direct impact of state and local pensions on budgets. But pensions could affect future budgets indirectly through the cost of their non-pension borrowing. In 2009, interest costs accounted for 5.5 percent of state and local revenues. In the private sector, numerous studies have shown that pension underfunding affects corporate bond ratings and thereby interest costs. [42] And Moody's reports that its analysts consider pension funding in the rating process. Despite the logic and the rhetoric, an earlier study found little relationship between state and local funding efforts and either the cost of state debt or the ratings conferred by Moody's.[43] However, the situation may have changed. Pensions have received a lot of negative attention in recent years, and in 2011 Moody's announced that it would combine unfunded pension liabilities with outstanding bonds when evaluating a state's leverage position. This section updates the earlier study to determine whether the relationship between pension funding efforts and borrowing costs has become more evident in the post-financial-crisis world.

The Rating of Municipal Bonds

The interest cost on municipal bonds is directly related to their rating.[44] The question is the extent to which pensions enter into the rating process. Rating agencies say that they take pensions into account when rating municipal bonds,

---

42. On the corporate side, a number of studies have examined the relationship between pension funding and equity prices, and a few have looked at the relationship between pension funding and corporate debt ratings. This literature reflects the assumption that while pensions are autonomous legally, investors view pension assets and liabilities as part of an expanded corporate balance sheet and thus take them into account when valuing a corporation's equities or bond rating. The evidence suggests that the status of the pension fund influences both the price of equities and corporate debt ratings. See Daley (1984); Dhaliwal (1986); Carroll and Niehaus (1998); Coronado and others (2008); Jin, Merton, and Bodie (2004); Landsman (1986); and Maher (1987).

43. Center for Retirement Research at Boston College (2011e).

44. Ratings for most bonds issued by states have been higher and more concentrated in the "A" categories than those issued by local governments. States have a larger and more diverse economic base and a sovereign right to tax that is not constrained by the Constitution (with the exception of interstate commerce or international trade). Localities have a much narrower base and derive their power to tax from the state. Moreover, a state's general obligation pledge is a very strong commitment, and states cannot go bankrupt.

and state officials express concern over how rating agencies will respond to pension developments.[45]

Moody's provides a detailed description of its rating methodology for state-issued bonds.[46] This methodology focuses on four aspects of each state: its economy, finances, debt, and management. Moody's tends to put more weight on finances and management than on the economy and debt. Nevertheless, Moody's analysts consider, as part of the debt category, both the funded status of the issuer's pension fund and the extent to which the issuer is making contributions to limit the growth of future unfunded liabilities. But historically, pension funding has been only one factor in a category that the analysts "underweight" in making their evaluations. This weighting may change in the wake of Moody's 2011 announcement that it will combine unfunded liabilities with outstanding debt to assess the leverage position of states.

An Empirical Analysis

The analysis is based on a Thomson Reuters dataset of municipal bonds issued between 2005 and 2011. The dataset tracks the bond sale date, duration, and yield at issue, as well as whether the bond is taxable, whether the rate is fixed or variable, and whether the bond is insured or credit enhanced. To have relevant economic/management information for each bond required limiting the sample to state bonds. For ease of interpretation, the analysis also focused on tax-exempt fixed-rate bonds. To control for differences in duration of the state-issued securities and fluctuations in interest rates over time, the dependent variable is defined as the spread between the rate of interest on our sample of a nontaxable state-issued bond and on a Treasury bond of the same duration issued in the same week (see figure 5-11).[47] The original analysis was conducted for the period 2005–09. The updated analysis has been repeated for the period before the financial crisis (2005–08) and the period after (2009–10).

The analysis was designed to determine whether pension funding status affected either: (1) the rating that Moody's assigned to a particular bond; or (2) the interest cost of the bond. The explanatory variables for both equations

45. See Mattoon (2006) for a discussion of the credit risks of pension underfunding.
46. Kutter and Blake (2004).
47. Before the 2008 financial collapse, state-issued municipal bond yields averaged about 60 basis points less than Treasuries of similar duration; since the financial collapse the pattern has reversed. The reversal can be attributed to two factors. First, Treasury yields dropped precipitously when investors rushed to safety, forcing Treasury rates down. Second, the required rates on municipal bonds rose as the percentage of new issues with insurance dropped sharply. The market collapse caused a decline in credit ratings of the bond insurers, making it difficult for municipalities to purchase a higher rating. Further, many insurers left the market; currently, only two large municipal insurers remain.

Figure 5-11. *Spread between Yields on State-Issued Bonds and Treasuries, 2005–10*[a]

Basis points

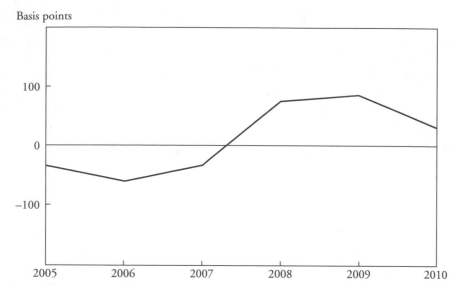

Sources: Thomson Reuters (2005–10); and Federal Reserve Bank of St. Louis (2005–10).

a. The municipal bond spread equals the yield of a municipal bond minus the yield on a U.S. Treasury of similar duration issued during the same week. The spreads are weighted by the dollar amount of each bond issue.

include the factors that Moody's indicated as important: management, finances, economy, and debt. They also include characteristics of the bond—general obligation and insured—and the tax treatment of municipal bond interest at the state level.

Management characteristics were represented by three variables:

—Economic advisers. States that had a council of economic advisers were assumed to be better managed, thereby reducing interest costs.

—Consensus forecast. States that based their revenue projections on realistic forecasts also would be viewed as more credible, thereby reducing interest costs.

—Carry deficit. States where it was possible to carry deficits from one year to another and thereby circumvent the balanced budget mandate would be viewed as less well managed, thereby increasing borrowing costs.

Financial status was captured by two variables:

—Growth in expenditures. States with rapid five-year growth in expenditures would have many competing demands for funds and therefore have to pay a higher rate.

—Fund balance. A positive balance in the General Fund and other key operating funds would reflect a consistent trend of balance sheet health and thereby reduce the cost of borrowing.

Economy was represented by two variables:

—Unemployment rate. At any moment in time, states with higher levels of unemployment face more financial stress and therefore would be forced to pay higher rates.

—Dependency ratio. States with a high proportion of the population under 17 and 65 and over would be more exposed to the budget pressures of education and Medicaid and therefore would have to pay more on their debt.

Debt was represented by two variables:

—Debt service as a percentage of revenue. States with an already high level of debt service would be viewed as more risky and thereby forced to pay higher interest rates.

—Percentage of ARC paid. States that pay a higher percentage of their pension plan's ARC would have lower demand on their resources going forward, requiring them to pay less to finance their debt.

Bond characteristics included two factors:

—General obligation. Since general obligation bonds are backed by the full faith and credit of the state, they would be expected to reduce the required interest cost.

—Credit enhanced/insured. Investors would require a lower yield on bonds that were accorded additional security through credit enhancement or insurance.[48]

Tax status: Most states exempt the interest on domestic bonds from the state income tax; some states (Illinois, Iowa, Kansas, Oklahoma, and Wisconsin) do not. All else equal, having the interest tax-exempt lowers the required premium. This effect is magnified by the magnitude of the marginal tax rate that bondholders face. This variable equals zero for those states that tax the interest of domestic bonds and equals the marginal tax rates for those that do not.

Results

The results of the two regressions—Moody's rating and interest cost for 2005–08 and 2009–10—generally show the expected direction, although the statistical

---

48. Municipal bond insurance, introduced in the United States in 1971, comes in two basic forms: nonpayment insurance, which ensures that the bond insurer will pay any principal and interest left unpaid by the issuer, and a purchase agreement, whereby the insurer purchases the bonds from the issuer. The insurer is then responsible for placing the bonds with investors and making payments on the bond. Bonds placed in this manner are accorded the healthy bond rating of the insurer, who is now responsible for the debt payments.

significance of the coefficients varies between the two equations and before and after the financial crisis. The key variable of interest is the coefficient of the percentage of ARC paid. The short story is that, before the crisis, pension funding played no role at all in Moody's ratings or interest costs (see appendix table 5A). For the period 2009–10, pension funding has a measurable impact on interest costs, but still no impact on Moody's rating. (In results *not* shown, Moody's new measure of outstanding debt and unfunded liabilities relative to expenditures was also tried and found to have no impact either before or after the crisis.)[49]

The impact of the other variables is also interesting. When Moody's rating is the dependent variable, four factors have a statistically significant effect.[50] The first is the bond characteristics—general obligation and/or credit enhanced. The second, as advertised in the description of Moody's ratings process, are the management factors (council of economic advisers, consensus forecasting, and ability to carry over a deficit). The third are factors related to the economy (the unemployment rate and dependency ratio). Finally, the ratio of debt service to revenue is also important. When interest cost is the dependent variable, all the variables have a statistically significant effect for one period or the other, with the exception of the council of economic advisers.

In short, although in conversation state officials frequently indicate that they are concerned about the impact of their pension decisions on their bond ratings and interest costs, no such impact is evident before 2009. Only after the financial crisis does pension funding have a meaningful effect on costs. Even then the effect is relatively modest—about 2 basis points—in comparison with other factors. This result is not surprising given that pension expense accounted for only 4.6 percent of state revenues in 2009. The magnitude could increase, however, to the extent that pensions become an increasingly important component of state budgets.

Conclusion

The funding shortfall of public pension plans has made national news since the 2008 financial collapse reduced asset values at the same time that state and local revenues dried up. The size of the funding hole differs depending on the

49. In actuality, correlation between any of the explanatory variables and the spread can only be inferred since there may be an omitted factor in the analysis that affects both the values of the explanatory variables and the spread. In this case, the effect of the omitted factor would mistakenly be attributed to the explanatory variables.

50. The results presented below are derived from ordinary least squares for ease of presentation. Because the relationships between the Moody's ratings are probably not linear, the correct approach is to use an ordered probit, but the coefficients from such an equation are very difficult to interpret. Fortunately, the two equations yield similar answers for the variables considered.

rate used to discount obligations, but regardless of assumptions, governments will eventually have to ante up. How much? In 2009, pension contributions amounted to about 4.6 percent of total state and local revenues. Assuming an 8 percent return on assets and thirty-year amortization beginning in 2014, this share would rise to only 5.1 percent. If funding were based on a lower assumed rate, the share would rise further. At 6 percent, pension contributions to fully fund benefit promises would increase to 9.5 percent of state and local budgets; at 4 percent, they would amount to 14.5 percent.

The burden that states will actually face has little to do with how liabilities are discounted for valuation purposes but a lot to do with the return actually earned on pension assets. If plans end up earning low nominal returns, their unfunded liabilities will increase and the ARC will rise. If low returns persist, sponsors may reduce their discount rate, thereby increasing the normal cost and further increasing the ARC. With a low return, pension contributions will take up a large share of state and local budgets. On the other hand, if they earn the assumed rate of return, their costs will continue to account for a relatively modest share of budgets.

Aggregate data, however, hide substantial variation. Many states will be just fine. They provide modest benefits, have a commitment to funding, and are recovering from the financial crisis. On the other hand, states that have systematically avoided funding, such as Illinois and New Jersey, face major challenges. Illinois may exhaust its pension assets and be forced to revert to pay-as-you-go. If New Jersey's recent legislation holds, it will end up in average shape. If, as in the past, it fails to make funding payments, the outlook will be bleaker. And California, which has one of the most generous pension systems in the nation and substantial underfunding due to a retroactive benefit increase in the late 1990s, is also facing severe budget problems. New York plans are well funded, but the expense is an increasing burden on the state and participating localities.

Solving the budget problems will require tough choices to allocate the burden equitably among all parties—current and future public employees, current retirees, and current and future taxpayers. Simply changing the rate used to discount liabilities or limiting union bargaining provides little guidance on how to make these tough choices. Some possible principles are discussed in chapter 8.

Appendix Table 5A. *OLS Regression Results on the Spread and Moody's Rating of State-Issued Bonds, 2005–08 and 2009–10*[a]

	Risk premium		Moody's rating	
	2005–08	2009–10	2005–08	2009–10
Council of economic advisers	−0.0366	−0.0848	−0.1650	−0.3722*
	(0.033)	(0.061)	(0.115)	(0.202)
Consensus forecasting	−0.1142***	−0.1006*	−0.3482***	−0.6953***
	(0.034)	(0.065)	(0.097)	(0.196)
Allowed to carry a deficit	0.0973**	0.3155***	0.5276***	0.7373**
	(0.037)	(0.074)	(0.179)	(0.285)
Expenditure growth (5 years)	0.0039***	−0.0012	0.0093**	0.0066
	(0.001)	(0.003)	(0.004)	(0.008)
Fund balance	−0.0034***	0.0069**	−0.0032	0.0005
	(0.001)	(0.003)	(0.005)	(0.008)
State unemployment rate	0.1405***	0.0494**	0.0892*	0.0361
	(0.034)	(0.022)	(0.046)	(0.056)
Dependency ratio	0.0643***	−0.0296	0.0328	−0.1759*
	(0.020)	(0.030)	(0.066)	(0.118)
Debt service to revenue	0.0127***	0.0082	0.0408***	0.0427*
	(0.005)	(0.009)	(0.014)	(0.031)
Marginal tax rate	−0.0219***	−0.0046	0.0076	0.0309
	(0.006)	(0.014)	(0.020)	(0.034)
Percentage of ARC paid	−0.0005	−0.0021*	−0.0007	−0.0027
	(0.000)	(0.001)	(0.001)	(0.003)
General obligation	−0.3054***	−0.6708***	−0.4320**	−1.5816***
	(0.052)	(0.055)	(0.208)	(0.236)
Credit enhanced	−0.3378***	0.1693*	−1.7487***	−1.0743***
	(0.029)	(0.095)	(0.162)	(0.263)
Constant	−5.2211***	5.2364***	0.0307	12.1390
	(0.830)	(1.141)	(2.351)	(4.388)
R-squared	0.3354	0.1961	0.2815	0.1815
Number of observations	30,681	13,113	30,979	12,356

Sources: Author's calculations from Thomson Reuters (2005–10); *Public Plans Database* (2005–10); U.S. Census Bureau, *State and Local Government Finances* (2005–10); U.S. Census Bureau and U.S. Department of Labor, Current *Population Survey* (2005–10); U.S. Census Bureau (2010a); Moody's Investors Service (2005–10); National Association of State Budget Officers (2008); and The Tax Foundation (2005–10).

a. Robust standard errors adjusted for state-level clustering are in parentheses. Coefficients are significant at the 1 percent level (***), 5 percent level (**), or 15 percent level (*). Variables not depicted include a control for observation year. The results presented below are derived from ordinary least squares for ease of presentation. Because the relationships between the Moody's ratings are probably not linear, the correct approach is to use an ordered probit, but the coefficients from such an equation are very difficult to interpret. Fortunately, the two equations yield similar answers for the variables considered.

6

Are Public Employees Overpaid or Underpaid?

The previous chapters focused on one component of compensation for state and local workers—namely, pensions. They explored the extent to which government employers had put aside money for future benefits and the extent to which shortfalls will require future contributions that squeeze out other priorities. The discussion showed that funded levels have declined sharply in the wake of the financial crisis and that the recession decimated state and local revenues, making it impossible for governments to compensate for the shortfall. As a result, politicians everywhere are looking for ways to reduce pension costs.

Proposals to cut pensions are usually based on the presumption that pensions are "too generous." But pensions are just one part of total compensation. The relevant question is not whether one component of compensation is excessive but whether the total compensation package—including both wages and fringe benefits—is appropriate for attracting and retaining state and local employees. The most obvious metric against which to assess the appropriateness of public sector compensation is pay in the private sector. As a result, the comparability of state and local versus private sector compensation has re-emerged as a major issue in the wake of the financial crisis.

This chapter explores what is known about public versus private sector compensation. The first section reports on some basic facts about the nature of public employees and their compensation. The second section reports on the existing literature—a luxury not available for the topics of earlier chapters—regarding the comparability of public and private compensation. The third section describes a rash of recent studies arguing that state and local workers are paid less or more than their private sector counterparts. Most agree that wages of state and local employees are lower than for private sector workers with similar education and experience, but researchers differ on the extent to which pensions and other benefits compensate for the shortfall.[1] The next two sections explore the relative outcomes for short-term versus long-term state and local employees compared to private sector workers. The fourth section, using household data from the *Health and Retirement Study* (HRS), asks whether, at the end of the day, state and local employees end up richer or poorer than their private sector counterparts and how that outcome varies by duration of employment. The fifth section narrows the issue back to pensions and uses the HRS to explore replacement rates for short-term versus long-term state and local employees relative to private sector workers.

A number of conclusions emerge. First, wages for workers with similar characteristics, education, and experience are lower for state and local workers than for those in the private sector. Virtually all researchers agree on this point. Second, pension and retiree health benefits for state and local workers roughly offset the wage penalty, so that, taken as a whole, compensation in the two sectors is roughly comparable. Most researchers agree on this point. The remaining issue is job security. Should it be viewed as a compensating differential, which perhaps offsets poor working conditions or a compressed wage structure, or should it be assigned a value and added to the compensation calculation? Third, the parity of compensation between the public and private sectors hides enormous variation by wage levels. State and local workers in the lowest third of the wage distribution are paid somewhat more than their private sector counterparts, those in the middle roughly comparable amounts, and those in the top third significantly less. Fourth, exercises using the *Health and Retirement Study* that relate lifetime employment patterns to outcomes at retirement show that those who spend *most of their career* in the state and local sector end up with more wealth and higher replacement rates than those who spend their entire career in the private sector. Short-term state and local workers actually appear to lose from the experience, ending up with less wealth and lower replacement rates than their private sector counterparts. Moreover, for households where the male is the public employee, the higher wealth appears to be attributable to the discipline imposed by being forced to save through a defined benefit plan.

In short, for the nation as a whole, the difference between public and private sector compensation appears modest. The relatively modest differential should make policymakers cautious about massive changes without carefully studying the specifics of their particular situation. This caution is particularly relevant in the case of teachers; many teachers currently fall within the top third of state and local workers in compensation and already earn significantly less than their private sector counterparts.

---

1. A recent exception is Gittleman and Pierce (2011).

Table 6-1. *State and Local Full-Time Equivalent Employees,*
by Function, 2010

Millions

Activity	State	Local	Total
Education	1.8	7.1	8.9
Elementary and secondary	0.1	6.8	6.9
Higher	1.7	0.3	2.0
Protective services	0.8	1.7	2.4
Health	0.6	0.8	1.4
Community development[a]	0.6	0.8	1.4
Transportation	0.3	0.5	0.8
Financial and other administration	0.2	0.5	0.7
Public welfare	0.2	0.3	0.5
Public utilities and waste management	0.0	0.5	0.5
Total	4.4	12.2	16.6

Source: U.S. Census Bureau (2010b).

a. Includes libraries, housing, community development, environment, recreation, and all other.

The Basic Facts

Many aspects of the public sector labor market are a source of great controversy, but some facts are undisputed. About 14 percent of American workers (nearly 17 million full-time equivalents) are employed by state and local governments. Nearly three-quarters of these people work for local governments. And more than half of all state and local workers are employed in education (see table 6-1). The share of those with at least a college degree is 52 percent in the public sector and 35 percent in the private sector. The share over age 45 is 51 percent in the public sector and 44 percent in the private sector. Fifty-seven percent are female in the public sector and 42 percent in the private sector (see figure 6-1). Median tenure in the public sector is eight years and five in the private sector.[2] These characteristics are likely driven by teachers, who constitute such a large portion of the public workforce.

While a full answer to the question of parity of compensation requires careful comparisons between people with similar skills doing similar jobs, some basic data set out the issues. Average wages for state/local workers between 25 and 64—even not controlling for education and other factors—are lower than those in the private sector, and the ratio of public to private sector wages has declined

2. U.S. Census Bureau and U.S. Department of Labor (1973–2010).

Figure 6-1. *Percent of Workers with at Least a College Degree, over 45, and Female, by Sector, 2010*

Percent

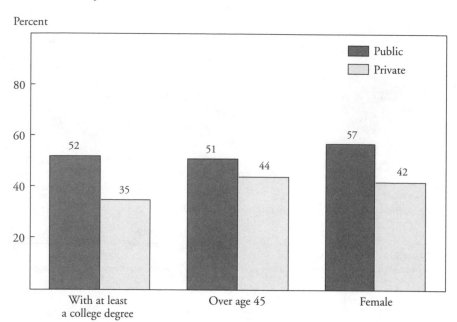

Source: Center for Retirement Research at Boston College (2011g).

over time (see figure 6-2).[3] On the other hand, pensions are more generous in the public sector. First, a greater percentage of workers—76 percent vs. 43 percent—have an employer-sponsored plan in the public sector than in the private sector. Second, among those employers who do sponsor plans, costs to the employer are higher in the state and local sector, despite significant employee contributions, than in the private sector (see figure 6-3). Finally, retiree health insurance is much more prevalent in the public sector than in the private sector.[4]

3. The relationship between public and private wages is sensitive to the selected *Current Population Survey* dataset. The Annual March Supplement shows state and local wages in recent years being lower than private sector wages, with or without controlling for education, experience, firm size, and other personal and job characteristics. In contrast, the Outgoing Rotation Groups show state and local wages as lower only when the controls are added.

4. Unfortunately, no data are readily available to confirm this pattern, so estimates are required. In the private sector, the *Medical Expenditure Panel Survey* (Agency for Healthcare Research and Quality, various years) provides information on retiree health insurance offerings by firm size, and the Census shows the distribution of workers by firm size. Combining the two pieces of information yields an estimate of private sector coverage of 18 percent. In the public sector, our assumption

Figure 6-2. *Ratio of Average Public to Private Sector Wages, Age 25 to 64, 1990–2010*

Percent

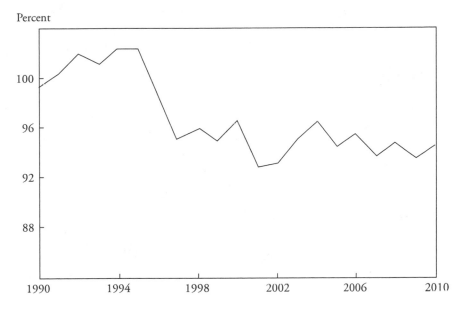

Source: Author's calculations from U.S. Census Bureau and U.S. Department of Labor (1990–2010).

The question is whether total compensation, including both wages and fringe benefits, is comparable between the public and private sector. Comparability is a desired goal for both equity and efficiency reasons. Equity considerations would dictate that a person not be paid more or less total compensation (including amenities) in the public sector than in the private. Efficiency considerations would dictate that the public sector pay no more than is necessary to attract and retain an adequate supply of labor, so the two sectors are in equal competition for talent.

The Literature to Date

The literature on public-private compensation differentials spans more than forty years. The focus of most studies can be categorized into four broad groups: (1) wages; (2) wages and fringe benefits; (3) sample selection; and (4) job queues.[5]

---

is that coverage for retiree health care is the same as coverage for pensions, in which case 76 percent of the state and local workforce is potentially eligible for retiree health care.

5. The following literature review is based on an essay written by Laura Quinby.

Figure 6-3. *Employer and Employee Pension Costs by Sector, 2010*[a]

Percent

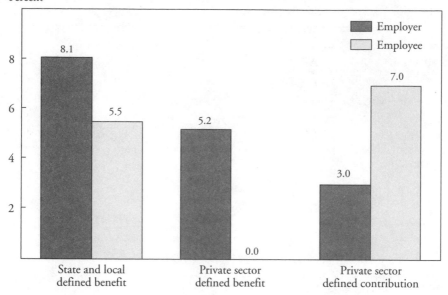

Sources: *Public Plans Database* (2010); Towers Watson (2009); and Vanguard Group (2011).

a. The costs for defined benefit plans represent the normal cost. In the public sector, the costs for those covered by Social Security averaged 8.5 percent (employer) and 4.7 percent (employee), while the cost for those without Social Security averaged 6.9 percent (employer) and 7.6 percent (employee).

The first group is the simplest empirically, as wages have long been observed in large micro datasets. Many of the researchers use the Blinder-Oaxaca decomposition technique to determine how much individuals with public sector characteristics would receive in wages if they worked in the private sector.[6] While each of these studies looks at a slightly different time period between 1979 and

6. See Blinder (1973) and Oaxaca (1973) for a discussion of the Blinder-Oaxaca decomposition technique. Smith (1976) used Census data, a human capital model, and the Blinder-Oaxaca decomposition technique to estimate the federal wage premium. The Blinder-Oaxaca method—which until Smith's paper had been primarily employed for measuring discrimination—was subsequently adopted by many public-private compensation studies. For example, Belman and Heywood (1989a) and Moore and Raisian (1991) employ the technique on data from the *Current Population Survey* (CPS) and *Panel Study of Income Dynamics* (PSID) to demonstrate that the public sector wage premium varies by occupation and gender, respectively. Katz and Krueger (1991); Poterba and Rueben (1994); Borjas (2002); and Belman and Heywood (2004) confirm the hypothesis that comparability differs across occupations.

2000, the consensus is that highly educated public sector workers are underpaid relative to their private sector counterparts, while workers with lower levels of education are overpaid. More recent studies all conclude that, on average, state and local workers experience a wage penalty of 6 to 12 percent.[7]

Wages, however, are only one component of total compensation, so a second branch of the literature attempts to account for fringe benefits. A study in the early 1980s, which calculates wealth from employer pension and Social Security contributions in the 1969 *Retirement History Study,* finds that public sector employees enjoy a significant contribution premium.[8] A 1990s study points to a significant decline in private sector pension coverage between 1979 and 1988, suggesting a relative increase in public sector compensation over this period.[9] A recent series of compensation studies, which are discussed below, first estimate a standard wage equation using *Current Population Survey* (CPS) data, then add the aggregate cost of benefits from the Bureau of Labor Statistics' *Employer Costs for Employee Compensation* (ECEC) database.[10] These studies fail to reach a consensus; most argue either for parity or for a state and local compensation penalty of between 2 and 10 percent.[11]

A third branch of the literature seeks to improve the traditional wage estimations by controlling for selection into the public sector. These researchers employ two-stage models where workers select into a labor market based on unobserved productivity characteristics.[12] The authors find evidence of selection into the public sector, controlling for which significantly alters the estimated public-private wage differential (although the direction and magnitude of the change are inconsistent across the two studies).

A fourth set of analyses takes a different tack entirely by looking at demand for government work as measured by "job queues." The premise underlying these studies is that any lack of parity could simply reflect compensating differentials for unquantifiable job characteristics, but a finding of excess demand for public sector jobs would suggest that these jobs pay more than the market wage. The two main studies focus on federal as opposed to state and local employment.

7. Allegretto and Keefe (2010); Bender and Heywood (2010); Keefe (2010); Schmitt (2010); Center for Retirement Research at Boston College (2011c); and Richwine and Biggs (2011).

8. Quinn (1982).

9. Belman and Heywood (1997).

10. See Allegretto and Keefe (2010); Bender and Heywood (2010); Keefe (2010); Center for Retirement Research at Boston College (2011h); and Richwine and Biggs (2011).

11. Meanwhile, Richwine and Biggs (2011) argue that state and local employees may actually enjoy a 30 percent compensation premium because the ECEC numbers fail to properly account for public pension benefits, retiree health insurance, and job security.

12. Gyourko and Tracy (1988); and Belman and Heywood (1989b).

Venti (1987) develops a stylized likelihood model to predict the probability that a worker who is offered a federal job will accept employment. Based on these predictions, he estimates that federal compensation exceeds that of the private sector by about 4 percent for men and 22 percent for women. Krueger (1988) looks at actual job applications for federal and private sector employment, demonstrating a 25 to 38 percent higher application rate for the government than for the private sector. These findings support the consensus that federal jobs pay more than the private sector.

Borjas (2002) looks at state and local as well as federal wages and employment relative to those in the private sector over the period 1960–2000. He first updates the relative wage literature, reporting that the pay gap between public and private sector workers has hovered around –5 to –10 percent for the past four decades, adjusting for socioeconomic characteristics. This stability, however, occurred against a background of dramatic changes in the wage structures of the public and private sectors. Wage dispersion, both across and within skill groups, increased much more dramatically in the private sector than in the public sector. Borjas analyzes the movement of workers between sectors in the matched Outgoing Rotation Groups of the CPS and finds that public sector wage compression during the 1980s and 1990s significantly reduced the likelihood of high-skilled workers entering and remaining in the public sector.

At this point in time, virtually all analysts agree that wages in the state and local sector—when adjusted for the higher educational attainment of public sector workers—are lower than those in the private sector. The big debate, as will become evident, is the extent to which fringe benefits—pensions, retiree health insurance, and other amenities—offset the lower wages. The debate is more than academic because efforts to cut back state and local pensions are based on the presumption that public sector employees are overpaid. If this presumption is correct, then cutbacks can be viewed as a proper realigning of public and private sector compensation. If it is not correct, then state and local actions will reduce public sector compensation to below that in the private sector, and, as Borjas demonstrates, relative compensation sharply affects the type of workers that state and local governments can attract.

Are State and Local Workers Overpaid?

A rash of recent studies has examined whether state and local workers are overpaid or underpaid relative to their private sector counterparts.[13] All start with

---

13. See Allegretto and Keefe (2010); Belman and Heywood (2004); Bender and Heywood (2010); Richwine and Biggs (2011); Borjas (2002); Braconi (2011); Keefe (2010, 2011); Schmitt (2010); and Thompson and Schmitt (2010).

an examination of wages, finding lower wages in the public sector, and then make adjustments for fringe benefits and, in one case, job security of public employment.

Comparing Wages in the Public and Private Sectors

The following repeats for the *nation* an analysis of wages in California undertaken by two groups—one on each side of the debate of whether public sector workers are overcompensated.[14] Like all other recent studies, both find wages lower in California's state and local sector.

So as to not introduce new issues, the dataset and variables for the nationwide analysis are the same as those used in the California studies. The data come from the Annual March Supplement of the *Current Population Survey* (CPS) for the years 2006–10. The analysis is limited to adult civilians working full time for a wage or salary during the whole previous year. The variables include whether the employer was federal, state, or local government and controls for hours worked per week, years of education, experience, experience squared, firm size, occupation, immigration status, race, gender, marital status, years to account for inflation, and some interaction terms.

Before reporting the results, it should be noted that two variables in these types of regressions are controversial. The first is firm size. The argument for including firm size is that most state and local workers are employed by large entities.[15] Including this variable means that public employees are being compared mainly to employees of large firms, which—for reasons not fully understood—tend to pay higher wages and benefits. Omitting the variable would make the wage penalty for working for a state or locality somewhat smaller.[16] Both California studies include firm size.

The other controversial variable is union status. One could argue that union status reflects the employee's preference, implying that should the employee leave public employment he would seek a union job. Therefore, union public sector workers should be compared only to union private sector workers. The problem is that only a small percentage of the private workforce is unionized, so the

14. See Allegretto and Keefe (2010); and Richwine and Biggs (2011).

15. Nearly 90 percent of state and local workers are employed by entities with 100 or more employees, based on calculations from the CPS. A recent study by Gittleman and Pierce (2011) omits the firm size variable because they view the higher pay in large firms as rent sharing rather than a reflection of workers' skills. Omitting this variable, they found that public employees earn considerably more than private sector workers.

16. The results presented in the text show a wage penalty of 9.5 percent. Omitting firm size from the equation reduces the penalty to 5.1 percent.

Figure 6-4. *Impact of Selected Factors on Wages of Full-Time Workers, 2006–10*[a]

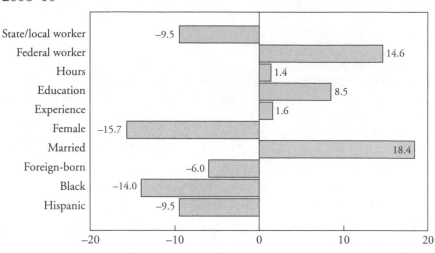

Impact on wage (percent)

Source: Center for Retirement Research at Boston College (2011h).
a. For "0/1" variables, the bars represent the relationship between the characteristic and wages; for continuous variables, the bars represent the impact of a one unit change on the wage.

exiting employee would be unlikely to find a union job. Therefore, controlling for union status does not seem relevant.[17]

The results of the wage regression for the nation are shown in figure 6-4. The coefficients for the continuous variables are the percentage increase in wages for a one unit increase in the variable. For example, an additional year of education is associated with an 8.5 percent increase in wages. For the 0/1 variables, the coefficient shows the percentage increase associated with having the characteristic. For example, women earn 15.7 percent less than men. The most important coefficient for this analysis is that associated with being a state or local worker. After controlling for firm size, education, experience, and numerous personal and job characteristics, the results show that state and local workers earned 9.5 percent less in wages than otherwise similar private sector workers. (Note, as the literature review suggested, that wages in the federal sector tend to be higher.)

17. Indeed, in equations not reported, including the variable has virtually no effect on the coefficient for state/local workers. Including union status in the equation increases the wage penalty from 9.5 percent to 9.7 percent.

Figure 6-5. *State and Local Relative to Private Sector Wages,*
by Wage Tercile, 2006–10

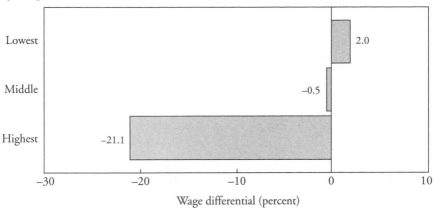

Wage differential (percent)

Source: Center for Retirement Research at Boston College (2011h).

To provide some sense of the heterogeneity of the wage penalty by type of worker, the wage equation was re-estimated by wage tercile. That is, a separate wage equation was estimated for the lowest paid one-third in each state, the middle one-third, and the highest one-third. The results show what other studies have found (see figure 6-5).[18] Public employees in the lowest one-third of the wage distribution are paid more than their private sector counterparts. Those in the middle third are paid about the same. And those state and local workers in the top one-third are paid about 20 percent less than private sector workers.

Despite the variation by wage level, the message from the wage analysis is clear: state and local workers as a group are paid less than their private sector counterparts. So far, most researchers have no real disagreements.

Comparing Benefits in the State/Local and Private Sectors

The controversy starts on the benefits side. The question is the extent to which the value of the benefits provided to state and local workers offsets the wage penalty. Several researchers who conclude that benefits do not cancel out the wage penalty base their case on the Bureau of Labor Statistics ECEC survey.[19] This survey shows that while benefits are much higher relative to wages for state

18. See Borjas (2002); Fogel and Lewin (1974); Katz and Krueger (1991); Poterba and Rueben (1994); and Schmitt (2010).
19. Allegretto and Keefe (2010); and Keefe (2010).

and local workers than for those in the private sector, they are not high enough to offset the wage penalty.[20] Therefore, they conclude that public sector workers receive less total compensation—wages and benefits combined—than their private sector counterparts.

The problem is that the ECEC survey understates state and local employee compensation in two ways:[21]

—It omits retiree health insurance since employers generally do not pre-fund these plans and therefore do not make payments for active employees. This omission is relevant because retiree health benefits are much more prevalent in the public sector than the private sector. Also, even those public sector retirees who receive little employer contribution toward their retiree health care can buy retiree health insurance at group rather than individual rates.

—Contributions to defined benefit pensions and to 401(k) plans are not comparable. Public sector plans in essence guarantee participants a return of 8 percent, whereas 401(k) plans provide no such guarantees. Taking this higher guarantee into account increases the value of public sector pension contributions.

RETIREE HEALTH INSURANCE. Clearly retiree health insurance should be added. Nationwide, the normal cost of retiree health insurance for state and local governments in 2009 was 7.6 percent of payrolls, assuming a discount rate of about 4.5 percent.[22] However, a 2011 survey of state and local governments reports that many respondents were cutting back on their commitments, shifting more costs to employees in the form of higher premiums, co-payments, and deductibles.[23] Given the uncertainty of eventual payment, the 2009 normal cost was re-estimated using a certainty equivalency factor of 50 percent, which reduced the applicable normal cost to 3.9 percent.[24] This figure was then

20. Benefits include paid leave, such as vacation, holiday, or sick pay; supplemental bonus pay, such as bonuses and overtime; insurance, such as life and health coverage; retirement and savings, which includes employer contributions to defined benefit and defined contribution plans; and legally required benefits, such as Social Security and Medicare.

21. Richwine and Biggs (2011).

22. Center for Retirement Research at Boston College (2011h). Appendix 2C in chapter 2, containing the most recent data, reports a lower aggregate normal cost of 7.1 percent. The decline since 2009 reflects retiree health cost reductions made by employers in response to budget pressures in the wake of the financial crisis.

23. Center for State and Local Government Excellence (2011).

24. Faced with a risky future payoff, most individuals would accept a lower payoff with no risk. The certainty equivalency represents the riskless payoff that has equivalent value to the risky payoff. The reduction factor in this case represents the probability of actual payment by the employer, or the number of cents on each dollar of normal cost that is expected to be paid. See Mas-Colell, Whinston, and Green (1995).

increased by 25 percent to reflect the fact that retirees could purchase in a group rather than in the individual market.[25] Finally, for lack of better data, it was assumed that the normal cost in the private sector is one-half that in the public sector.[26] Adding retiree health insurance increases public sector compensation much more than private owing to the higher cost and more extensive coverage in the public sector.

PENSIONS. Comparing ECEC pension data across the public and private sectors involves two problems. First, the ECEC contributions to defined benefit pension plans include both the normal cost and an amortization payment to reduce unfunded liabilities. As the employee only earns the normal cost, the ECEC contribution number, which includes the amortization payment, *overstates* public sector compensation. Second, contributions to private sector 401(k) plans and public sector defined benefit plans are not comparable. The public sector contribution essentially guarantees a return of about 8 percent, whereas no such guarantee exists for 401(k)s. Thus the public sector contribution *understates* public sector compensation.

Given the limitations of the ECEC data, total normal cost was assumed to equal 13.6 percent (liabilities discounted at 8 percent) of payrolls as reported in the *Public Plans Database* (PPD). This number was then multiplied by the state/local payroll coverage rate of 85 percent to reflect the fact that the PPD relates to *covered* payroll while the ECEC number refers to *total* payroll.[27] The recent academic literature suggests that a defined contribution account can earn a certainty equivalency return of 1.23 percentage points more than the risk-free interest rate by allowing for investment in equities.[28] Therefore the public plan normal cost was recalculated using an interest rate of 6.23 percent (5 percent riskless rate + 1.23 percent).[29] The employee contribution was then subtracted,

25. This adjustment was suggested by Richwine and Biggs (2011).

26. The 50 percent reduction may be excessive. A survey of limited data in the *Public Plans Database* showed that the average retiree-only individual premium was $300 to $400 monthly for three plans that reported between 2006 and 2010. Meanwhile, the private sector premium was $270 monthly according to McArdle and others (2006).

27. Author's calculations from U.S. Census Bureau and U.S. Department of Labor (2010).

28. Gollier (2008); and author's conversation with Peter Diamond, emeritus professor at MIT, in 2011. The Gollier model assumes a portfolio that is rebalanced annually over a forty-year investment period to maintain a constant equity allocation of 40.4 percent. The risk-free rate is assumed to remain constant over time, and future stock returns are completely independent.

29. See Center for Retirement Research at Boston College (2011h) for a description of this calculation.

Figure 6-6. *Total Compensation of State and Local and Private Sector Workers, as a Percentage of Private Sector Wages, 2010*

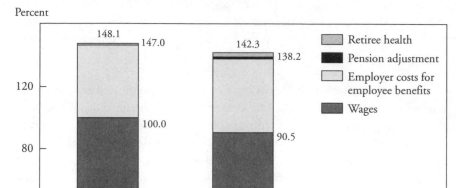

Source: Center for Retirement Research at Boston College (2011h).

and the amount by which the re-estimated employer normal cost exceeds the ECEC contribution number was added to employee benefits.[30]

The calculations show that state and local benefits nearly offset the private sector wage premium, so that compensation in the public sector is only slightly less than that in the private sector (see figure 6-6). Given all the assumptions required, the best way to describe the respective compensation levels is that they are roughly equal. Surprisingly, researchers do not differ greatly in their view of the findings up to this point.[31] The remaining disagreement is over the issue of job security and the extent to which it should be quantified and included in the compensation calculation.

---

30. The original ECEC contribution number includes amortization payments on unfunded liabilities in addition to the normal cost. This number is adjusted so that it reflects only the estimated normal cost component, or the increase in lifetime benefits earned by one more year of service.

31. An exception is Gittleman and Pierce (2011), who find that state government workers have compensation costs 3–10 percent greater than their private sector counterparts and that local government workers have compensation costs 10–19 percent greater. This study differs from other compensation studies in three ways: it uses microdata from the Bureau of Labor Statistics that are not readily available to other researchers; it includes extremely detailed occupation controls that other studies do not use; and it does not include a control for firm size.

Job Security

The argument is that job security, like wages and benefits, is a major goal of collective bargaining. To the extent that workers have security, they should be willing to accept less in wages or benefits.[32] The issue of job security raises three questions. First, is it correct that state and local workers have more job security than their private sector counterparts, or does their apparent security reflect the fact that they are better educated and older? Second, to the extent to which job security is a factor, should it be considered as part of the work environment or quantified as part of compensation? Third, if it is to be quantified, how best should it be measured?

To answer the first question requires an exploration of the importance of state and local employment, as opposed to employee characteristics, in explaining job security. Indeed, an equation relating the probability of those age 25 to 64 being unemployed for the period 2001–10, controlling for education and age, shows that state and local employment reduces the likelihood of being unemployed by 2 percentage points.[33] This difference is meaningful given that the unemployment rate averaged about 6 percent over the period 2000–10. Whether job security will remain a tenet of public sector employment is slightly less clear. Since the onset of the recession in 2007, by June of 2012 employment in the state and local sector was down 3.4 percent since its peak compared to 3.9 percent for the private sector.[34] And whereas the private sector has ceased dropping jobs, the state and local sector is continuing to contract.

The second question is how to think about greater job security in the public sector. One could argue that it is just one of many nonquantifiable factors that characterize public sector employment. State and local workers also have several negative aspects to their work environment. Anyone who has visited a state or local employment site knows that the accommodations are often cramped and grim. In addition, public employees operate in an environment where wages are compressed, so they have little chance of ever earning a lot of money.[35] Moreover, since the financial crisis, public employees are the target of derision and blamed for the budget shortfalls facing state and local governments.

But say one wants to quantify the value of job security and incorporate that measure into the compensation calculation, how should the exercise proceed?

---

32. To the extent that state and local workers are more risk averse than the average worker, as is discussed in chapter 7, job security would be a particularly valuable benefit.

33. This finding is consistent with Biggs (2011a).

34. The private sector peak was January 2008; the public sector peak was August 2008. The decline in employment was measured from each peak to June 2012.

35. See Borjas (2002).

A recent study gave this advantage a baseline value of 6 percent.[36] On the other hand, the difference in the cost for supplemental unemployment insurance suggests that the premium for job security in the public sector amounts to only 2.4 percent of private sector wages.[37] Either estimate is unlikely to overturn the general conclusion that private sector and state and local workers receive about the same level of compensation, including both wages and fringe benefits. This equality on average, however, hides the fact that lower-paid state and local workers receive more than they could earn in the private sector, whereas the higher-paid receive less.

Do State and Local Workers End Up Rich?

Given that a direct look at total compensation shows little difference between private sector and state and local workers, this section attempts to measure whether, at the end of the day, state and local employees end up with more wealth at retirement than their private sector counterparts. That is, it looks at the wealth of couples where the head is age 65 and tests, controlling for many other factors that could affect the outcome, whether state and local employment has a positive or negative effect on wealth and how that effect is related to tenure in the state and local sector. By definition, this approach is an indirect way to measure compensation; many factors could affect lifetime saving and wealth. So the results need to be interpreted with caution. But they do provide some evidence for those who think state and local workers end up a lot richer than those with careers in the private sector.

The analysis uses data from the *Health and Retirement Study* (HRS), a nationally representative panel of older American households.[38] This study began in 1992 by interviewing about 12,650 individuals from about 7,600 households ages 51–61 and their spouses (regardless of age), and the survey has been re-administered every two years since 1992. Over time, other cohorts have been added to the survey, substantially increasing the sample size. The strategy here is to focus on the original 1992 cohort and limit the analysis to retired married couples. Given the age range of the original sample, the first group reaches 65 in 1996 and the last group in 2006. The final sample includes 1,100 households, roughly 20 percent of which had spent some time in the state and local sector.

36. For California, the value increases to 15 percent because California public employees are assumed to be highly risk averse and enjoy a substantial compensation premium compared to their private sector counterparts. See Biggs (2011b and 2011c) for a more detailed discussion of the value of public sector job security.

37. Biggs (2011b).

38. Center for Retirement Research at Boston College (2011i).

Figure 6-7. *Distribution of HRS Respondents and Spouses by Percent of Career Spent in the State and Local Sector, 1996–2006*

Percent

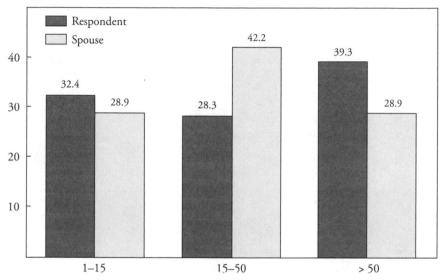

Percent of career in state/local employment

Source: Center for Retirement Research at Boston College (2011i).

The estimated equation relates total household wealth when the respondent is 65 to the percentage of the respondent's and the spouse's career spent as a state/local worker.[39] Because defined benefit plans are backloaded—delayed vesting, increasing benefit factors, and benefits based on final earnings—the relationship between state and local tenure and wealth would not be expected to be linear. Thus tenure is broken into three periods: 1 percent to 15 percent of career spent as a state/local employee; 15 percent to 50 percent; and over 50 percent. Figure 6-7 shows that roughly equal numbers of state and local workers fall in each category.[40]

Before proceeding with the analysis, it is interesting to see how the wealth of households with a state/local worker compares to that of households with a history of private sector employment. Figure 6-8 shows that the relationship varies

39. The sample is constructed so that all the respondents are men and all the spouses are women.

40. As one would expect, those with less tenure tend to have left state/local employment early in their careers, while those with longer tenure left at older ages. The average age of departure for short-tenured workers was about 33; the average age of departure for long-tenured workers was 46.

Figure 6-8. *Percent Difference between Age-65 Wealth for Couples with State/Local versus Private Sector Employment, by State/Local Tenure, 1996–2006*

Percent of career in state/local employment

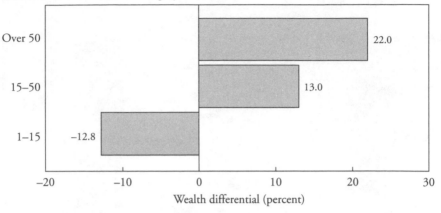

Wealth differential (percent)

Source: Center for Retirement Research at Boston College (2011i).

with how long the individual worked in state and local employment. Couples with a long-tenured state/local worker have 22 percent more wealth, while those with a short-tenured worker have 13 percent less. The question is how much of these differences can be explained by the nature of the individuals and the nature of the jobs.

The Analysis

In order to isolate the impact of tenure in the state/local sector, it is necessary to control for personal and job characteristics that could affect wealth accumulation. The focus is on married couples at 65, so no controls are required for marital status or age of the respondent. The control variables included in the equation fall into four groups: demographics; personality factors; other sources of wealth; and job characteristics.

Demographic variables include:

—*Education.* More years of schooling for either the husband or wife should be associated with more wealth.

—*Race.* The literature suggests that nonwhites would be expected to have less wealth.

—*Age of spouse.* Although the respondent is 65, the spouse can be any age. The hypothesis is the older the spouse, the shorter the expected life of the couple and therefore the less need for wealth.

—*Life expectancy.* This variable is the self-reported probability of living to age 75. A higher probability would be expected to be correlated with more wealth. The nature of the couple could also have an impact on wealth accumulation.

—*Percentage of wealth held in stocks.* Households with a greater taste for high-risk/high-return investments would be expected to have more wealth.

—*Risk aversion.* The HRS asks participants to choose between pairs of jobs where the pay is more or less risky. Based on their responses, they are assigned levels of risk preference ranging from 1 being least risk averse to 6 being most risk averse. Risk aversion is defined as being in level 5 or 6. Risk aversion and wealth would be expected to be positively related.

—*Long horizon.* Households with a longer financial planning horizon are more likely to save and end up with wealth.

Other factors that could affect wealth accumulation include whether the household consists of one or two earners and whether the household has received or expects to receive an inheritance.

—*Career spouse.* Two-earner households, especially at high education levels, would be expected to have more wealth than a single earner.[41]

—*Expect inheritance*: All else equal, households expecting to receive an inheritance would have lower wealth. However, if taste for saving is correlated among generations, and not fully accounted for in the regression, then households expecting to receive an inheritance could have higher wealth.

—*Received inheritance*: Households having already received an inheritance would have higher wealth.

Job characteristics include occupation, firm size, and region.

—*Occupation.* The ten job categories are: management, professional, service, sales, administrative support, agriculture and forestry, construction and extraction, maintenance and repair, production, and transportation occupations.[42]

—*Firm size.* Firm size consists of five groups: 24 employees or fewer; 25 to 99; 100 to 499; 500 to 999; and 1,000 or more.[43]

—*Census region.* The nation is divided into five regions: Northeast, Midwest, South, West, and Other.

Note that the list of control variables does not contain any measure of lifetime earnings. The reason is that we are *not* asking, "For a given level of earnings, what is the impact on wealth of being a state/local worker?" It is widely

---

41. The variable is equal to one if the spouse worked at least ten years and retired no earlier than age 50. To reflect the hypothesis that the impact on wealth of a second earner will vary with education, the equation includes another variable that interacts education and career-spouse.

42. Members of the armed forces are excluded.

43. This variable is the number of employees at the respondent's location from the individual wave data. However, a large number of missing values requires imputations based on occupational averages from the *Current Population Survey* for public and private sector workers separately.

Figure 6-9. *Impact of State/Local Tenure on Percent Difference between Age-65 Wealth for Couples with State/Local versus Private Sector Employment, 1996–2006*[a]

Percent of career in state/local employment

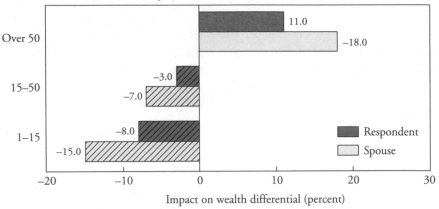

Impact on wealth differential (percent)

Source: Center for Retirement Research at Boston College (2011i).

a. Solid bars indicate the coefficient is statistically significant at least at the 10 percent level. The bars represent the relationship between the characteristic and total wealth.

acknowledged that equivalent individuals would have different lifetime earnings depending on whether they worked in the public or private sector. The question of interest here is, "Given personal characteristics, occupation, enterprise size, and region of the country, does it matter in terms of household wealth at 65 whether an individual spends his/her career in the private or public sector?" This broader question does not require controlling for earnings.

In the regression equation, the coefficients of all the control variables come in with the expected signs and are statistically significant.[44] The impact of state/local employment is presented in figure 6-9. The results show that spending more than 50 percent of one's career as a state or local worker is associated with 11 percent (respondent) to 18 percent (spouse) more household wealth at age 65, and the coefficients are statistically significant. About one-third of those with some state or local employment fall into this category.

The relationships between shorter periods of state/local tenure and wealth are consistent with expectations, although the coefficients are not always statistically significant. Those who spend only a brief time in state or local employment

44. The coefficient of expected inheritances, whose expected sign was ambiguous, turned out to be positive, suggesting that it captures an inherited taste for saving.

appear to end up with less wealth than those who never work as a public employee. About a third of those with public sector employment fall into this group. This finding is not surprising, given that many leave without vesting in the pension and receive only a refund of their contributions and some small interest payment. And those who work for employers without Social Security leave with much less than they would have accrued in the private sector where coverage is universal. The wealth of those who spend an intermediate portion of their career (15 to 50 percent) in state or local employment looks very similar to that of private sector employees at age 65.

Some Further Questions

The results presented above raise a number of questions. How does one account for possible early retirement of state and local workers? Does simply being covered by a defined benefit plan force people to save more? Are 1996–2006 results applicable in 2012?

EARLY RETIREMENT. The analysis implicitly assumes that state/local and private sector workers retire at the same time. But what if state and local workers had been retired for a significant period of time before they were observed at age 65? To take an extreme example, suppose they had retired from a state or local job and had received a pension and retiree health insurance for fifteen years, from age 50 to age 65. Such a pattern requires addressing two issues: (1) the value of pensions and retiree health insurance received during that period; and (2) the value of the leisure enjoyed. The financial aspect of such a situation is captured in the analysis. The pension can be viewed as equivalent to a wage, and to the extent that it is saved or avoids the drawdown of accumulated assets, it will be reflected in the final wealth figure. Similarly, savings from not having to purchase retiree health insurance will show up in the wealth at 65. The really troublesome issue would be the fact that someone had fifteen years of leisure. Valuing such leisure would be important in any final assessment of comparability of public versus private compensation.

As it turned out, the leisure issue was not a major problem. Most of the respondents who had spent time in the state/local sector ended up retiring from a private sector job. The retirement age of those public sector employees who moved to the private sector was actually higher than that of workers who had spent their entire careers in the private sector. Those who retired directly from state/local jobs did retire early, but they accounted for only a small fraction of those with state and local employment. In short, an issue that could have complicated the analysis turned out to not be particularly important.

A related issue is the treatment of the income received by state and local employees who leave their public sector jobs and move to the private sector.

These individuals would be earning wages from their private employer and (if eligible) could be simultaneously receiving a pension from their former state or local employer. Again, to the extent that any of this income is saved, it will be reflected in the final wealth figure.

ROLE OF DEFINED BENEFIT PLANS. That households with a long-tenured state/local worker end up with greater wealth than households with a history of private sector employment could reflect that either: (1) they received more in total compensation; or (2) they worked in a defined benefit environment where they were forced to save. Indeed, 78 percent of state and local households in the sample received a defined benefit pension; only 59 percent of private sector households did.

To test the importance of being covered by a defined benefit plan, the equation was re-estimated including a variable indicating the receipt of a defined benefit pension. The results show that the advantage of being a long-tenured state and local worker disappears totally for men, as the coefficient is not significantly different from zero.[45] In the case of women, the effect remains, but is reduced. This finding is not surprising given that women's relative wages are higher in the public sector than in the private sector.[46] In any event, the results suggest that wealth comparisons between state and local and private sector workers are influenced by the discipline imposed by the pension structure.

APPLICABILITY TO TODAY. The analysis covers the period 1996–2006, and the question is the extent to which it reflects circumstances after that date. A number of changes have occurred in the intervening period. For example, at this writing in 2012, private sector retirees are less likely to have a defined benefit plan and retiree health insurance than their counterparts in the past, which would suggest that their situation has worsened in comparison with that of public employees. On the other hand, public sector wages relative to those in the private sector have declined over time, and recently government sponsors have increased employee contributions to pensions, cut cost-of-living adjustments, reduced benefits for new employees, and raised employee premiums and co-payments for retiree health, which works in the other direction. On balance, it is unclear how recent developments would affect the picture.

In short, as a group, households in which one or both members worked in the state/local sector do not end up richer than couples with private sector

45. The addition of the defined benefit control had virtually no impact on the magnitude or significance of the other coefficients.
46. Borjas (2002).

careers. This analysis is an indirect contribution to the debate over state/local versus private sector compensation.

Do State and Local Workers End Up with "Too Much" in Pensions?

A widespread perception is that state and local government workers receive high pension benefits that, combined with Social Security, provide more-than-adequate retirement income.[47] The perception is consistent with multiplying the 2 percent benefit factor in most plan formulas by a thirty-five- to forty-year career and adding a Social Security benefit. But this calculation assumes that individuals spend enough of their career in the public sector to produce such a retirement outcome. The following analysis uses the HRS to test the hypothesis that state/local workers have more than enough money for retirement.[48]

The "Replacement Rate" Concept

Replacement rates are used to gauge the extent to which older people can maintain their pre-retirement levels of consumption once they stop working.[49] The most direct approach would be a comparison of household consumption while working with consumption after retirement. But such data are rarely available. An indirect approach is to compare pre- and post-retirement income.[50]

People clearly need less than their full pre-retirement income to maintain their standard of living once they stop working. One big difference before and after retirement is the extent to which income is taxed. When people are working, their earnings are subject to both Social Security and Medicare payroll taxes and federal personal income taxes. After retirement, they no longer pay payroll

47. Beshears and others (2011).

48. Center for Retirement Research at Boston College (2011f).

49. Technically people are interested in smoothing marginal utility, not consumption. To the extent that they get pleasure from leisure in retirement, they can maintain overall utility with lower levels of consumption after they stop working. The enjoyment of leisure may explain what the literature calls the "retirement-consumption puzzle"—namely, the fact that consumption appears to drop as people retire. See Bernheim, Skinner, and Weinberg (2001); Banks, Blundell, and Tanner (1998); and Hurd and Rohwedder (2003).

50. In an extension of the replacement rate approach, to test whether people are saving optimally for retirement, two studies (Engen, Gale, and Uccello (1999) and Scholz, Seshadri, and Khitatrakun (2004)) compare people's actual behavior with the behavior that comes out of simulation models. In these simulations, households attempt to smooth their consumption over their remaining lives as they are buffeted by shocks to their wages, employment, and health. Because of these shocks, households with very similar characteristics can end up with very different levels of wealth. Most of these simulations have produced results where households' actual level of preparedness looks very much like the numbers generated by the simulations, suggesting that people respond rationally to life events.

taxes, and they pay lower federal income taxes because only a portion of Social Security benefits are taxable.[51]

A second major reason why retirees require less than their full pre-retirement income is that they no longer need to save a portion of that income for retirement. In addition to contributing to 401(k) plans, many households try to pay off their mortgage before they retire. In retirement, these households no longer need to save and, in fact, can draw on their accumulated reserves. Thus a greater share of their income is available for consumption.

The RETIRE Project at Georgia State University has been calculating required replacement rates—that is, retirement income as a percentage of pre-retirement earnings—for decades.[52] As of 2008, the project estimated that a couple with an income of $50,000 required 81 percent of pre-retirement earnings to maintain the same level of consumption (see table 6-2). Couples earning $90,000 needed 78 percent, and couples earning $20,000 needed 94 percent because they save very little before retirement and after retirement enjoy less in the way of tax reduction.

Constructing Replacement Rates

Constructing actual replacement rates for individual workers raises a number of issues. The first question is the relevant measure of pre-retirement earnings. Social Security—the primary source of monthly cash income for today's elderly Americans—replaces a portion of "average indexed monthly earnings" (AIME), which is essentially the thirty-five highest years of earnings indexed to the present by wage growth.[53] Employer-sponsored defined benefit plans—the other source

---

51. The percentage of Social Security benefits subject to personal income taxation is as follows. Individuals with "combined income" between $25,000 and $34,000 pay tax on 50 percent of benefits; over $34,000 they pay on 85 percent. Couples with "combined income" between $32,000 and $44,000 pay tax on 50 percent of benefits; over $44,000 they pay on 85 percent. "Combined income" is adjusted gross income as reported on tax forms plus nontaxable interest income plus one-half of Social Security benefits.

52. For an array of pre-retirement earnings levels, they calculate federal, state, and local income taxes and Social Security taxes before and after retirement. They also use the U.S. Bureau of Labor Statistics *Consumer Expenditure Survey* to estimate consumer savings and expenditures for different earnings levels.

53. In the case of retirement, the AIME is determined in two steps. First, the worker's annual taxable earnings after 1950 are updated, or indexed, to reflect the general earnings level in the indexing year, which is age 60. Earnings in years after age 60 are not indexed but instead are counted at their actual value. A worker's earnings before age 60 are indexed by multiplying them by the ratio of the average wage in the national economy for the indexing year to the corresponding average wage figure for the year to be indexed. Second, the AIME is calculated by taking the highest thirty-five years of wage-indexed earnings between ages 22 and 62 and dividing that total by the number of months in that period.

Table 6-2. *Percentage of Pre-retirement Salary Required to Maintain Living Standards, 2008*

Pre-retirement earnings	Two-earner couples (percent)	Single workers (percent)
$20,000	94	88
$50,000	81	80
$90,000	78	81

Source: Palmer (2008).

of monthly income—typically replace a portion of the worker's annual earnings during the last three or five years of employment, which tend to be the worker's highest-earning years with that employer. Thus pre-retirement income could be defined as: (1) some measure of lifetime earnings; (2) earnings with a particular employer; or (3) earnings just before retirement. This analysis uses earnings just before retirement, defined as the highest five in the last ten years adjusted for inflation, because it provides a measure of the end-of career standard of living that workers seek to maintain in retirement.

A second consideration is defining when "pre-retirement" ends and retirement begins. With the growth of bridge jobs, it is often impossible to precisely define the work/retirement divide. For this reason, this analysis focuses on the first year that workers start receiving Social Security benefits. In the case of couples, retirement is defined as when both members of the household are receiving benefits.

A third consideration is the unit of analysis. Replacement rates have largely been calculated on an individual worker basis, even though the great majority (roughly 80 percent) of Americans enter retirement as part of a married-couple household. The usual presentation of replacement rates for individual workers no doubt reflects the fact that Social Security and employer pension benefits are based on individual worker earnings. However, given that households consume on a joint basis, the following presents replacement rates for couples.

Replacement Rates for Households

The calculation of replacement rates relies on data from the HRS, the nationally representative longitudinal survey of older Americans described earlier. Again, the analysis uses the original HRS sample and follows this group through the 2008 survey.[54] The final sample consists of 4,469 newly retired households.

---

54. The HRS expanded the sample dramatically in 1998 and 2004, with the addition of the War Babies (born between 1942 and 1947) and Early Boomers (born between 1948 and 1953), respectively. The latest sample addition, made in 2010, was the inclusion of the Mid Boomers (born between 1954 and 1959). Like the original sample, these three additional cohorts are interviewed every two years.

For this sample, the task is to calculate replacement rates first for Social Security and then for Social Security and employer-sponsored defined benefit and defined contribution plans, and to present the results for households that spent their entire career in the private sector and those that worked in the state/local sector. As in the discussion of wealth at age 65, replacement rates are reported by the percentage of career spent in the state/local sector: 1–15 percent, 15–50 percent, and more than 50 percent.[55] As shown in figure 6-10, roughly one-third of households are in the middle group, somewhat more in the short-tenure group, and somewhat fewer in the long-tenure group.

The first step is to calculate *total* earnings just before retirement for each worker in the household. Since reported earnings in the HRS are top-coded at the Social Security maximum taxable earnings for each year, the calculation of actual career-average earnings for some individuals requires imputations. For individuals with coded earnings at the cap, their total earnings are imputed using regression results from an estimated wage equation.[56] The total earnings history is then used to calculate the highest five in the last ten years adjusted for inflation for each individual.

Each household's Social Security replacement rate is determined by dividing household Social Security benefits calculated at the relevant retirement age by the earnings before retirement. The results are shown in table 6-3. Social Security alone provides a median replacement rate for private workers of 32 percent and for state and local workers of 29 percent.

The next step is to include income from defined benefit and defined contribution plans. In both cases, income was calculated as the annuitized value of pension wealth. The argument for taking this approach in the case of defined benefit as well as defined contribution plans is that simply reporting the first-year benefit would understate the value of state and local defined benefit pensions since these benefits are adjusted annually—at least partially—for inflation.

Both defined benefit and defined contribution wealth come from data posted on the HRS website. The data are presented at ages 50, 55, 60, 62, and 65, and the observation selected was the one closest to the individual's

---

55. The HRS reports the year the individual began work in the state/local sector and the year state/local employment ended. Subtracting one year from the other provides the total years spent in the state/local sector; those years are then divided by the total length of the individual's career, as reported in the version of the HRS data maintained by the RAND Corporation. For couples with two state/local workers, the household is classified by the tenure of the longest tenure worker.

56. About 15 percent of the final sample of individuals used in this study required imputations for at least one year of earnings. To impute earnings for those at the maximum taxable earnings, a random-effects, Tobit regression is applied to all of the available data, with earnings below the cap as the dependent variable. The explanatory variables include age, age square, categorical variables for gender, college degree and race, and dummies for each decade.

Figure 6-10. *Distribution of Households with State and Local Workers in the Health and Retirement Study, by Tenure*

Percent

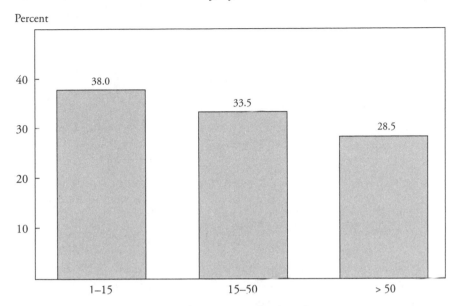

Percent of career in state/local employment

Source: Center for Retirement Research at Boston College (2011f).

retirement age.[57] Unfortunately, the wealth data are available for only a portion of the sample, so defined benefit pension wealth had to be calculated from reported benefits for the remaining individuals using the same assumptions about inflation and asset returns.[58]

Individuals are identified as having a defined contribution plan in one of two ways—either they have defined contribution wealth or they indicated in the first (1992) wave that they were covered by an employer-sponsored defined contribution plan. For those with coverage but without a measure of defined contribution wealth, Individual Retirement Account (IRA) balances are set equal to pension wealth because most of the assets in these accounts are rollovers from

57. A small fraction (about 2 percent) of respondents in the HRS sample indicated having a pension plan with both defined benefit and defined contribution characteristics. Data on defined contribution assets in these "combined" plans were often not available, so they are grouped together with defined benefit plans.

58. The resulting numbers for both defined benefit and defined contribution plans are comparable to those reported by Gustman and Steinmeier (1999).

Table 6-3. *Median Replacement Rates for Households by Employment History*[a]

Retirement income source	Private sector			State/local sector			
					Percent of career spent in state/local sector		
	All	*Without pensions*	*With pensions*	*All*	*1–15*	*15–50*	*>50*
Social Security	32.0	35.7	30.9	29.3	29.7	29.4	28.3
Social Security + pensions[b]	46.9	35.7	52.0	57.4	47.6	57.0	71.8
Addendum: Percent of sample	67	24	43	33	13	11	9

Source: Center for Retirement Research at Boston College (2011a).

a. The denominator is based on each individual's top five years of earnings in the last ten years indexed for inflation.

b. For those with pension coverage, IRA assets are included in defined contribution wealth; for those without pension coverage, IRA assets are classified as part of financial assets.

401(k) plans and the earnings on those rollovers.[59] For those with wealth, IRA balances are combined with defined contribution assets. For those without pension coverage, IRA assets are included in total financial wealth.[60]

The next step is to derive a stream of annual income by applying annuity factors to the defined benefit and defined contribution wealth. The annuity factors vary by gender and marital status. In addition, an 18 percent increase in cost due to adverse selection, marketing, and other factors is applied to annuities purchased in the private market.[61] Married men are assumed to opt for a joint-and-survivor annuity that provides 50 percent of the benefit to the surviving spouse. The replacement rates reported are based on nominal annuities, under which the purchasing power of benefits will decline over time; replacement rates based on real (inflation-adjusted) annuities would produce lower initial levels of replacement.

59. Increasingly, IRA accumulations will also include rollovers from defined benefit and cash balance plans.

60. Median defined contribution wealth for those with coverage is $67,000 (excluding IRA assets) and median defined benefit wealth is $80,000. These results are fully consistent with those from other studies.

61. Premium loads on annuities vary with annuity type and with the age of purchase. They also vary between companies and over time, and are somewhat sensitive to the choice of interest rate used to calculate expected present values. Mitchell and others (1999), table 3, report loads that are typically on the order of 18 percent.

Household income from the annuitized value of defined benefit and defined contribution assets is summed for individuals in the households. As before, household replacement rates are estimated at the first year in which both members of the household are retired.[62] Dividing these values by the earnings measure produces pension replacement rates.

Table 6-3 shows the impact of income from employer-sponsored plans on the replacement rates of households for private sector and state and local workers. Adding the annuitized value of defined benefit and defined contribution wealth to Social Security brings the median replacement rate to 47 percent for private sector workers and to 57 percent for workers with some state and local employment.

Replacement rates are higher in the state/local sector than in the private sector, primarily because almost 40 percent of private sector households have no employer-sponsored pension benefits. Within the public sector, replacement rates increase with tenure from 48 percent for households with a short-tenured employee to 72 percent for those with a long-tenured worker. Again, median replacement rates do not reach the 80 percent target for most households with state and local employment.

The Impact of Non-Pension Financial Assets

The final exercise with the HRS explores the impact of non-pension financial assets on replacement rates. Financial wealth includes stocks, bonds, savings and checking accounts, certificates of deposit, and any other account, minus non-housing debt.

In order to make the calculations economically meaningful, the definition of pre-retirement income needs to be expanded to include a measure of pre-retirement income from financial assets. Non-pension financial wealth was not annuitized; rather, income was derived by applying a nominal return to asset values. The nominal return on financial assets was 5.1 percent, consistent with the assumptions used throughout the analysis. The results are shown in table 6-4. Adding income from financial assets closes the gap somewhat, but still leaves most state and local households short.

The major finding from the HRS analysis is that most households with state and local employment end up with replacement rates that, while on average higher than those in the private sector, are well below the 80 percent needed to maintain pre-retirement living standards. Even those households with a

---

62. This calculation is done by estimating the annuity value for defined benefit and defined contribution pensions for each member of the household starting at his or her retirement age and then projecting this value to the year in which the second member of the household retires.

Table 6-4. *Median Replacement Rates for Households, Including Financial Assets, by Employment History*[a]

Retirement income source	Private sector			State/local sector			
					Percent of career spent in state/local sector		
	All	Without pensions	With pensions	All	1–15	15–50	>50
Social Security	30.3	34.0	29.1	27.1	27.8	27.3	25.8
Social Security + pensions[b]	44.8	34.0	50.0	53.1	43.4	54.2	67.5
Social Security + pensions[b] + financial assets[c]	51.0	40.5	55.6	60.2	50.9	61.3	72.7

a. The denominator is based on each individual's top five years of earnings in the last ten years indexed for inflation plus income from financial assets.

b. For those with pension coverage, IRA assets are included in defined contribution wealth; for those without pension coverage, IRA assets are classified as part of financial assets.

c. The real return on financial assets is assumed to be 2.3 percent.

Source: Center for Retirement Research at Boston College (2011f).

long-service state/local worker—those who spend more than half of their careers in public employment—have a median replacement rate, including Social Security and financial assets, of only 73 percent. And this group accounts for less than 30 percent of households with a state/local worker. The remaining 70 percent of households with a short- or medium-tenure state/local worker have replacement rates of 51 percent and 61 percent, respectively.

Conclusion

Wages for workers with similar characteristics, education, and experience are lower for state and local workers than for those in the private sector. Most researchers agree on this point. Pension and retiree health benefits for state and local workers roughly offset the wage penalty, so that total compensation in the two sectors is roughly comparable. But the parity of compensation between the public and private sectors hides enormous variation by wage levels. State and local workers in the lowest third of the wage distribution are paid somewhat more than their private sector counterparts, those in the middle roughly comparable amounts, and those in the top third significantly less. Outcomes at retirement are related to lifetime employment patterns. Those who spend *most of their career* in the state/local sector end up with more wealth and higher replacement rates than their private sector counterparts. Short-term state and local workers actually end up with less wealth and lower replacement rates than similarly situated private sector employees.

The overwhelming conclusion is that, for the nation as a whole, the difference between state/local and private sector compensation is modest. The implication of this relatively modest differential is that policymakers need to be cautious about massive changes without carefully studying the specifics of their particular situation. This caution is particularly relevant in the case of teachers, who constitute more than half of state/local employees and who often fall within the top third of state/local workers and already earn significantly less than private sector workers with similar socioeconomic characteristics.

7

Do Defined Contribution Plans Have a Role in the Public Sector?

The financial crisis and its aftermath generated two types of responses from sponsors of state and local government pensions. The first was to cut back on existing defined benefit plan commitments by raising employee contributions, reducing benefits for new employees, and in some cases suspending the cost-of-living adjustment for existing retirees. The second response was to initiate proposals to shift some or all of the pension system from a defined benefit to a defined contribution plan. This chapter explores the implications of such a shift for the employer and the employee in order to answer the question whether defined contribution plans have a role to play in the public sector.

The discussion is organized as follows. The first section offers some explanations for why defined benefit plans have lasted so long in the public sector, when 401(k) plans now dominate the private sector. The second section discusses the strengths and weaknesses of public sector defined benefit plans. The third section reports on the results of the thirty-year experiment in the private sector with increasing reliance solely on defined contribution plans. The fourth section describes the extent of the shift to defined contribution plans in the public sector both before and after the financial crisis. The fifth section discusses various pension redesign options available to state and local governments.

The main conclusion that emerges from this discussion is that defined contribution plans do have a role to play in the public sector. While defined benefit plans provide the most predictable retirement income for long-service employees, sole reliance on these plans in a political arena puts states and localities at considerable financial risk and creates a reward structure that provides little for shorter-term workers. At the same time, the 401(k) experiment in the private sector suggests that a wholesale shift to such plans would transfer too much risk to public sector workers. In order to balance risks and to provide some benefits for mobile workers, some combination of defined benefit and defined contribution plans would enhance the benefit structure in the public sector.

Why Have Defined Benefit Plans Lasted So Long in the Public Sector?

In the 1970s, the nature of pension coverage in the public and private sectors was quite similar. In both sectors, the overwhelming majority of those with pensions were covered by a defined benefit plan. These plans provided employees with lifetime retirement income based on a formula that accounted for service and final average salary; the assets were held in trust and managed by professional investors. The public sector plans differed from their private sector counterparts in two ways: public sector plans adjusted benefits, at least partially, for inflation after retirement and employees as well as employers generally contributed. But in both cases, the employer bore the investment risk and provided guaranteed lifetime income.

By 2010, however, the picture was quite different (see figure 7-1). While the vast majority of public sector workers remained in defined benefit plans, only one quarter of private sector employees with coverage had such a pension. Most private sector workers were covered by a 401(k) plan. These plans are like savings accounts, where both the employee and the employer contribute to the account, the employee selects the investments, and the benefit at retirement depends on the value of the assets. The question is why the pattern of pension coverage evolved so differently in the two sectors. What role was played by the employer, the employee, and the regulatory environment?

The Employer

Employers in the public sector are different from those in the private sector: they are perpetual entities, and they are much less sensitive to financial market volatility. Each characteristic has had both a direct and an indirect effect on the likelihood of having a defined benefit plan.

PERPETUAL ENTITIES. In the private sector, the shift from defined benefit plans to 401(k)s occurred primarily through the decline of companies with defined benefit plans and the establishment of 401(k) plans at new companies. Thus the demise of old firms in manufacturing and other industries and the rise of new firms in services and high tech provided an automatic mechanism for pension change in the private sector. Not until the post-2000 round of "pension freezes" did large employers shut down a defined benefit plan and open a successor

Figure 7-1. *Percentage of Workers with Pension Coverage with Defined Benefit Plan, by Sector 1975 and 2010*

Percent

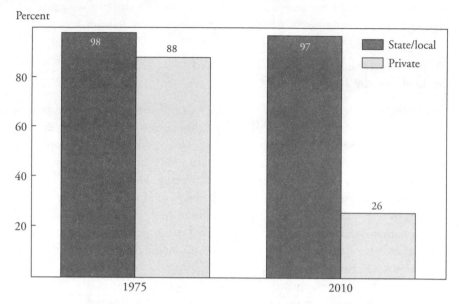

Source: Author's calculations from U.S. Congress (1978); U.S. Board of Governors of the Federal Reserve System, *Survey of Consumer Finances* (2007); U.S. Department of Labor, *Current Employment Statistics* (2009); and *Public Plans Database* (2009).

401(k) or expand an existing one.[1] No such "organizational churn" occurs in the public sector, since most governmental units exist in perpetuity, so conversions must occur through the political process. Public employees and employee unions usually resist such change.

In addition to this direct effect, the perpetual nature of state and local governments also leads to higher levels of unionization, further strengthening support for defined benefit plans. As just noted, in the private sector, a portion of the growth in 401(k) plans involves the demise of old firms and the creation of new firms. Since all new firms are created union-free, unionization will decline without new organization. In contrast, in the public sector, employment tends to grow steadily in line with population, so when the growth occurs in jurisdictions already unionized, the number of unionized workers increases automatically.[2]

1. For a discussion of the factors underlying recent pension freezes, see Munnell and Soto (2007).

2. Farber (2005). The author offers two additional explanations for the different unionization patterns in the two sectors. First, the products produced by the two sectors differ. The private sector

Finally, public sector employers have an organizational interest in maintaining defined benefit plans. State and local governments are perpetual entities that deliver stable services. Because public sector jobs may be quite specialized, both employees and employers benefit from long job tenure. Defined benefit plans serve to attract and retain a high-skilled workforce needed to provide these specialized and stable services.

LESS SENSITIVITY TO VOLATILITY. Public employers do not have to worry nearly as much as those in the private sector about the fluctuations in defined benefit pension expense and unfunded liabilities caused by financial market volatility. The implications of market volatility for private sector employers have increased dramatically since the early 2000s: financial markets have been particularly turbulent and firms have been subject to increasing regulation and disclosure. The Pension Protection Act of 2006 required underfunded plans to dramatically increase their contributions, and accounting changes forced fluctuations in pension finance onto the income statement.[3] This volatility generates substantial movement in the company's cash flow and stock price, with the latter benchmark often directly affecting executive compensation.

---

produces tradable goods, where competition can limit the ability of unions to increase compensation. The public sector produces primarily nontradable goods, such as police and fire protection and education, which makes it easier for public sector unions to raise compensation without the loss of jobs. Finally, public sector unions can produce more membership benefits than their private sector counterparts. In addition to bargaining directly for compensation and workplace administration, union members can work for the election of union-friendly candidates, who can be helpful in contract negotiations. These greater potential membership benefits make unions relatively more attractive in the public sector. Also see Freeman (1988).

3. The Pension Protection Act of 2006 (PPA) represents the most significant change in pension regulation since the Employee Retirement Income Security Act of 1974. The funding rules significantly reduce the leeway that companies have in making contributions to their plans. Plans must now be 100 percent funded, and most sponsors of underfunded plans have only seven years to pay off any existing shortfall. Moreover, sponsors will have less ability to smooth the value of assets or liabilities, making cash contributions significantly more volatile. Originally intended to take effect in 2008, the funding rules were eased by three years in response to the financial downturn with the passage of the Worker, Retiree, and Employer Recovery Act. At the same time as the PPA, the Financial Accounting Standards Board (FASB) instituted the first step of a two-step pension reform project by requiring sponsors to show pension surpluses or deficits directly on the balance sheet. This change could introduce volatility to the balance sheet, which could seriously cut into shareholder equity. In the second step, FASB is expected to require companies to mark-to-market the value of pension assets and liabilities, eliminating the smoothing available under current rules. Given the enormous volatility in the stock and bond markets in recent years, marking-to-market could introduce significant additional volatility in reported earnings. Such volatility is not acceptable to corporate managers, and may in large part explain why large healthy companies have taken steps to end their defined benefit plans.

Fluctuations in pension assets and liabilities do occur in the public sector, as the bursting of the dot.com bubble and the 2008 financial collapse demonstrated. But the smoothing of gains and losses dampens reported fluctuations, and underfunded public plans do not have to comply with the legislated funding requirements that apply to private plans. As a result, until the Governmental Accounting Standards Board's (GASB's) 2012 standards take effect, a severe drop in the stock market and/ or interest rates will have less of an impact on public sector pension assets.

In addition to these accounting considerations, government has an advantage over the private sector in being able to enforce intergenerational risk sharing.[4] In that sense, it has an additional tool for managing volatility. The volatility is still present and important, but losses and gains can be spread over a larger number of people and a longer period of time. Thus the economics, like the accounting, enable public plans to better manage fluctuations in asset prices.

The Employee

A second contributor to the continued presence of defined benefit plans in the public sector may be the nature of the workforce itself. Fundamentally, public sector workers tend to be more risk-averse than their private sector counterparts. To evaluate risk preferences of individuals, economists often use the coefficient of relative risk aversion (CRRA). The *Panel Study of Income Dynamics* in 1996 asked respondents whether they would give up their current job for one with a 50-50 chance of doubling their income but also a 50-50 chance of cutting it by some percentage. The questions were asked in a sequence so that individuals could be placed into one of six categories of risk aversion. Higher values of the coefficient indicate greater aversion to risk. The results show that public employees are less comfortable with uncertainty than employees in the private sector; they have a CRRA of 5.4 compared to 2.8 for their private sector counterparts.[5] A regression equation that estimated the probability of being employed in the public sector suggests that—even after controlling for gender, race, and family status—the measure of relative risk aversion increases the probability of being a public employee by about 8 percentage points (see figure 7-2).[6] And risk-averse employees would surely want a defined benefit pension where the employer absorbs investment, longevity, and inflation risk.

Consistent with being risk-averse—and also consistent with the incentives in a defined benefit plan—public sector workers tend to have longer job tenure

---

4. Gollier (2008).

5. Individuals were assigned the mean coefficient for their risk aversion group following the methodology described by Barsky and others (1997) and Hryshko, Luengo-Prado, and Sorensen (2011).

6. This magnitude is consistent with Bellante and Link (1981), who found an effect of 7.5 percentage points.

Figure 7-2. *Relationship between Risk Aversion and Probability of Being Employed in the Public Sector*

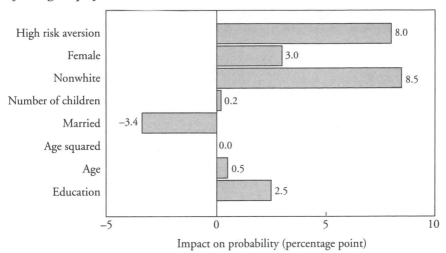

Impact on probability (percentage point)

Source: Author's calculations from University of Michigan, *Panel Study of Income Dynamics* (1996).

and be older than their private sector counterparts. While private sector workers have become more mobile over time, the median tenure of the public sector workforce actually increased over the 1973 to 2010 period (see figure 7-3). The longer tenure in the public sector results in an older workforce. As noted in the previous chapter, the percentage of the workforce over age 45 is 51 percent in the state/local sector and 44 percent in the private sector. Older workers are more likely to care about their retirement than younger workers and, not surprisingly, favor defined benefit plans.

Longer tenure, older age, and a preference for defined benefit plans are also likely to make unions more attractive to employees in the public sector. And indeed, as discussed in chapter 4, the union picture for the two sectors has diverged dramatically. While union membership in the private sector fell from 35 percent in the 1950s to 7 percent in 2010, the rate in the public sector increased from relatively low levels in the 1950s to over 35 percent in 2010.[7] And, as noted above, unions support defined benefit plans.[8]

---

7. Union membership, of course, varies by region and type of job. For example, public safety employees and teachers tend to be more unionized than others.

8. In the private sector, 58 percent of union members were covered by a defined benefit plan in 2008, but only 16 percent of nonunion workers. Author's calculations from the *Panel Study of Income Dynamics* (2009).

Figure 7-3. *Median Years of Tenure of Wage and Salary Workers Ages 25–64, by Sector, 1973–2010*[a]

Number of years

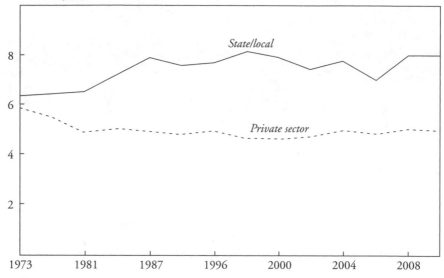

Source: Author's calculations from U.S. Census Bureau and U.S. Department of Labor, *Current Population Survey* (1973–2010).

a. The median tenure shown for state and local workers before 1983 is for all government workers.

The Regulatory Environment

A final factor contributing to the different pension profile between the public and private sectors is the regulatory environment. In the private sector, the Employee Retirement Income Security Act of 1974 (ERISA) imposes minimum standards for participation, vesting, and funding. ERISA also established the Pension Benefit Guaranty Corporation (PBGC), which collects premiums from plan sponsors and pays benefits (within limits and subject to certain restrictions) in the event of plan termination. Public plans are not covered by ERISA, which results in lower administrative costs and allows later vesting, two factors that would make defined benefit plans more attractive to public sector employers.[9]

9. Plans in both the public and the private sector operate under a common set of rules spelled out in the Internal Revenue Code. On the accounting side, standards governing public sector pensions were established by GASB in 1994. As with the Financial Accounting Standards Board (FASB) in the private sector, GASB acts as a standard-setter but does not actually enforce compliance. However, compliance with GASB standards is necessary for the plan to receive a statement that its financial statement is in accordance with generally accepted accounting principles (GAAP).

It was not only the original enactment of ERISA that raised the costs of running a private defined benefit plan, but also subsequent legislation that Congress enacted every few years during the 1980s.[10] Congress also repeatedly raised PBGC premiums and imposed an excise tax on employers who claim the excess assets of terminated defined benefit plans. The cumulative impact of the legislative changes increased the costs of defined benefit plans relative to those for defined contribution plans.[11] A number of studies have identified regulatory costs as a factor in the decline of private sector defined benefit plans.[12]

In addition to the administrative and regulatory costs, critics have charged that forcing plan sponsors to pay benefits to departing employees through accelerated vesting contributed to the demise of defined benefit plans in the private sector.[13] To the extent that this view is accurate—studies in the 1970s suggested that these payments to short-service employees would not be a significant burden[14]—the later vesting in the public sector would make defined benefit plans more attractive to employers.

One final factor that affects the relative cost of defined benefit and defined contribution plans is that employees contribute to defined benefit plans in the public sector. One implication of these contributions is that state and local governments are unlikely to save much by converting to a defined contribution plan with comparable benefits. Moreover, public plan sponsors can raise contribution rates on employees to manage costs, which has helped hold state and local government costs in check.

In short, defined benefit plans dominated both the private and state and local sectors in the 1970s. In the early twenty-first century they are disappearing in the private sector but remain dominant in the state and local sector. The reasons for these divergent trajectories reflect the different nature of the public employer—a perpetual entity less sensitive to the fluctuations in pension expense caused

10. For example, the Omnibus Budget Reconciliation Act of 1987 reduced the full funding limits for defined benefit plans from 100 percent of projected plan liability to the lesser of that value or 150 percent of benefits accrued to date. Basing funding limits on benefits already accrued means that funding contributions no longer include any provision for anticipated pay increases. See McGill and others (2005). This funding restriction exposes the sponsor to higher costs in the future.

11. The biggest increase in both absolute and relative costs of defined benefit versus defined contribution plans occurred in the late 1980s as plans adjusted to the Retirement Equity Act of 1984 and the Tax Reform Act of 1986. See Hustead (1998).

12. Kruse (1995) found that rising administrative costs contributed to the decline in defined benefit pension coverage over the period 1980–86.

13. See Macchia (2007). Before ERISA, it was not unusual for plans to lack vesting provisions. ERISA incorporated minimum vesting rules. Originally, ERISA set a maximum of ten years (cliff vesting) or fifteen years (graded vesting). The Tax Reform Act of 1986 reduced the limits to five and seven years, respectively. See Graham (1988).

14. Sass (1997).

by market volatility; the different nature of the public sector workforce—older, more risk-averse, less mobile, and more unionized; and a different regulatory environment—free from the administrative costs and vesting requirements of ERISA, with the ability to adjust employee contributions to control employer costs. Now, however, many state and local officials are considering or have already introduced a defined contribution plan for new employees. Therefore, it is important to understand the strengths and weaknesses of each type of plan.

The Strengths and Weaknesses of Public Sector Defined Benefit Plans

Any type of retirement plan involves both financial and human resource considerations. On the financial side, the questions are whether the sponsor is positioned to bear the investment, longevity, and inflation risks and to prefund the commitments in an orderly fashion and whether the plans provide an adequate stream of retirement income to participants. On the human resource side, the question is whether the structure of benefits attracts and retains the desired workforce.

Financial Considerations for Sponsors

One certainty is that defined benefit plans in the public sector are likely to be "big." That is, as discussed in earlier chapters, pensions account for a much larger share of compensation in the public sector than in the private sector, so the accrual rate and the ultimate benefit are larger than are found in the private sector. As discussed in chapter 4, it is simply easier to offer employees a dollar of future pension benefits than to pay a dollar of wages, given the flexibility that public sector employers have in funding their pension obligations. The net result is that these pensions create an enormous commitment.

At the same time, politicians have every incentive to hold down the annual pension contributions. They are often under pressure to address short-term priorities rather than put money aside for long-term funding needs. Participants who believe that they will be paid regardless of funding may not push for government contributions. Similarly, legislatures sometimes make unfunded benefit improvements in good times, such as California in the 1990s, that further aggravate the funding shortfall. As a result of all these forces, taxpayers face the political risk that benefit promises will not be funded. Underfunding means that future taxpayers and employees will be required to contribute not only to cover the accruing cost of benefits for current workers but also to cover benefits for retirees for whom no funds have been put aside.

It is probably a mistake, however, to overstate this risk of underfunding. With the incentives not to fund and without the funding requirements of ERISA, one might conclude that states and localities would not put aside *any* money to fund future benefits. Indeed, pre-1980, a number of plans operated on a pay-as-you-go basis. In the wake of ERISA, however, the Financial Accounting Foundation and ten national associations of state and local government officials established the Governmental Accounting Standards Board (GASB) specifically to set standards of accounting and reporting for state and local governments. As discussed in earlier chapters, in the mid-1990s GASB issued Statements No. 25 and 27 that defined an acceptable amortization period for the unfunded liability and an annual required contribution (ARC). These standards—plus a robust stock market—produced funded ratios in 2000 in excess of 100 percent. Of course, the ratios were calculated using an 8 percent discount rate, and funding levels would have been much lower using a riskless rate. But if one assumes that sponsors were taking their lead from the actuaries in selecting the discount rate, and if one leaves aside bad actors, such as Illinois and New Jersey, then a reasonable argument could be made that states and localities are serious about funding their pensions.

The two financial crises threw states and localities—as well as everyone else with assets—seriously off course. Some critics object to characterizing state and local plans as victims. They argue that states and localities made a *choice* to invest their portfolios in a manner that made them vulnerable to a financial crisis, and enjoyed the benefits—the ability to justify higher discount rates and lower contributions in good times—that come along with that risk. Had they immunized their liabilities by investing in duration-matched securities, they would not have enjoyed the benefits of equity investment but would have been insulated from the financial crisis. A more sympathetic reading of the situation is that public plans should hold some equities because such a portfolio offers young workers who should hold some risky assets an indirect way to secure such investments and provides a hedge against benefits based on final wages.[15] Given some equity holdings, public plans—like their private sector counterparts—rode the bull market and ended up with 66 percent of their holdings in risky investments in 2000. The challenge then was to reduce their holdings of equities, which would have lowered the expected rate of return and required a large increase in contributions. Without pressure from their financial advisers to rebalance, plan sponsors retained their equity holdings and lost money with the bursting of the dot. com bubble. This behavior may not have been optimal, but it is hard to characterize it as reckless.

The response to the bursting of the dot.com bubble provides some support for the notion that public plan sponsors are committed to funding. Between 2001 and 2008, the ARC nearly doubled, increasing from 6.4 percent to 11.8 percent of payrolls. Over the same period, the portion of ARC paid declined from

15. See discussion in chapter 3.

100 percent in 2001 to 83 percent in 2006 but then rose to 92 percent in 2008 just as the second crisis hit. Thus public plans were moving back to paying 100 percent of a significantly larger number. The second financial crisis, which hit in 2008, was accompanied by a prolonged recession that depleted state and local budgets and, as a result, the portion of ARC paid declined to 80 percent. Based on past behavior, the most likely scenario is that states and localities—with some notable exceptions—will increase the percentage of ARC paid as the economy recovers.

The conclusion that emerges from this discussion is nuanced. On the one hand, the pressures in the public sector are toward generous pension benefits and holding down annual pension contributions. On the other hand, states and localities are more committed to funding than is generally acknowledged. On balance, given the complex cross currents, taxpayers would face less uncertainty if states and localities relied somewhat less on defined benefit plans to compensate public employees.

Financial Considerations for Employees

For employees who remain with their employer until retirement, defined benefit plans are wonderful. They provide a predictable stream of lifetime retirement income; participants know how much they are going to receive when they stop working and can plan accordingly. Defined benefit plans traditionally shield employees from major risks that are difficult for individuals to absorb; the sponsor bears the investment risk during the accumulation phase and then longevity risk and, in the public sector, much of the inflation risk after retirement. Two issues are relevant in considering the financial implications of defined benefit plans for public employees. First, they have never been good for mobile workers. Second, the employer did not bear all the costs from the financial crisis.

MOBILE EMPLOYEES. Defined benefit plans are designed to attract and retain qualified employees. As such, these plans become more valuable the closer the employee gets to the full retirement age because accrual rates often increase with age and the salary base is usually an average of the last three to five years of earnings. Vested employees who leave early forfeit significant retirement income because their accumulated credits are applied to their salary at termination rather than their salary at retirement.[16]

Consider two workers with forty-year careers: one works for four employers for ten years each and one works forty years for the same employer. Both are cov-

16. Under several state plans, vesting does not occur for ten years, and employees who leave receive only their contributions and some minimal amount of credited interest.

ered by defined benefit plans that provide a benefit equal to 2 percent of final pay for each year of service. If wages did not grow at all, the mobile employee and the forty-year employee would receive identical benefits. But if wages increased 4.5 percent annually, the pension of the worker who held four jobs would equal only 58 percent of the annual pension of the worker who remained continuously employed by one firm. The more wages rise with productivity growth and inflation, the relatively lower the benefits received by the mobile employee. Thus, for mobile employees, final earnings defined benefit plans are not a mechanism for providing predictable and adequate retirement income.

RESPONSE TO THE FINANCIAL CRISIS. How defined benefit promises have actually played out in the public sector in the wake of the financial crisis is an interesting story. On the one hand, public plan participants were thought to have a higher degree of protection than their private sector counterparts. Whereas ERISA protects benefits earned to date, participants may end up with less than expected if their employer closes down the plan for reasons of economy or bankruptcy. In such cases, the factors in the benefit formula are applied to today's earnings rather than to the higher earnings at retirement. In contrast, in many states the constitution prescribes or the courts have ruled that the public employer is prohibited from modifying the plan.[17] This prohibition means that employees hired under a public retirement plan have the right to earn benefits as long as their employment continues. Thus if the employer wants to reduce the future accruals of benefits, such a change usually applies only to new hires.

On the other hand, in the wake of the financial crisis, in many instances the "pension wealth" of both current employees and retirees has been reduced. The most direct way this reduction occurred for current workers is through increases in required employee contributions. Such increases were possible because while constitutions and state laws preclude benefit changes, they usually place no restrictions on how much the state can ask the employee to pay.[18] Thus the employee continues to accrue the expected benefit, but the net contribution from the employer has been reduced.

The diminution of employer-provided benefits has not been limited to active workers. In some states, retirees have seen the reduction or suspension of their cost-of-living-adjustments (COLAs). In four states—Colorado, Minnesota,

17. See Steffen (2001).

18. The ability to increase contributions for current employees is not universal. For example, in 2012 a New Hampshire judge ruled that it is unlawful to increase the contribution rate of vested employees. A Florida judge ruled similarly that same year, but the state appealed the decision, and the suit is currently under consideration by the Florida Supreme Court.

New Jersey, and South Dakota—the suspension has been challenged in court and the court upheld the change.[19] In three states—Maine, Rhode Island, and Washington—suspensions have been put in place, and challenges are in court. In Colorado, the judge argued that the COLA is separate from the core promised benefits and that retirees had signed documents acknowledging that the COLA was subject to change. In Minnesota, the judge ruled both that the COLA was not a core benefit and that the COLA suspension was necessary to prevent the long-term fiscal deterioration of the pension plan. If one perceives the COLA as an integral part of the benefit, then the suspension would violate the ERISA provisions, which protect all benefits earned to date. Of course, almost no private sector defined benefit plans have COLAs, so a direct comparison is not possible.

The key point is that the defined benefit promises in the public sector are not as secure as one would have thought before the financial crisis. It was the belief that they were guaranteed that led economists to argue that the liabilities should be discounted by the riskless rate for valuation purposes.[20] But when the stock market collapsed, benefit promises were in many cases reduced.

Human Resource Issues

Defined benefit pension plans for public employees almost universally compute benefits based on final pay. That is, employees' initial pension benefits are based on their age at retirement, their years of service, and their average earnings in a small number of years. While most economists attribute this structure to the desire to reward long-service employees,[21] it could also be due to record-keeping

19. In Colorado, 2010 legislation reduced the COLA for 2010 from 3.5 percent to the lesser of 2 percent or the average of the CPI-W for the 2009 calendar year (which resulted in a zero COLA for 2010) and a maximum of 2 percent thereafter (linked to investment returns) for current and future retirees. In Minnesota, in 2010 the state reduced the COLA for the State Employees' Retirement Fund from 2.5 percent to 2 percent and for the General Employees' Retirement Plan from 2.5 percent to 1 percent. The COLA for the Teachers' Retirement Association was suspended between 2011 and 2012 and reduced from 2.5 percent to 2 percent thereafter. In New Jersey, the COLA is eliminated until the pension funds reach 80 percent funding and the new board, established under the 2011 legislation, agrees to reinstate the COLA. Given that New Jersey is phasing in its funding contributions, an 80-percent funded ratio is not expected until 2040. In South Dakota, the decline of the funded ratio to 76 percent triggered a requirement to make immediate reforms to return to 100 percent funded. In response, legislation reduced the COLA from 3.1 percent to 2.1 percent for current and future retirees in 2010. Future adjustments will depend on the funded ratio as follows: 3.1 percent if the funded ratio is 100 percent or greater; between 2.9 and 2.1 (CPI-linked) if the funded ratio is between 90 and 100 percent; between 2.4 and 2.1 (CPI-linked) if the funded ratio is between 80 and 90 percent; and 2.1 if the funded ratio is less than 80 percent.

20. Brown and Wilcox (2009).

21. Lazear (1985).

constraints before the age of computers or an interest in relating pre-retirement to post-retirement income in a seemingly transparent way. Whatever the initial motivation, final pay plans have three distinct characteristics: (1) they severely "backload" benefits; (2) they treat workers on different career trajectories very differently; and (3) they invite mischief, such as sudden late-career promotions that substantially boost retirement benefits.[22]

To illustrate the effects of final pay provisions, the following analysis uses a plan with a constant 2 percent benefit factor, a three-year averaging period, a full retirement age of 65, actuarially fair adjustments for early retirement, and a COLA that fully compensates for inflation after the start of benefits.[23] Employees may claim a pension as early as 55, provided they have accumulated at least ten years of service. No cap is imposed on the replacement rate. Employee pension contributions are 6 percent of salary, the most typical rate found among the *Public Plans Database* (PPD) sample of plans.[24]

BACKLOADING OF BENEFITS. Participants in a final pay plan earn most of their benefits in the last few years of employment, which means that they face a very strong incentive to keep working until full benefits are available.[25] As shown in figure 7-4, an employee starting at age 35 with a thirty-year career will earn about one-third of lifetime pension benefits in the last five years of employment; those leaving with ten years of service receive about 14 percent of the possible lifetime benefits.[26]

A full career in the public sector may be optimal for both the employer and the employee in some situations, but in other instances shorter periods of employment may be more desirable from the perspective of both parties. For example, social workers, who face burdensome caseloads and constant stress, are often exhausted long before retirement age. These workers need to move to new jobs

22. The following discussion focuses on the impact of final pay plans on short-term workers. These plans also affect the retirement patterns of long-term employees. See Friedberg (2011).

23. The calculation assumes 4.5 percent annual earnings growth and 3 percent inflation.

24. This analysis focuses on the problems of the average earnings formula at the core of the final pay pension. For an analysis that illustrates other erratic patterns of benefit accrual associated with common features of teacher retirement systems, see Costrell and Podgursky (2009). For an analysis that focuses on one state in detail, see the Technical Appendix to the Final Report of the Special Commission to Study the Massachusetts Contributory Retirement Systems (2009).

25. If the plan caps the replacement rate, the strong incentive to continue working stops when the cap is reached.

26. Backloading also makes the comparison of compensation across workers with different salaries opaque and makes the cost of employing a worker today depend on past employment. The system also creates a large incentive for employees who left public service at a young age to return to covered public employment for a short period immediately before retirement.

Figure 7-4. *Percentage of Lifetime Pension Benefits Earned over an Employee's Thirty-Year Career, Starting at Age 35*

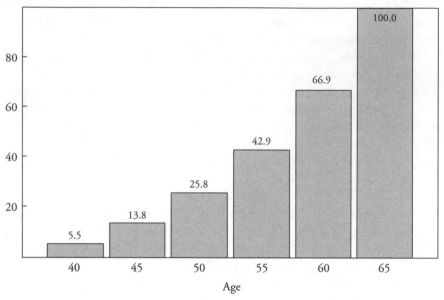

Percent

Source: Center for Retirement Research at Boston College (2010d).

in either the public or private sector. Therefore, a plan that disproportionately rewards long-service workers does not provide the right incentives in all cases.

IMPACT OF RATE OF EARNINGS GROWTH. Another issue with final pay plans is the extent to which they reward individuals with rapid earnings growth, who tend to be the higher-paid. Since a final pay formula links pension benefits only to compensation at the end of the career, it rewards workers whose earnings grow rapidly. The 4.5 percent growth rate assumed to this point results in a pension value of 26 percent of accumulated salary for an individual who works from age 25 to age 65. However, an employee who has a constant earnings growth rate of only 3 percent over the same forty-year career would receive a pension value of 19 percent of lifetime salary. An employee with more rapidly rising earnings (6 percent) would receive benefits equal to 33 percent of lifetime earnings (see figure 7-5).

INCENTIVES FOR "PROMOTION." In similar fashion, a worker who receives a promotion in his final years of employment ends up with a much larger

Figure 7-5. *Lifetime Pension Benefit at Age 65 as a Percentage of Accumulated Earnings, by Wage Growth*

Percent

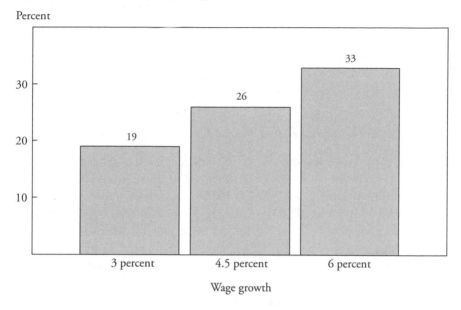

Wage growth

Source: Center for Retirement Research at Boston College (2010d).

pension than a worker who does not. If an employee is promoted at age 60 and receives a 20 percent pay raise (rather than the 4.5 percent trend), his lifetime salary will be only 2 percent greater than it would have been without a promotion, but his initial pension benefit will be 15.5 percent larger. Thus the total value of a late promotion or sudden salary increase is substantially larger than the pay raise itself.

About 40 percent of state and local plans have introduced "anti-spiking" provisions, limiting the amount of a pay raise that counts for pension calculations in order to prevent this type of pay boost immediately before retirement. Without such a provision, which can create administrative difficulties of its own, the incentive to inflate late-career pay is very strong in final pay plans.[27]

27. Instances of suspicious salary increases in the years just before retirement are all too common. In Illinois, a police sergeant of the Village of Steger Police Department took a 25 percent pay increase in pensionable earnings on the condition of immediate retirement. He worked one full day and then retired at the increased pay rate. See Puchalski (2002). Illinois courts eventually ruled against awarding the pension benefit at the increased pay rate. In northern California, a retiring chief of fire for Orinda and Moraga municipalities earning $186,000 was granted an increase in his salary largely by enabling him to sell unused vacation days and holidays. That helped boost his

In short, the final pay formula produces strongly backloaded benefits that favor workers with rapidly rising earnings and that produce an enormous payoff to salary increases in the final years of employment.[28] These incentives may be consistent with the human resource goals of state and local governments for some types of employees, but it is unlikely that they are appropriate for all types of employees. Thus human resource considerations, like the financial issues, argue for less reliance on final pay defined benefit plans. The question is whether the public sector should undertake a wholesale shift to defined contribution plans.

Strengths and Weaknesses of Defined Contribution Plans

From the perspective of sponsoring governments and taxpayers, shifting to a defined contribution plan would get them out of bearing investment, infla- tion, and longevity risk. These plans would be funded by definition, and when things go wrong in financial markets, the taxpayer would not be responsible for covering the shortfall. In theory, defined contribution plans could provide as much income as defined benefit plans. They also offer several advantages for the worker. Unlike defined benefit plans, they do not penalize mobile employees; benefits accrue at a steady pace so that young workers can move to a new job without forfeiting any accumulation. Defined contribution plans do not pro- vide incentives for early retirement, which, given improvements in health and life expectancy, can be an advantage for both the employer and the employee. And defined contribution plans offer individuals a sense of control over their retirement planning.

Despite all the potential advantages of defined contribution plans, the pri- vate sector's increasing reliance on these plans since the 1980s has not produced encouraging outcomes. The defining characteristic of defined contribution plans is that they shift the responsibilities and the risk to the employee. The shift has been particularly pronounced in the design of the main type of private sector defined contribution plan—the 401(k). When 401(k) plans emerged in the early 1980s, they were viewed mainly as supplements to employer-funded pension

---

annual pension to $241,000. See Borenstein (2009). In Boston, pension spiking was so rampant that it prompted a federal investigation. More than a hundred Boston firefighters claimed career-ending injuries while they were filling in for superiors at higher pay grades, enhancing their tax-free disability pensions by an average of $10,300 a year. See Slack and Robinson (2008).

28. Moreover, while the calculations have focused on a determinate environment, workers face significant risks from final pay plans. The excessive pension value of a promotion represents a risk to a worker who may or may not receive a promotion. Employees who are terminated before retire- ment also face the loss of substantial pension benefits. And periods when inflation rises faster than wage growth, such as the 1970s, can erode the value of pensions even for plans based on a few years of final pay.

Figure 7-6. *Private Sector Workers with Pension Coverage by Type of Plan, 1980, 1994, and 2008*

Percent

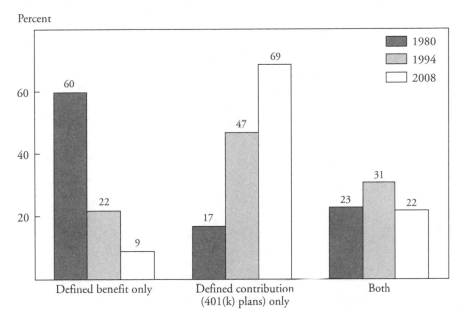

Source: Author's calculations using U.S. Department of Labor, *Annual Return/Report Form 5500 Series* (1980, 1994, and 2008).

and profit-sharing plans. Since 401(k) participants were presumed to have their basic retirement income security needs covered by an employer-funded plan and Social Security, they were given substantial discretion over 401(k) choices, including whether to participate, how much to contribute, how to invest, and when and in what form to withdraw the funds.

Over the past thirty years, the pension landscape in the private sector has changed dramatically. In the early 1980s, most workers lucky enough to work for an employer providing a pension were covered by a defined benefit plan. Today most workers have a 401(k) as their primary or only plan (see figure 7-6). Yet 401(k)s still operate under the old rules. Workers continue to have almost complete discretion over whether and how much to contribute, how to invest, and how and when to withdraw the funds.

Since employees shoulder all the risks in a 401(k) system, they have to make good decisions for these plans to work well. But employees make mistakes at every step along the way (see figure 7-7).[29] Twenty-one percent do not join the

29. Liang and Weisbenner (2002).

Figure 7-7. *Percentage of Individuals Who Make Various Mistakes in 401(k) Plans, 2010*

Percent

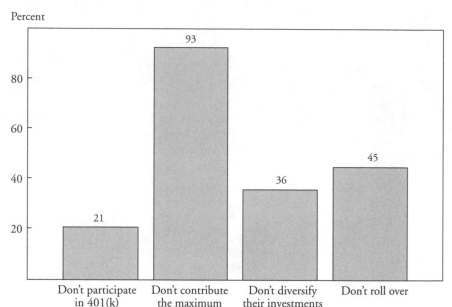

Source: Munnell (2012).

plan; more than 90 percent do not contribute the maximum; most make bad investment decisions (over one-third do not diversify; many overinvest in company stock; and none reduce their equity holdings as they age); and 45 percent cash out when they change jobs. So their 401(k) balances end up way below their potential.

Figure 7-8 shows simulated and actual amounts of 401(k) balances by age. The simulated amounts are for a typical worker who ends up at retirement with earnings of about $65,000. The worker, who begins contributing at age 30, pays in 6 percent of earnings and the employer matches with 3 percent—the typical contribution pattern under a 401(k). The actual amounts are those reported for households in the Federal Reserve's 2010 *Survey of Consumer Finances*. The balances include holdings in IRAs as well as 401(k) accounts because such a large portion of IRA balances are rollovers from 401(k)s. As shown, actual balances for households are far less than what an Excel spreadsheet would suggest for an individual.

One could argue that 401(k)s are still relatively new, but the same pattern of falling short of projected accumulations is evident at younger ages. One could also argue that the encouragement provided for automatic enrollment under the Pension Protection Act of 2006 should improve the private sector results.

Figure 7-8. *Median 401(k)/IRA Balances for Households with 401(k) Plans and Simulated Accumulations, by Age Group, 2010*

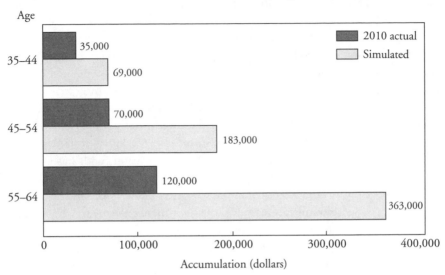

Source: Munnell (2012).

But this innovation has not been widespread enough to solve the problem; less than half of large firms have adopted automatic enrollment, and most apply the provision only to new employees (as opposed to a one-shot re-enrollment of all workers). Moreover, only about a third of those firms with automatic enrollment have adopted auto escalation in the default contribution rate.[30] Without auto escalation, workers who are enrolled with a 3 percent contribution—a popular auto-enrollment rate—tend to stay at that low contribution level. The bottom line is that the experience with 401(k) plans in the private sector suggests that reliance on a 401(k)-type defined contribution plan as the sole employer pension will leave public sector workers with insufficient resources to ensure a secure retirement.

Moreover, some arguments for shifting from a defined benefit to a defined contribution plan are simply not correct. For example, a common justification for such a shift is the magnitude of the state's or locality's unfunded liability.[31] The reality is that even with a new defined contribution plan, states and localities are still left to deal with past underfunding. A new plan only addresses pension costs going forward; it does not help close the current gap between pension

30. Plan Sponsor Council of America (2011).
31. For example, see Gottleib (2005); Klas (2011); Summers (2009); and Whaley (2012).

assets and liabilities.[32] Although new employees will not accrue any benefits under the old plan, the state must still cover the cost of accrued benefits from past service. Thus, even if the introduction of a new plan—either defined benefit or defined contribution—reduces pension costs going forward, such a step does nothing to solve the current funding problem.

Similarly, some contend that switching to a defined contribution plan would save money in the future. But for any given level of benefits, defined benefit plans—particularly in the public sector—have lower administrative expenses than defined contribution plans.[33] As discussed earlier, public plans are relatively free from regulatory costs, since they do not face the administrative expenses or PBGC premiums associated with ERISA. The freedom from regulatory costs combined with the economies of scale achieved by large state pension funds has kept the cost of administering public sector defined benefit plans very low. According to the 2009 Census of Governments, the weighted average administrative cost (including cost of administration and investment management) for the nation's public defined benefit plans is 0.42 percent of assets.[34] The costs of administering defined contribution plans, which maintain individual accounts and typically update these accounts daily, are considerably higher. In addition, most defined contribution plans use mutual funds or similar instruments as investment options—with an average expense ratio that ranges from about 0.60 percent for a bond mutual fund to about 0.75 percent for a stock fund.[35] As a result, the annual cost of a defined contribution plan usually exceeds 1 percent of assets.[36]

32. In many cases, closing an existing defined benefit plan to new hires and switching to a defined contribution plan increases short-term costs. The Governmental Accounting Standards Board (GASB) Statement No. 25 states that closed plans using the level percent of payroll method for calculating the Annual Required Contribution (ARC) must acknowledge that covered payroll is decreasing. This recognition frontloads costs. As a result, most closed plans use the level dollar method of amortizing the unfunded liability. However, the ARC under the closed plan is still frontloaded relative to the ARC under the ongoing plan. Moreover, market gains from future new hire contributions that would have been used to offset the unfunded liability are now sequestered in the new defined contribution plan. See California Public Employees' Retirement System (2005), Michigan House Fiscal Agency (2009), Retirement Systems of Minnesota (2011), and The Segal Company (2010) for more information.

33. For a more detailed discussion of the cost efficiencies of defined benefit pension plans, see Almeida and Fornia (2008).

34 Author's calculations from U.S. Census Bureau, *State and Local Public-Employee Retirement Systems* (2009).

35. The estimates of investment management expenses are from personal communication in 2006 between Lipper company employee Derek D. Lewis and CRR.

36. Some studies estimate considerably higher costs for public defined contribution plans. For example, the Illinois Municipal Retirement Fund (1999) estimated that replacing the defined benefit plan with a defined contribution plan would increase the administrative costs from 0.44 percent of assets a year to about 2.25 percent.

Advocates may think that even if total costs increased, taxpayers could gain by shifting contributions from the government to the employee. Transferring the burden to the employee provided a major economic incentive in the private sector to move from defined benefit plans (where employees make no contributions) to 401(k) plans (where employees make the bulk of the contributions). But, as noted above, in the public sector most employees already make substantial contributions to their defined benefit pensions, and these contributions have increased in the wake of the financial crisis.[37] It is unlikely, then, that state and local governments will be able to save money simply by shifting more of the cost of comparable benefits to the employee. Of course, moving to a defined contribution plan could be used as a mechanism to cut retirement benefits and thereby lower total employee compensation.

Finally, some proponents of defined contribution plans contend that participants will be able to match their portfolio to their preference for risk and perhaps earn higher returns than under a defined benefit plan. The preference argument is correct in theory, but studies show that individuals put little thought into structuring their portfolios and rarely rebalance them.[38] With respect to higher returns, such an outcome would contradict the experience in the private sector.[39] Over the period 1988–2004, the return on 401(k) assets averaged about 1 percent less than the return on private sector defined benefit assets, even though a greater percentage of 401(k) assets were invested in equities during the stock market boom of the 1990s.[40]

In short, the reason for considering defined contribution plans for the private sector has nothing to do with providing a solution to current unfunded liabilities, lowering administrative costs, or earning higher returns. Rather, the argu-

37. In states where employees are covered by Social Security, the median contribution rate is 5 percent of earnings. In states without Social Security, the median employee contribution rate is 8 percent.

38. See Agnew, Balduzzi, and Sundén (2003); Benartzi and Thaler (2001, 2002).

39. Munnell and others (2006). The results of a 2011 Towers Watson study are more ambiguous because the study does not control for asset allocation.

40. The expectation of higher returns also is belied by the experience of Nebraska. In the 1960s, the Nebraska legislature wanted to provide pensions for its state and county workers. But instead of instituting a defined benefit plan similar to that covering teachers and judges, it created a defined contribution plan. In the early 2000s, however, Nebraska officials became concerned that the defined contribution plan was producing lower returns than the defined benefit plans. The Nebraska Public Employees Retirement Systems reported in a 2002 newsletter that "On average, the investment returns in the School Employees, State Judges and State Patrol defined benefit plans were 11% for the past 20 years while state and county employees returned between 6% and 7% on average." Faced with such an enormous disparity, the state legislature replaced the defined contribution plan with a cash balance plan—a defined benefit plan where assets are managed by the employer but participants have separate accounts.

ment for a defined contribution component rests on the desire to better balance the financial risks between taxpayers and participants and to provide a benefit structure that offers some reward to short-term employees. But the experience in the private sector shows that total reliance on defined contribution arrangements can lead to poor outcomes. Fortunately, as described below, few states have taken such an approach.

Defined Contribution Activity in the Public Sector

The public sector has seen a movement toward defined contribution plans since the turn of the century and accelerated interest in these plans in the wake of the financial crisis. This section reports separately on what has happened with defined contribution activity before and after the financial crisis.[41]

Before the Crisis

Before the financial crisis, only a smattering of states had introduced defined contribution plans. Only two states, Michigan and Alaska, introduced plans that require all new hires to participate solely in a defined contribution plan (see figure 7-9).[42] The Alaska reform applied to both general government workers and teachers, while the Michigan reform was limited to general state workers. Two states, Indiana and Oregon, adopted hybrid plans, where employees are required to participate in both a defined benefit and a defined contribution plan. Another six states retained their defined benefit plans and simply offered the defined contribution plan as an option to their employees.[43]

The time line of the introduction of these defined contribution plans is interesting (see figure 7-10). Some of the changes may have been a response to

41. Public sector workers often have an optional 403(b) and/or 457 defined contribution plan that allows them to put aside a portion of their pay on a tax-deferred basis to augment their public pension. These supplementary plans are not the topic of this discussion. Rather, the focus is on states where the nature of the *primary* plan has changed.

42. The District of Columbia also requires its general government employees to join a primary defined contribution plan, but the analysis here is limited to states. Other states have considered moving to a primary defined contribution plan. For example, California's governor proposed such a switch in 2004, but this plan generated substantial opposition from public employee unions and the proposal was dropped in 2005. For more details on other attempts to move into defined contribution plans, see American Federation of State, County and Municipal Employees (2007).

43. These states were Colorado, Florida, Montana, Ohio, South Carolina, and Washington. Except in Washington and Ohio, the options are either a traditional defined benefit plan or a defined contribution plan. Washington offers a choice of a defined benefit plan or a hybrid plan. Ohio employees can choose from a defined benefit plan, a defined contribution plan, or a hybrid plan. In all cases, the defined benefit plan is the default for those who do not actively make a selection.

Figure 7-9. *Adoption of Defined Contribution Plans, by State, before 2008*[a]

☐ Mandatory defined
   benefit plan
■ Mandatory defined
   contribution plan
▨ Mandatory hybrid plan
☐ Choice of primary plan

Sources: Various retirement systems' annual reports and websites of state legislatures.

a. Mandatory defined benefit plans are primary plans that require employees to join. Mandatory defined contribution plans are primary plans that require employees to join. Mandatory hybrid plans require employees to join a plan with both a defined benefit and a defined contribution component. "Choice" plans typically allow employees to pick either a primary defined contribution plan or a primary defined benefit plan. In all cases, the defined benefit plan is the default for those who do not actively make a selection.

economics or politics, but much of the activity occurred in the wake of the fantastic performance of the stock market during the 1990s.

In order to assess why some states adopted defined contribution plans before the financial crisis, an empirical analysis was used to identify possible factors that may either encourage or discourage states from introducing a defined contribution plan. These factors included the funded status of the existing defined benefit plan, the current level of employee contributions to that plan, the extent to which participants are unionized,[44] whether government employees are covered by Social Security, and the political climate.

44. Public sector unions largely support the retention of defined benefit plans. Therefore the hypothesis is that the greater the degree of unionization, the less likely the state is to switch from a defined benefit to a defined contribution plan. The problem is that the only readily available data are the percentages of public sector employees who are unionized by state. Unionization, however, varies significantly by type of plan. For example, a far greater percentage of teachers are unionized than are general employees. Therefore a proxy for the role of unions is whether the plan covers teachers. The hypothesis is that when a plan includes teachers, the state is less likely to introduce a defined contribution plan.

Figure 7-10. *Introduction of State Defined Contribution Plans, by Year, 1990–2012*[a]

Number of states

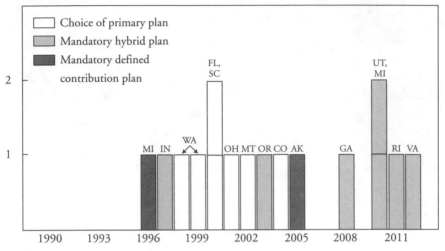

Sources: Various retirement systems' annual reports and websites of state legislatures.

a. Indiana's hybrids were put in place in 1955, but were not allowed to invest in equities until 1996.

The analysis included data on each state-administered plan from 1992 through 2006. The dependent variable was set equal to zero if no action was taken; 1 if the state introduced a defined contribution plan as an option; 2 if the state replaced the defined benefit plan with a "combined" defined benefit/defined contribution plan; and 3 if the state replaced the defined benefit plan with a mandatory defined contribution plan. To capture historical data, the exercise was limited to seventy-seven plans; once a state introduced a defined contribution plan, the observation was removed from the sample.[45]

The results are displayed in figure 7-11. The figure shows the effect on the probability of introducing a defined contribution plan in a single year. The effects are quite large given that only 20 percent of sponsors introduced some form of defined contribution plan over the fifteen-year period. The results generally, but not universally, confirm expectations. The funded ratio and the accrual

45. Before 2003, Nebraska was excluded from the analysis because it has always had a defined contribution plan and therefore was not in a position to switch. In 2003, Nebraska switched to a cash balance plan. The West Virginia TRS plan was excluded from the analysis since it was switched to a defined contribution plan in 1991, which is outside the period of analysis. It was later switched back to a defined benefit plan in 2005.

Figure 7-11. *Impact on the Probability of Introducing a Defined Contribution Plan*[a]

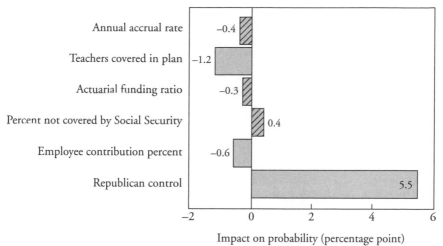

Impact on probability (percentage point)

Source: Center for Retirement Research at Boston College (2008b).
a. Solid bars indicate the coefficient is statistically significant at least at the 10 percent level. For the binary variables, teachers covered in plan and Republican control, the bars represent the change in the probability derived from a 0 to 1 change (no teachers in the plan to teachers in the plan, no Republican control to Republican control). For the other variables, the bars represent the change in probability derived from going from the 25th percentile to the 75th percentile in each variable. For each variable, these calculations hold all other variables constant at their means.

rate do not seem to be important factors for the introduction of a defined contribution plan.[46] But if the plan includes teachers—that is, it is a highly unionized plan—or if employee contributions are high, the state is less likely to introduce a defined contribution plan.

Two aspects of these results are surprising. First, the fact that states with a large percentage of workers not covered by Social Security did not have a lower probability of introducing a defined contribution plan is unexpected. The results are clearly driven by Colorado, Ohio, and Alaska, three states with a very high proportion of noncovered workers. In Colorado and Ohio, the defined

46. The expected coefficient on the funded ratio is ambiguous. On the one hand, persistently low levels of funding might highlight the need for some action to prevent further underfunding. On the other hand, some experts contend that the closer the system is to pay-as-you-go, the more expensive the transition. The government would have to contribute both to the defined benefit plan to cover annual benefit costs for current retirees as well as to the new defined contribution plan. This issue arose explicitly in Michigan. When the new defined contribution plan was introduced, the legislation explicitly stated that school employees could not make the transition until the $3 billion unfunded liability in their retirement system was erased. See Fore (2001).

contribution plans are optional and the take-up has been modest. Thus most of these workers will continue to have the protection against investment risk and the promise of an annuity that comes with a defined benefit plan. In Alaska, however, the majority of newly hired state workers and teachers, who do not have Social Security coverage and who are required to join the defined contribution plan, will not have any form of defined benefit protection.

The second interesting aspect of the results is the importance of Republican control.[47] Its impact is larger and more robust than any of the other factors. Having a Republican governor and a Republican legislature increases the probability of introducing some type of defined contribution plan by 6 percentage points.

The general picture before the financial crisis is that defined contribution activity was modest. Excluding the six states that simply added a defined contribution option, only five introduced any form of mandatory defined contribution plan. The primary motivation appeared to be political philosophy. Republicans value the control over investments and portability offered by defined contribution plans, and when they have dominated the political scene they have changed the nature of public pensions.

Defined Contribution Activity since the Financial Crisis

In the wake of the financial crisis, discussion of shifting in whole or in part from a defined benefit to a defined contribution plan became more widespread (see figure 7-12).[48] Five states—Georgia, Michigan (teachers' plan), Utah, Rhode Island, and Virginia—have taken action, joining the eleven states that had introduced some form of defined contribution plan before 2008. Interestingly, none of the five has followed the earlier Alaska-Michigan model of relying solely on a defined contribution plan. Rather, each has adopted a plan in which new employees accumulate retirement income under both a defined benefit and defined contribution plan. The Rhode Island experience, which covers current as well as new employees, is discussed in chapter 8; the other four states are described below.

GEORGIA. General state employees hired after January 1, 2009, are covered under the new hybrid (defined benefit/401(k)) plan; existing employees had the option to join the new plan. New hires are automatically enrolled in the 401(k) plan (unless they affirmatively elect not to participate) and contribute

47. The importance of political philosophy in the move to defined contribution plans in the public sector was first suggested by Wiles (2006).

48. At this writing in 2012, the issue is under discussion in Alabama, Connecticut, Nevada, North Carolina, Tennessee, and Wisconsin. In Illinois and Kentucky, legislation is under consideration to create defined contribution plans for new hires. A similar proposal was defeated in North Dakota and withdrawn in Oklahoma in 2011. See Frazier (2010); Fehr (2010); National Conference of State Legislatures (2011); Steyer (2010); and Preston and McNichol (2010).

Figure 7-12. *Adoption of Defined Contribution Plans, by State, after 2008*

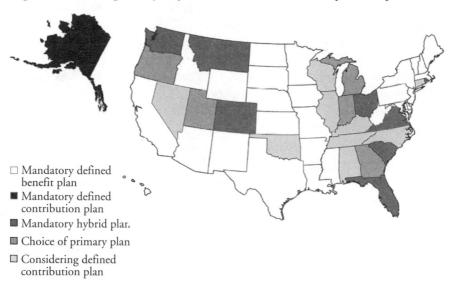

☐ Mandatory defined
   benefit plan
■ Mandatory defined
   contribution plan
■ Mandatory hybrid plan.
▣ Choice of primary plan
☐ Considering defined
   contribution plan

Sources: Various retirement systems' annual reports and websites of state legislatures.

1 percent of salary with additional contributions up to 5 percent eligible for an employer match.[49] The match is 100 percent of the automatic contribution and 50 percent of optional contributions, for a maximum match of 3 percent of salary. Employees can contribute up to the Internal Revenue Service (IRS) limit but will receive no further employer match.

The defined benefit plan will pay 1 percent for each year of service on the annual average of the highest twenty-four months of earnings.[50] Members contribute 1.25 percent of salary to the defined benefit plan, and the state contributes an actuarially determined rate, which is 11.54 percent of payroll in 2013.

System communiqués indicate that the change was driven primarily by the preference of young workers, who constitute 62 percent of the state's workforce, for wages over benefits. In response, the state raised wages and introduced the smaller hybrid plan with a 401(k) component, so that young mobile workers would have something to take with them when they left state employment.

49. In the public sector, the only 401(k)s are grandfathered plans that were established by May 6, 1986, or before, so Georgia had originally established a 401(k) plan before 1986 as an optional supplement to its primary defined benefit plan. See Plan Member Financial Corporation (2010).
50. The board of trustees can increase the benefit factor in the future up to 2 percent if funds are available.

MICHIGAN. As discussed above, since 1997 all new Michigan general state employees have been enrolled in a 401(k) plan. But when the time came to revamp the system for public school employees, the state decided to adopt a hybrid. Employees hired after July 1, 2010, automatically contribute 2 percent of salary to the 401(k) (unless they affirmatively elect not to participate), with optional contributions up to the IRS limit. The sponsor matches 50 percent of the employee's first 2 percent of contributions.[51]

The defined benefit plan for new hires will pay 1.5 percent for each year of service on the annual average of the highest sixty months of earnings. Employees will contribute 6.4 percent of salary to the plan. Whereas the accrual rate is the same as it was under the two existing defined benefit plans for school employees, the age and service requirements for retirement in this plan have been increased and the COLA eliminated.

Press reports suggest that future employer costs (including required contributions for retiree health insurance) were a major motivation for the new plan.[52] Broadly speaking, the new plan reduces the benefits provided by the existing defined benefit plan, and the defined contribution plan involves an extremely modest contribution from the employer.

UTAH. State and local government employees hired after July 1, 2011, have the option to participate in either a defined contribution plan or a hybrid. In the case of the defined contribution plan, the employer will automatically contribute 10 percent for most public employees and 12 percent for public safety and firefighter members.[53] Employees can contribute up to the IRS limit. Employee contributions vest immediately, and employer contributions vest after four years. Members can direct the investment of their contribution immediately, and those of the employer after four years.

Under the hybrid plan, the employer will pay up to 10 percent of an employee's compensation toward the defined benefit component; employees will contribute any additional amount to make the required contribution.[54] When the cost of the defined benefit plan is less than 10 percent, the difference is deposited into the employee's defined contribution account. The defined benefit plan for new employees is less generous than the former plan: the accrual rate was reduced from 2.0 percent a year to 1.5 percent; the period for calculating final average salary was increased from the highest three years to the highest five; and

51. Michigan House Fiscal Agency (2010).
52. GovMonitor (2010); and Michigan Association of School Boards (2010).
53. Liljenquist (2010).
54. Employers are also required to pay 5 percent of payroll to the Utah Retirement System to amortize legacy unfunded pension liabilities.

the employee contribution increased from zero to the cost above 10 percent. In 2012, the plan's cost is 8.4 percent, so 1.6 percent will be contributed to the defined contribution component.

VIRGINIA. Virginia is the most recent state to adopt a hybrid plan. Employees beginning employment in January 2014 will be required to participate in the new plan, and current employees will be given the option of remaining in the (scaled back) defined benefit plan or joining the hybrid.[55]

Under the hybrid plan, the defined benefit component will provide 1 percent of final salary (average of the last 60 months) for each year of service, financed by an employee contribution of 4 percent and an actuarially determined employer contribution. The defined benefit plan includes a cost-of-living adjustment, capped at 3 percent. On the defined contribution side, the employee is required to contribute 1 percent, but the employer will match contributions up to 5 percent—100 percent on the first 2 percent and 50 percent on the next 3 percent. The adequacy of the retirement income generated by the new hybrid will depend critically on how much more than the mandatory 1 percent employees contribute to the defined contribution plan.

Table 7-1 summarizes the provisions of the new hybrid plans. The pattern is quite similar in several respects. First, the combined cost of each new plan is significantly less than the pre-existing defined benefit plan. Second, the employer commitment to the defined contribution plan is minimal and the default employee contribution rate is low. Experience with 401(k)s in the private sector suggests that participants tend to stay where they are put.[56] So if automatic contributions are set at 1 percent or 2 percent of earnings, participants are likely to keep their contributions at that level. Low saving in the defined contribution component means that employees will be forced to rely on the now-reduced defined benefit plan in retirement. A reduced defined benefit plan would not be a major concern if the lower benefit factors were paired with later retirement ages. But several of the hybrid reforms retained the ages in the old defined benefit plan.

Table 7-2 reports the number of participants and amount of assets in the defined contribution plans created both before and after the financial crisis. Because both sets of plans are still relatively new, the compulsory plans apply only to new hires, and the others are optional, participants and assets are

55. The legislation establishing the hybrid plan also scales back the existing defined benefit plan by lowering the accrual rate from 1.70 to 1.65 percent, calculating final compensation on the last sixty months instead of the last thirty-six, and capping the cost-of-living adjustment at 3 percent. In addition, any person with less than twenty years of service who takes general retirement would not be eligible for a COLA until one year after reaching normal retirement age.

56. Madrian and Shea (2001); Choi and others (2004); and Gale, Iwry, and Orszag (2005).

Table 7-1. *Provisions of New Hybrid Plans*[a]

Hybrid plan components	Georgia	Michigan	Utah	Virginia	Rhode Island
Defined benefit plan					
Accrual rate	1	1.5	1.5	1	1
COLA	Ad hoc	None	CPI up to 2.5%	Capped at 3%	Based on returns
Contributions					
Employer	11.54%	17.65%	10% cap	TBD	20.02%
Employee	1.25%	6.4 %	DB cost more than 10%	4%	3.75%
Defined contribution plan					
Employee contribution	1%	2%	None	1%	5%
Employer contribution	100% on first 1% 50% on next 4%	50% on first 2%	10% minus DB cost	100% on first 2% 50% on next 3%	1%

Sources: Various retirement systems' annual reports, legislation, and websites of state legislatures.

a. Employer contribution rates are for 2012–13. The annual COLA in Rhode Island is suspended until the system is 80 percent funded. Intermittent COLAs will be granted at five-year intervals based on investment returns. Employee contribution rates in Rhode Island vary based on occupation, employer, and Social Security coverage. The rates shown are for state employees covered by Social Security.

modest.[57] In 2009, participants accounted for 6 percent of all state and local active members, and assets amounted to less than 1 percent of total state and local pension assets.[58]

Options for Public Sector Pensions

Introducing 401(k)-type defined contribution plans is not the only path to achieving a better balance of risks and compensation patterns in the public sector. Alternatives include changing the nature of defined benefit plans, introducing explicit risk-sharing rules, designing better defined contribution plans, and finally,

57. In the private sector, when a new plan is adopted, the existing defined benefit plan is usually frozen. Existing employees can retain the benefits earned but are not permitted to accrue any further service credits. In the public sector, when a new plan is adopted, existing employees usually have a legal right to continue to participate in the previous plan, and only employees hired after the date the plan is adopted are required to participate in the new plan.

58. Author's calculations from the U.S. Census Bureau (2007); U.S. Board of Governors of the Federal Reserve System (2007); and *Public Plans Database* (2001–10).

Table 7-2. *Characteristics of Primary Defined Contribution Plans,*
2007 and 2009

Plan name	Legislative date	Participants (number) 2007	Participants (number) 2009	Assets ($ in millions) 2007	Assets ($ in millions) 2009
Mandatory defined contribution plans					
Alaska PERS	2005	2,862	7,516	9	41
Alaska TRS	2005	646	1,997	6	27
Michigan SERS	1996	24,043	25,540	2,547	2,750
Mandatory hybrid plans					
Georgia—GSEPS	2008	0	2,105	0	311
Indiana PERF—ASA	1997[a]	213,984	223,561	2,707	2,669
Indiana TRF—ASA	1997[a]	122,107	164,590	4,605	3,901
Michigan—MPSERS	2010	0	0	0	0
Oregon PERS—IAP	2003	43,541	59,073	1,877	2,109
Rhode Island —ERSRI	2011	0	0	0	0
Utah—Tier II contributory hybrid	2010	0	0	0	0
Virginia RS—hybrid	2012	0	0	0	0
Choice of primary plan					
Colorado PERA—PERAChoice	2004	489	3,039	3	37
Florida RS—PEORP	2000	98,070	121,522	3,687	4,075
Montana PERS—DCRP	2002	1,999	2,345	41	44
Ohio PERS—combined plan	2002	6,905	7,354	157	223
Ohio PERS—member-directed plan	2002	8,579	9,824	124	201
Ohio STRS—member directed and combined plans	2001	11,863	12,829	283[b]	297[b]
South Carolina—ORP	2000	26,873	31,968	502	561
Utah—Tier II defined contribution	2010	0	0	0	0
Washington PERS—3	1999	27,605	31,123	1,348	1,188
Washington SERS—3	1998	37,854	38,585	1,052	918
Washington TRS—3	1998	57,667	60,146	3,971	3,419
Total		715,775	840,833	22,919	22,771

Sources: *Public Plans Database* (2007 and 2009); and various financial and actuarial reports.

a. The Indiana hybrid plans were established in 1955, but equity investment only became possible in 1997.

b. Ohio STRS does not separate assets for the member-directed and combined plans in its financial reports.

Table 7-3. *Saving Rate Required for a Medium Earner to Attain an 80 Percent Replacement Rate with a 4 Percent Rate of Return*
Percent

Retire at age	Start saving at age		
	25	35	45
62	22	35	65
65	15	24	41
67	12	18	31
70	7	11	18

Source: Munnell, Golub-Sass, and Webb (2011).

creating a "stacked" hybrid defined benefit/defined contribution arrangement. Whatever the form taken, the total cost of providing retirement benefits will be high if public sector employees continue to retire in their early 60s, because spending twenty or thirty years in retirement costs a lot of money. Therefore the retirement age should be an important part of any conversation on plan restructuring.

Importance of Retirement Age

The following exercise is couched in a defined contribution plan framework, but the question is how much needs to be put aside each year for a secure retirement through employee or employer contributions to either a defined benefit or defined contribution plan. Experts say that a secure retirement requires total income from Social Security and employer-sponsored plans to equal 80 percent of pre-retirement income.[59] The required savings rate then depends on four main factors:

—Earnings level. The lower the earnings, the greater the portion provided by Social Security and the lower the individual's required saving rate.

—Rate of return. The higher the rate of return on assets, the lower the required saving rate.

—Age when savings begins. The earlier the individual starts saving, the lower the required rate for any given retirement age.

—Age of retirement. The later the individual retires, the lower the required rate.

The required saving rates for the medium earner assuming a real (inflation-adjusted) rate of return of 4 percent, which would be about 6.5 percent nominal, are presented in table 7-3.[60] The rates are shown for different starting and retirement ages. The rates are very high for people retiring at age 62; even the steady saver or defined benefit participant who begins at age 35 would need to

59. Palmer (2008).
60. It is also assumed that Social Security benefits remain as promised under current law and people draw down their accumulations at 4 percent a year.

Table 7-4. *Saving Rate Required for a Medium Earner to Attain an 80 Percent Replacement Rate with a Starting Age of 35, by Rate of Return*
Percent

Retire at age	Real rate of return		
	2	4	6
62	46	35	26
65	32	24	17
67	26	18	13
70	16	11	7

Source: Munnell, Golub-Sass, and Webb (2011).

save 35 percent of earnings a year. Retiring at age 70 reduces the required contribution rate by two-thirds.[61]

Table 7-4 shows the impact of lower and higher rates of return for individuals who start at age 35. The 2 percent return is slightly less than the inflation-adjusted long-run rate of return on intermediate-term government bonds and the 6 percent return is slightly less than the inflation-adjusted long-run rate of return on large cap stocks. While higher returns require smaller contribution rates, they also come with increased risk. Even ignoring risk, the required saving differentials are less than those associated with dates for starting to save and the age of retirement. In fact, an individual can offset the difference in accumulation between a 2 percent return and a 6 percent return by retiring at 67 instead of 62.

The required saving rates for low earners would be lower and for maximum earners would be higher because of Social Security; under current law, at age 67 Social Security will replace 55 percent of pre-retirement earnings for low earners and 27 percent for those earning the taxable maximum. The story, however, remains the same. Retirements that begin in the early 60s are very expensive. Higher returns help, but the most potent lever is a later retirement age. This factor needs to be considered as public sector employers redesign their plans. The following discusses some of the design options.

Career Average Defined Benefit Plans

Several alternatives to final pay defined benefit plans are available. One approach adopted in the private sector is to shift to a cash balance plan, which is a defined

61. In the private sector, retiring later is an extremely powerful lever for several reasons. First, because Social Security monthly benefits are actuarially adjusted, they are over 75 percent higher at age 70 than at age 62. Second, by postponing retirement, people have additional years to contribute to their 401(k) and allow their balances to grow. Finally, a later retirement age means that people have fewer years to support themselves on their accumulated retirement assets.

benefit plan that maintains notional individual accounts throughout the asset accrual phase. As in traditional private sector defined benefit plans, the employer makes the contributions, owns the assets, selects the investments, and bears the risk. The employer typically contributes 4 or 5 percent of the worker's pay to a "notional" account and provides an interest credit (usually based on U.S. Treasury securities) on the balance. Employees receive regular statements and can withdraw the balance as a lump sum when they retire or terminate employment.

Four public sector systems—Nebraska (for state and county workers), the Texas Municipal Retirement System, the Texas County and District Retirement System, and the California State Teachers' Retirement System for part-time instructors at community colleges—have adopted cash balance plans. The assets in these plans are pooled and managed by the employer, while participants have separate accounts. Unlike cash balance plans in the private sector, these public plans involve employee as well as employer contributions, and at retirement the Texas plan annuitizes the balances in the individual member accounts.

An alternative to a cash balance plan is a defined benefit plan that bases benefits on a measure of career earnings. Of course, a career average system would require some indexing procedure so that earnings early in life are restated in units relevant at retirement.[62] Thus career earnings plans and cash balance plans can be viewed as similar; a cash balance plan adds up each year's earnings weighted by the cumulative interest credited, while a career average plan follows the same procedure but the weighting is based on the growth in either prices or wages.

One example of a movement away from a final pay plan for public employees occurred recently in the United Kingdom. In 2007, the British government closed its final pay plan for civil service employees to new hires and replaced it with "nuvos," a career average salary plan. A career-indexed average system changes several outcomes. First, a system that adjusts earnings histories for inflation sharply reduces the age-induced backloading in the plan. As a result, younger workers who leave early receive relatively larger benefits. Second, a career-average system largely eliminates the bias in favor of those with rapidly growing earnings, who, as noted earlier, tend to be the higher-paid. The lifetime pension benefit as a percentage of lifetime earnings is virtually equivalent for the low and high earner. Third, an indexed career earnings plan like nuvos largely eliminates the incentive for late-career salary increases.[63] Such a reform, done

62. Such a system is essentially equivalent to a notional defined contribution system with a benefit calculation that does not rely on a mortality calculation for determining benefits at full retirement age and no adjustments over time as mortality changes.

63. A 20 percent increase in salary in the last three years of a career increases lifetime pension benefits by only 2 percent under an indexed career average plan compared to 15 percent under a three-year final pay plan. Such a small increment provides little incentive for either the employer or employee to distort career patterns and personnel priorities.

with no change in total cost, necessarily affects different workers differently. But from the perspective of workers uncertain about their future career paths, a career average system is less risky.

Explicit Risk Sharing

Another approach is to introduce explicit risk sharing into existing defined benefit plans. In the wake of the 2000 perfect storm, when falling stock returns and falling interest rates hit pension funds, the Dutch changed the structure and risk sharing of their quasi-public, employer-based, supplementary defined benefit plans, which cover 90 percent of workers.[64] Most of the defined benefit plans moved from basing benefits on final earnings to indexed career average earnings.[65] That is, individuals accrue pension rights annually based on the salary earned each year, and earnings are usually revalued upward each year to take account of inflation or wage growth. After retirement, benefits are mostly inflation-indexed or wage-indexed. The indexed career average plans are like traditional defined benefit plans in that accrued pension rights are based on an employee's wages and years of service, and contribution rates can be raised in response to a funding shortfall. But they are also like defined contribution plans in that benefits are not strictly defined, but are tied to the fund's financial status—and therefore to investment returns—via the annual indexation factor, which is applied to both the accrued rights of active workers and the benefits of retired workers.

As a result of the redesign, these hybrid defined benefit/defined contribution plans have two mechanisms—contribution rates and indexation—to respond to any underfunding created by a financial and economic crisis. For moderate underfunding, a so-called policy ladder suggests equal parts from higher contributions and reduced indexation of benefit accruals and benefits in payment. Unfortunately, the rules had not specified how to return to solvency in the case of the severe underfunding that occurred in the wake of the 2008 financial collapse.[66] This situation led to inertia as policymakers attempted to figure out whether the employer should make additional contributions, whether retirees should absorb nominal cuts in benefits, whether workers should accrue less in benefit rights, or

64. Ponds and van Riel (2007).

65. In an average-wage plan, individuals accrue pension rights annually based on the salary earned in each year of their working life (rather than the final year, as in a final pay plan). The accrual rate is 2 percent or even higher because a total pension equal to 80 percent of the average wage corresponds to approximately 70 percent of final pay.

66. The Dutch government requires that a nominal funding ratio of 105 percent be restored by the end of five years. The nominal funding ratio is the ratio of assets valued at market to accrued liabilities discounted by the nominal yield curve. In other words, the nominal liability is the value of liabilities when no indexation is provided.

whether all parties should do nothing and hope the financial markets rebounded.[67] The Dutch experience highlights the need to have rules for how to allocate the burden in extreme, as well as moderate, underfunding situations.

Better Defined Contribution Plans

To the extent that the public sector decides to move away from defined benefit plans to defined contribution plans, it can profit from the 401(k) experience in the private sector. For example, coverage can be by default or even mandatory, instead of voluntary. The default contribution rate can be higher than the 3 percent usually applied in the private sector. Individuals do not need to manage their assets independently; they can be managed professionally by the fund. And at retirement, accruals do not have to be distributed as a lump sum.

Oregon's Individual Account Program (IAP) seems like a positive step in the design of defined contribution plans. Members automatically contribute 6 percent of salary to an individual account. They do not contribute to the defined benefit plan (PERS). Once contributed, the assets are invested with those of PERS and receive the same investment return. Members do not have control over IAP investments. Upon retirement, members may receive the account balance as a lump-sum or fixed-period annuity. The annuity period is either five, ten, or twenty years. Upon death, the remaining account balance is transferred to beneficiaries (even if the annuity option is chosen). All these design features are more likely to lead to a secure retirement income than the private sector 401(k). This type of defined contribution plan could be combined with a defined benefit plan in any number of ways; one new suggestion follows.

A "Stacked" Option

The emergence of hybrid plans reflects an attempt to balance employee and taxpayer risk. But, to date, states are achieving this goal by reducing the government's contribution across the board rather than considering how best to use each plan type.

An alternative approach to limiting taxpayer risk is to lower the cap on the income covered by the defined benefit plan.[68] Such a cap would avoid the situation where the typical taxpayer, earning $50,000, is forced to pay higher taxes when the stock market plummets to cover benefits for highly paid public employees, such as university presidents. Therefore the proposal would be to limit coverage under the defined benefit plan to earnings below, say, $50,000

---

67. Kortleve and Ponds (2010) explore various policy options and their distributional effects.

68. Effective January 1, 2012, the limitation on compensation eligible for defined benefit plans under section 415(b)(1)(A) is $250,000.

Figure 7-13. *"Stacked" Hybrid Plan versus "Parallel" Hybrid Plan*[a]

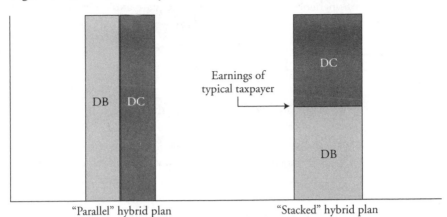

"Parallel" hybrid plan   "Stacked" hybrid plan

Source: Author's illustration.
a. DB = defined benefit plan; DC = defined contribution plan.

(indexed for inflation).[69] Many public sector workers would still be covered in full under the defined benefit plan.

Earnings above $50,000 would be covered by a defined contribution plan. Thus, someone earning $100,000 would receive benefits based on the first $50,000 from the defined benefit plan and benefits on the second $50,000 from the defined contribution plan. That is, instead of "parallel" plans where employees contribute to both a 401(k) and a defined benefit plan from the first dollar of earnings, "stacked" plans would maintain the defined benefit plan as a base and provide defined contribution coverage for earnings above some cutoff (see figure 7-13). The stacked approach could be wed with any desired size of the plan.

The advantage of the "stacked" approach is that it allows employees with modest earnings to receive the full protection of a defined benefit plan. This group would be the most vulnerable if required to rely on a 401(k) for a portion of their core retirement benefit. Indeed, the private sector experience discussed earlier illustrated the potential problems. So maintaining a full defined benefit plan for public employees such as sanitation workers would be preferable. More highly paid public employees would still have the protection of a defined benefit plan as a base and would then rely on the 401(k) for earnings replacement that

69. The Internal Revenue Code contains a maximum compensation limit for defined contribution plans. This limit was $245,000 in 2011. It is indexed for inflation and increases in $5,000 increments. A similar procedure could be used for stacked plans.

exceeded the earnings of a typical private sector worker.[70] This overall arrangement offers a reasonable balance by providing adequate and secure benefits targeted to public employees who need them most while limiting the risk to taxpayers of covering large pension shortfalls.[71]

Conclusion

Defined contribution plans may well have a role in the public sector, but in combination with, not as an alternative to, defined benefit plans. Continued reliance solely on final earnings defined benefit plans raises both financial and human resource issues. On the financial side, the risk is that these plans are not funded on a timely basis, shifting costs to future taxpayers. The financial crisis has also demonstrated that fluctuations in the financial markets put benefits at risk for both current workers and retirees. On the human resource side, final earnings plans produce strongly backloaded benefits that favor workers with rapidly rising earnings and that produce an enormous payoff to salary increases in the final years of employment. These incentives may be desirable for some types of employees, but are not appropriate for all. Thus, human resource considerations, like the financial issues, argue for less reliance on final pay defined benefit plans.

On the other hand, the thirty-year experiment with 401(k)s in the private sector cautions against a wholesale shift to defined contribution plans. The balances in these plans fall way below potential, and the shortfall can be traced to the decisions of participants. Moreover, such a shift from defined benefit to defined contribution plans is not a panacea for the sponsor. It would not eliminate the current unfunded liabilities associated with defined benefit plans, it would not reduce costs, and it would not lead to higher returns.

Therefore, some redesign that combines elements of both defined benefit and defined contribution plans would better balance the financial risks between taxpayers and participants and provide a benefit structure that offers some reward to short-term employees. The options extend beyond simply cutting back on the

---

70. A well-designed defined contribution plan would set the combined employee-employer contribution at a level that would achieve, in combination with a defined benefit plan, a targeted replacement rate. It would also have the default payment at retirement be an annuity, with the ability of participants to opt out if such an arrangement did not meet their needs. One reviewer also suggested that the plan might guarantee the employee's contribution regardless of investment performance as a way of encouraging participation.

71. One question is whether such a stacked approach would violate IRS nondiscrimination rules. The legal answer is that tax-qualified governmental plans are not normally subject to nondiscrimination provisions. On a substantive level, the government contribution for the defined contribution plan could be less than for the defined benefit plan, so that the two plans taken as a whole do not favor higher-paid workers.

defined benefit plan and adding a 401(k) plan. Sponsors can consider modified defined benefit plans, such as cash balance or indexed career average, the introduction of explicit risk sharing, the construction of better defined contribution plans, or a stacked approach. But to provide meaningful retirement income, any approach will require significant contributions from either the employer or the employee if public employees continue to retire in their early 60s. Hence later retirement should be considered as states and localities think about redesigning their pension systems.

8

Making State and Local Pensions Better

This chapter looks to the future. The first section recaps the main findings of this book to provide context for discussing the major challenges facing sponsors of state and local pensions going forward. The key point is that while a few bad actors exist, many public plans are functioning well, create little risk to the state or local sponsor, and offer benefits that, together with cash wages, provide total compensation comparable to that in the private sector. The second section then identifies the three major challenges facing almost all public plans—excessive holdings of equities, sharp cuts in benefits for new employees, and the difficulty state officials face when they need to reduce *future* benefits for current employees. The third section discusses the path forward when reform is needed, highlighting the importance of fairness, and, using Rhode Island as an example, shows how reform is possible when the process is open and equitable. Neither discounting liabilities by a riskless rate for reporting purposes (albeit correct) nor fighting unions holds much promise for solving problems where they exist. The fourth section discusses the inevitability of pressure to cut back public plans as long as retirement protection remains inadequate in the private sector. Public pension reform should not be based on comparisons with the private sector but rather on identifying the size and characteristics of the desired workforce and then constructing a competitive compensation package, with the appropriate mix of wages and benefits, to achieve it.

A Recap

The most important conclusions from the previous chapters are that state and local plans are a heterogeneous lot and that all public plans are not in trouble.

States with seriously underfunded plans, such as Illinois, Kentucky, Louisiana, New Jersey, and Pennsylvania, have behaved badly. They have either not made the required contributions or used inaccurate assumptions so that their contribution requirements are not meaningful. An equally large number of states—Delaware, Florida, Georgia, Tennessee, and North Carolina—have done a good job of providing reasonable benefits, paying their required contribution, and accumulating plan assets. Some states with poorly funded plans will see enormous pressure from pensions on their budgets; others with fairly well funded plans will not.

Critics have identified two major sources of problems in the public pension arena: (1) discounting promised benefits by the long-run expected rate of return instead of the riskless rate; or (2) the collective bargaining activities of unions. These factors certainly cannot explain the variation across plans or why some plans are poorly funded. Bad actors did not come close to surmounting the lower hurdle associated with a high discount rate; raising the hurdle is unlikely to have improved their behavior. And, consistent with other research, union strength did not show up as a statistically significant factor in any of the empirical analysis. Pension funding is simply a story of fiscal discipline.

Whereas using a high discount rate is not the source of the problem in states with underfunded pensions, adopting a discount rate for *reporting* purposes that reflects the riskiness of the benefits has clear advantages. It would increase the credibility of public sector accounting with private sector analysts and could well forestall unwise benefit increases when the stock market soars, as occurred in California in the 1990s. And while using the riskless rate may not change the behavior of the bad actors, higher *reported* liabilities could create pressure for all plans to increase their funding. Adopting the riskless rate could also avoid aggressive portfolio allocations to justify high discount rates.

Interestingly, in the early 1980s, the riskless rate exceeded the expected return on assets, and if inflation should take off, the liabilities of states and localities would once again appear to be minuscule. Thus the issue is not whether liabilities should be larger or smaller, but rather whether they are measured correctly. The rationale behind discounting by a riskless rate applies only to reporting; it does not carry over to funding and investing. Several arguments support some equity investment in public plans; and the amount set aside each year need not be based on the riskless rate.

The other important question pertaining to pensions is the appropriateness of the level of benefits. It is important to remember that the average pension benefit in 2010 was $24,000. Whether that level is too high or too low cannot be judged in a vacuum, but must be considered in concert with wages to gauge whether total compensation in the public sector is comparable to that in the private sector. The evidence shows that wages for workers with similar characteristics, education, and experience are lower for state and local workers than for those in the private sector. However, pension and retiree health benefits are higher for state and local workers and almost offset the wage penalty, so that, taken as a whole, compensation in the two sectors is roughly comparable. Most researchers agree on this point. Some argue that job security tilts the scale toward state and local workers, but, in the end, any discrepancy is small.

The parity of compensation between the public and private sectors hides enormous variation by wage levels and amount of time spent in public service. State and local workers in the lowest third of the wage distribution are paid somewhat more than their private sector counterparts, those in the middle roughly comparable amounts, and those in the top third significantly less. Similarly, those who spend *most of their career* in the state and local sector end up with slightly more wealth and higher replacement rates than their private sector counterparts. Short-term state and local workers actually appear to end up with less wealth and lower replacement rates than those who spend their entire career in the private sector.

These different outcomes by tenure are one reason to consider whether sole reliance on final earnings defined benefit plans is desirable. The other concern is the distribution of risk. It is hard to maintain a stable system where the employer bears all the risk. At the same time, the thirty-year experiment with 401(k) plans in the private sector suggests that a wholesale shift to defined contribution plans would leave public sector workers with inadequate retirement income. In order to balance risks and to provide some benefits for mobile workers, some combination of defined benefit and defined contribution plans would enhance the benefit structure in the public sector.

In short, most public plans are in reasonable shape. They were on a road toward full funding when they were thrown off course by the bursting of the dot.com bubble at the turn of the century and the financial collapse in 2008 and ensuing recession. As noted in chapter 7, critics object to characterizing state and local plans as victims, arguing that they should not have been so invested in equities. But good arguments exist for some equity investment, and every indication is that plans will increase their funded ratios as the economy and the stock market recover. In general, plans provide reasonable benefit levels, although the retirement age should be increased and risk sharing could be improved. But state and local plan sponsors do face some real challenges, and three troublesome issues facing even responsibly managed plans are discussed below.

Three Major Challenges Facing Public Plans

The three major challenges facing public pension plan sponsors are the share of their assets allocated to risky assets, the implications of recent benefit cuts for new employees on their ability to hire quality workers in the future, and the

Figure 8-1. *Distribution of Investments in Risky Assets by State and Local Pension Plans, 2010*[a]

Percent

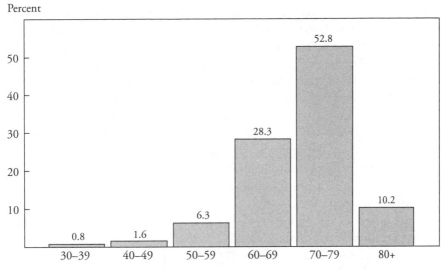

Percent of investments in risky assets

Source: *Public Plans Database* (2010).
a. Risky assets equal all assets that are not held in bonds or cash.

constraints they face in adjusting future benefits for current employees. These issues apply across the board; the next section explores how severely troubled plans might approach reform.

Allocation in Risky Assets

In 2011, state and local pension plans held about two-thirds of their assets in equities, hedge funds, real estate, and other alternative investments. These assets have higher expected returns, but they also carry more risk. The concern here is not that public plans invest in equities and other high-risk assets, but that they have such a large share of their portfolio in these investments (see figure 8-1). The returns on risky investments fluctuate substantially; some times are good, some times are bad. If the abnormally high returns during the good times were stockpiled, they most likely would offset the low returns or losses during bad times. But the politics of state and local plans make it difficult to keep contributions or benefits steady when pension plan returns exceed the assumed rate year after year as they did in the 1990s. Thus the most compelling practical reason for reducing equity holdings is the asymmetry in the treatment of the surpluses and deficits that results from abnormally high and low returns. The cost of reducing equity holdings is the acceptance of lower returns—and the need to levy higher taxes or pay lower benefits—over the long term. The question is how much of the portfolio should be allocated to high-risk investments.

One possible benchmark is private sector defined benefit plans. In 2011, private defined benefit plans in the United States held 49 percent of their investments in equities and other risky assets. But the situation of private plan sponsors is quite different from that of sponsors in the public sector. In the private sector, two developments—FASB Statement No.158 and the Pension Protection Act of 2006—increased the pain associated with a sudden drop in funded status and created incentives to match pension assets with liabilities.[1] The incentives for matching assets and liabilities were accentuated by the widespread freezing of defined benefit plans following the perfect storm of 2001–02. Given that liabilities are discounted by the prevailing market yield on AA-rated corporate bonds, firms can reduce mark-to-market volatility by selecting a portfolio whose fair value is positively correlated with the fair value of the pension liability. With a frozen plan and a finite time horizon, matching assets and liabilities essentially takes the pension plan out of the financial picture.

Another possible benchmark is the Dutch quasi-public, employer-based, supplementary defined benefit plans, discussed in chapter 7, which cover 90 percent of workers. The Dutch plans in 2011 held 46 percent of their total portfolio in risky assets.[2] Their situation is more analogous to state and local pensions.

In comparison with either private defined benefit plans or the Dutch plans, state and local pension plans have a very high allocation to risky investments. Such a high share is most likely *not* the result of deliberate policy decisions. Rather, it appears that public plans, like private plans, rode the bull market and ended up with equities accounting for 70 percent of plan assets by the market peak in 2007. At that time, a striking divergence occurred. Public plans allowed their share in equities to rebound in the wake of the 2008 financial crisis, whereas private plans reduced their equity holdings to about 42 percent.

---

1. FASB 158, which became effective for financial statements issued in December 2006, was designed to improve financial reporting through three major changes: (1) measure assets and liabilities at market value at the end of the fiscal year; (2) recognize on the firm's balance sheet the overfunded or underfunded status of the plan as a liability or asset; and (3) recognize changes in the funded status of the plan due to gains/losses and prior service costs/credits. These changes introduce substantial volatility into reported income and shareholder equity. See Amir, Guan, and Oswald (2010). In addition to the change in accounting, the Pension Protection Act of 2006 dramatically shortened the period (from thirty years to seven for single-employer plans) over which plans must amortize the unfunded liability. Thus a shortfall in funding could lead to a large increase in required contributions.

2. The Dutch funds held 32 percent in equities, 10 percent in real estate, 3 percent in hedge funds, and 1 percent in commodities (author's calculations from De Nederlandsche Bank 2011).

At this point, all the incentives in the system encourage sponsors to engage in high-risk investing. Given that the Governmental Accounting Standards Board (GASB) says that sponsors should value liabilities using (at least in part under the new standards) the expected long-run return, any move to reduce equity holdings would have a major impact on reported outcomes. Lower equity holdings would reduce the expected return, resulting in higher unfunded liability, higher normal cost, and therefore higher annual required contributions. The investment community also makes a lot of money by selling high-risk products to public plans. And a continued focus on peer rankings leads to sponsors "chasing each other up the ladder of high risk."[3]

The challenge is how to break out of the existing pattern. In conversation, investment managers of public plans have said that they are compelled to take on more risk than they would otherwise because they are given a "bogie" that they need to hit by the actuaries. A recent survey of plans notes that asset allocation objectives typically are chosen to meet a numerical goal for ex-post investment returns, rather than a desire to hedge the risk of liabilities.[4] On the other hand, actuaries are required by professional standards to set the expected return based on the asset allocation. The situation resembles that of a dog chasing its tail.

Investment decisions in public plans need to be made with an eye to two factors—the tolerance for risk of plan sponsors and plan members and a recognition of the asymmetrical treatment of gains and losses. Year after year of higher-than-assumed returns will inevitably lead to reduced contributions or benefit expansions, so surpluses will not be there when the lean years hit.

In terms of risk tolerance, plan sponsors do not want to see their contributions reach unsustainable levels, and plan members do not want to see their benefits cut. Plan boards need to determine how much risk they are willing to accept in the form of contribution volatility and benefit security, and then investment managers should try to maximize the portfolio return for a given level of risk. Actuaries would then recommend the expected discount rate based on the portfolio.

Inevitably, an assessment of the financial and political risks will lead to lower desired holdings of equities and alternative assets. While such a reduction would produce a better balance of risk and sustainability, it would also result in lower assumed rates of return for both reporting and funding.[5] (Discounting obligations by the riskless rate for reporting purposes would make the shift away from equities easier because such a shift would have no impact on reported

---

3. Comment by actuary Gene Kalwarski, CEO of Cheiron Inc., as reported in Keegan (2012).

4. Peng (2009).

5. The Dutch plans assume a long-run return of 6 percent, according to e-mail correspondence in 2011 between the author and Eduard Ponds, a pension expert affiliated with APG (a pension administrator), Tilburg University, and Netspar.

liabilities.) But whatever the increase in liabilities, the share of the portfolio allocated to risky assets needs to be lower. The current allocation, combined with the asymmetrical treatment of gains and losses, will continue to endanger funding in the state/local sector.

Cutting Pension Benefits for New Employees

The second major issue facing state and local governments is the potential impact of cutting pension benefits for new employees on the quality of future workers. The studies reviewed in chapter 6 show that wages for public employees are lower than those in the private sector and that the addition of benefits makes total compensation roughly equal in the two sectors. If compensation is equal today, and benefits are being cut for new workers, then—in the absence of a wage increase—compensation for new workers will be lower in the public sector than in the private sector. And lower compensation will reduce the quality of workers attracted to the public sector.

In response to the 2008 financial crisis and the ensuing recession, states have introduced four types of changes (see figure 8-2).[6] Nine states suspended the cost-of-living adjustments (COLAs) for current and future retirees, and some have linked future COLAs to the funded status of the plan or to returns on assets held in the fund. Twenty-one states raised employee contributions for current and future employees and five for new employees only, which diminishes the net compensation received in the form of pensions for these workers. Thirty-one states reduced benefits for new employees, primarily by increasing the age when full benefits are paid, and five states introduced a less expensive hybrid defined benefit/defined contribution system for new employees.[7] In all cases, new employees will receive diminished pension compensation.

The point here is not to criticize the retrenchment. In fact, retirement ages in the public sector are much lower than those in the private sector. As discussed earlier, offering full benefits at age 60 creates a prohibitively expensive system.

6. *Suspended COLAs*: Colorado, Maine, Minnesota, New Jersey, Oklahoma, Rhode Island, South Dakota, Washington, and Wyoming. *Raised employee contributions*: Alabama, Arizona, Colorado, Delaware, Florida, Hawaii, Iowa, Kansas, Louisiana, Maryland, Minnesota, Missouri, Montana, Nebraska, Nevada, New Hampshire, New Jersey, New Mexico, North Dakota, Oklahoma, Pennsylvania, Texas, Virginia, Vermont, Wisconsin, and Wyoming. *Reduced benefits for new hires*: Arizona, California, Colorado, Connecticut, Delaware, Florida, Georgia, Hawaii, Iowa, Illinois, Kansas, Louisiana, Massachusetts, Maryland, Michigan, Minnesota, Missouri, Mississippi, Montana, North Carolina, Nevada, New Hampshire, New Jersey, Oklahoma, Pennsylvania, Rhode Island, Texas, Virginia, Vermont, West Virginia, and Wisconsin. *Introduced a hybrid plan:* Georgia, Michigan, Rhode Island, Utah, and Virginia.

7. Rhode Island, which is discussed later, is an exception in that it has also introduced a hybrid for current employees.

Figure 8-2. *States Making Changes to State or Local Pension Plans in the Wake of the Financial Crisis*

Number of states

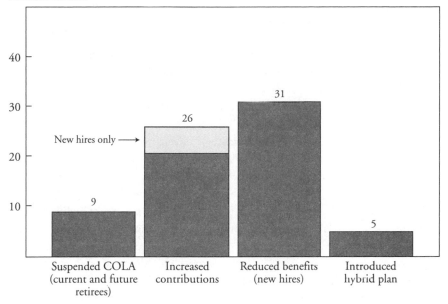

Source: National Conference of State Legislatures (2008–12).

Given the improvements in health and longevity, requiring employees to delay retirement is a sensible reform. Similarly, as discussed in chapter 7, some mixture of defined benefit and defined contribution plans can offer a better sharing of risks between public sector employees and taxpayers and improved protection for shorter-term workers. But even if all the changes are good policy, they will diminish the total compensation that new workers will receive, making public sector jobs less attractive and reducing the quality of applicants.

Economists have shown that changes in relative wages between the public and private sector have a real effect on individual job decisions. A particularly persuasive study focused on the impact on job choice of changing patterns of wage dispersion between the public and private sector.[8] Between 1970 and 2000, wage dispersion rose sharply in the private sector, while the wage structure in the public sector remained relatively compressed. In the face of such a change, one would expect that high-skilled private sector workers (such as college graduates) would have declining interest in entering the public sector and high-skilled

8. Borjas (2002).

public sector workers would have increased interest in moving to the private sector. To test this hypothesis, the author merged data from the U.S. decennial Censuses and from the *Current Population Surveys* (CPS) and identified two groups of private sector workers: (1) those who had just entered the private sector; and (2) those who were leaving the private sector. Examining the characteristics of these two groups revealed that as public sector wages became relatively compressed, high-skilled private sector workers became increasingly less likely to quit their jobs to enter the public sector and high-skilled public sector workers became increasingly more likely to switch to the private sector. In short, with a more compressed wage structure, the public sector found it harder to attract and retain high-skilled workers.

Thus, large pension cuts, in the absence of offsetting wage increases, will discourage workers from entering public sector employment. The potential damage is particularly worrisome because while compensation is comparable on average, the pattern varies by earnings level. The lowest paid one-third of employees in the public sector earn more than their private sector counterparts, while the top one-third earn less. And the level of compensation of many teachers falls within that top third of state and local workers. Therefore, current actions, without any compensating changes in wages, have the potential to adversely affect the quality of people willing to teach in public schools.

In the public sector, a disproportionate share of cuts has fallen on new employees. Two factors contribute to this outcome. First, new employees do not have a seat at the table. Most often, the sponsor negotiates with representatives of current employees, many representing the interest of those with long service. These representatives inevitably exert most of their effort in protecting the benefits of current public sector workers and concede more readily when the discussion turns to future employees. The second factor is unique to the public sector. Many states are severely constrained from changing future benefits for current employees and are thereby forced to focus their efforts on future workers. The need to bring benefit protection in line with the private sector is discussed next.

Legal Constraints on Pension Changes

Many states are severely constrained in their ability to change *future* pension benefits for current employees. This constraint not only ties the hands of public officials when it comes to making substantial changes in their pension plans, but also accords public employees greater protections than their private sector counterparts. The Employee Retirement Income Security Act of 1974 (ERISA), which governs plans in the private sector, protects benefits earned to date but allows employers to change future benefits in response to economic conditions.

The legal constraints on changing future benefits are largely a reaction to a period when pensions were viewed as a gratuity that could be withdrawn or changed by the state at any time.[9] Since the two federal laws that regulate pensions do not apply to public sector plan changes, states are responsible for providing protection for their public employees.[10] The legal approaches to protect public pensions vary significantly from one state to another.

Most states protect pensions under a contracts-based approach. The federal Constitution's Contract Clause and similar provisions in state constitutions prohibit a state from passing any law that impairs existing contracts, whether public or private. To determine whether a state action is unconstitutional under the Contract Clause, the courts undertake a three-part test. First, they determine whether a contract exists. This part of the test involves determining when the contract is formed and what the contract protects. Second, the courts determine whether the state action constitutes a substantial impairment. Third, if the impairment is substantial, then the court must determine whether the action is justified by an important public purpose and if the action taken in the public interest is reasonable and necessary. This approach sets a high bar for changing future benefits, presenting a serious obstacle to pension reform.

A handful of states that protect pensions under the contract theory also have state constitutional provisions that expressly prevent the state from amending the plan in any way that would produce benefits lower than participants expected at the time of employment. Illinois and New York have such a provision. Alaska has language that specifically applies only to accrued benefits, but the courts have interpreted the provision to protect all benefits from the time participants enroll. Arizona's language is less clear, but prior court rulings suggest that the protection extends to future as well as accrued benefits. In these states, changing benefits for existing employees is virtually impossible without amending the constitution. In contrast, Hawaii, Louisiana, and Michigan have constitutional provisions that have been interpreted as protecting only benefits earned to date.

Table 8-1 categorizes the states by the extent to which core benefit accruals are protected and the legal basis for that protection.[11] It is necessary to separate

9. This discussion is based on Center for Retirement Research at Boston College (2012b).

10. ERISA does not cover state and local plans at all. While the Internal Revenue Code does specify—for public plans as well as private plans—the requirements that plans must meet to qualify for favorable tax treatment, it specifically exempts state plans from the "anti-cutback" rule, which precludes amendments that would decrease benefits already accrued.

11. The sources of information used to construct table 8-1 in some cases provided conflicting guidance on how to classify a given state. To offer a clear standard for the reader, the hierarchy among the sources is as follows. Preference was given to information provided by a plan's legal counsel when accompanied by a decisive court ruling. If no information was provided, Monahan (2010) was the primary source. For states not covered in Monahan and where no information was received from the plans, the National Conference on Public Employee Retirement Systems' (NCPERS) 2007 analysis was the primary source. The only exception was New Hampshire, where more recent developments suggest that the NCPERS information is now outdated (see Associated Press 2012).

Table 8-1. *Legal Basis for Protection of Public Pension Rights under State Laws*

	Accruals protected			
Legal basis	Past and future	Past and maybe future	Past only	None
State constitution	Alaska Illinois New York	Arizona	Hawaii Louisiana Michigan	
Contract	Alabama California Georgia Kansas Massachusetts Nebraska Nevada New Hampshire North Dakota Oregon Pennsylvania Tennessee Vermont Washington West Virginia	Colorado Idaho Maryland Mississippi New Jersey Rhode Island South Carolina	Arkansas Delaware Florida Iowa Kentucky Missouri Montana North Carolina Oklahoma South Dakota Utah Virginia	
Property	Maine Wyoming	Connecticut New Mexico Ohio	Wisconsin	
Promissory estoppel[a]	Minnesota			
Gratuity				Indiana Texas[b]

Sources: Cloud (2011); Monahan (2010); National Conference on Public Employee Retirement Systems (2007); Mumford and Pareja (1997); Reinke (2011); Staman (2011); Simko (1996); and consultations with plan legal counsels when accompanied by a decisive court ruling.

a. Promissory estoppel is the protection of a promise even where no contract has been explicitly stated.

b. This gratuity approach applies only to state-administered plans. Accruals in many locally administered plans are protected under the Texas constitution.

core benefits from the COLA because recent court decisions suggest that the two components should be treated differently. Most states that protect core benefits under the contract theory do not have a state constitutional provision, but rather have statutes that expressly adopt the contract theory or judicial decisions that have ruled the relationship to be contractual. Interestingly, for thirteen states the protections apply only once benefits are vested.[12] Eight states protect benefits only once the employee is eligible for retirement.[13] While New Jersey and Rhode Island have been classified in table 8-1, they have court cases pending regarding changes in core benefits.

California and several other states that fall in the contract group have attempted to introduce some flexibility by expanding the interpretation of the third part of the three-part test for Contract Clause constitutionality—that the change be "reasonable and necessary." Under the expanded test, the change could be reasonable and necessary either to achieve an important public purpose—the conventional test—or if the disadvantages are accompanied by new advantages. In the end, however, the ability to modify pensions in these states hinges on when the contract is deemed to exist. States where the contract is found to exist at the time of employment have little freedom to change benefits. States where the contract is found to exist at retirement have considerably more flexibility.

Six states have adopted a property-based approach to protecting pensions. To the extent that pension benefits are considered property, they cannot be taken away without due process according to the Fifth and Fourteenth Amendments to the Constitution. Due process has both a procedural and a substantive component. Most of the challenges to state action are based on substantive due process and have not been successful. Courts have usually found amendments to public pension plans to be "an adjustment to the benefits and burdens of economic life" rather than the taking of private property without just compensation.[14] Thus state officials have much more freedom to adjust pensions in states that have taken the property-based approach to pension rights.

For the vast majority of states, however, changing future benefits for current employees is extremely difficult. The exception appears to be the COLAs, which the courts have recently interpreted as having a different status than "core" benefits. The early decisions in Colorado and Minnesota laid out the rationales for allowing COLA suspensions.[15] In Colorado, where the decision is currently

12. The thirteen states that protect only vested benefits are: Alabama, Alaska, California, Connecticut, Florida, Indiana, Louisiana, New Hampshire, New Mexico, North Carolina, Ohio, Oklahoma, and Tennessee. Vesting usually occurs within five years. In Indiana, protections apply only to the state's voluntary contributory plans; accruals under the state's mandatory noncontributory plans are not protected since they are viewed as a gratuity.

13. The eight states that protect benefits only once the employee is eligible for retirement are: Arkansas, Delaware, Iowa, Kentucky, Missouri, Montana, Utah, and Virginia.

14. *Pineman v. Fallon*, 842 F.2d 598 (2nd Cir. 1988).

15. In Colorado, 2010 legislation reduced the COLA for 2010 from 3.5 percent to the lesser of 2 percent or the average of the CPI-W for the 2009 calendar year (which resulted in a zero COLA for 2010) and a maximum of 2 percent thereafter (linked to investment returns) for current

under appeal, the judge found that the plaintiffs had no vested contract right to a specific COLA amount for life without change and that the plaintiffs could have no reasonable expectation to a specific COLA given that the General Assembly changed the COLA formula numerous times over the previous forty years. In Minnesota, the judge ruled both that the COLA was not a core benefit and that the COLA modification was necessary to prevent the long-term fiscal deterioration of the pension plan. Both these decisions clearly imply that core benefits are protected.

The protection of future accruals of core benefits serves to lock in any benefit expansions, limiting policymakers' ability to respond to changing economic conditions. For example, California public employees covered by CalPERS will continue to be able to claim substantial benefits at age 55, an age introduced in a benefit expansion during the heady days of the 1990s. Few argue that core benefits earned to date based on retirement at that age should be changed. Current workers accepted public employment with the understanding that they were accruing pension benefits at a certain rate, and remained employed with that understanding. But future benefits, much like future payroll, should be allowed to vary based on economic conditions. That is, public officials should be able to change future benefits for current CalPERS workers.

Such increased flexibility for public employers would accord their employees the same protections as workers in the private sector. ERISA, which governs private plans, protects accrued benefits but allows employers to change the terms going forward. In Illinois and New York, such a change could not be made without a constitutional amendment, because future benefits are protected explicitly. In other states, the challenge is to narrow the definition of the contract. Here the burden would fall on the legislature and the courts. This goal could be achieved by enacting legislation that the contract is created when the employee performs the service, which would create an ERISA-type standard. If this legislation is challenged, the courts would then need to be persuaded to adopt a more flexible standard in light of changed conditions, just as they once abandoned the gratuity theory in favor of a contract-based approach. In fact, adopting a more flexible contract approach would be less dramatic than shifting theories.[16]

In summary, virtually all public plans face three challenges: the need to reduce their holdings of risky assets, the need to ensure that compensation for new

---

and future retirees. In Minnesota, in 2010 the state reduced the COLA for the State Employees' Retirement Fund from 2.5 percent to 2 percent and for the General Employees' Retirement Plan from 2.5 percent to 1 percent. The COLA for the Teachers' Retirement Association was suspended between 2011 and 2012, and reduced from 2.5 percent to 2 percent thereafter.

16. Monahan (2010).

workers is competitive, and the need to change the legal environment so that sponsors can adjust future benefits for current employees. A better balancing of investments, an increase in wages for new employees to offset pension cuts, and more flexibility to adjust benefits would make the public pension system better for both public employees and for taxpayers. The positive aspect of these challenges is that while solutions are not simple or cheap, the problems are solvable. The next section explores what to do when the financial challenges are so great that marginal adjustments are not an option.

The Importance of "Fairness"

Some states, such as Illinois and California, where pension costs could well approach 15 percent of state and local revenues even without any new financial crisis, will require a dramatic restructuring of their pension system. Without changes, the state will have to cut back on its support for roads and other infrastructure, universities and colleges, health services for low-income individuals, and other expenditures that contribute to the quality of life within the state. Dramatic restructuring is a polite way to say that public employees will receive less and taxpayers will have to pay more. The required changes will involve pain; people will end up with less than they had planned on. The question is how to go about solving pension problems when the situation is dire. The following discussion pursues the notion that the process needs to be "fair," defines what fairness means, and offers Rhode Island's experience as a model for success.

Defining "Fairness"

Although the goal to establish a fair process seems uncontroversial, it is not always clear how it should be implemented. Interestingly, a 2011 panel on reforming Illinois public pensions included Anthony Laden, a professor of philosophy at the University of Illinois at Chicago. Laden attempted to flesh out what it means for a process to be fair. He argued that fairness is a value that needs to shape conversations from the very beginning, not a criterion against which to measure outcomes at the end. Laden used a quote from the political philosopher John Rawls to help define how fairness would shape the conversation:

> Persons engaged in a just, or fair, practice can face one another openly and support their respective positions, should they appear questionable, by reference to principles which it is reasonable to expect each to accept.[17]

17. Rawls (1999).

In other words, a process is fair if participants can and do face each other openly: one party does not try to manipulate or bully the other. Those putting forth proposals must be prepared to offer reasons that they think others might accept. And those who are asked to accept the proposals must understand that being a citizen in a democracy requires the acceptance of loss. Laden also quoted Danielle Allen, the author of a book about democracy:

> Communal decisions inevitably benefit some citizens at the expense of others. . . . Those people who benefit less than others . . . but nonetheless accede to those decisions, preserve the stability of political institutions. Their sacrifice makes collective democratic action possible.[18]

The challenge then is, how do policymakers face their fellow citizens openly when their decisions require that everyone sacrifice for the common good? Allen suggests three criteria for sacrifice to be fair, and Laden developed their relevance to debates about pension reform:

—First, the sacrifice has to be voluntary, so no actions will be taken without the acceptance of those who will bear their costs. It has to be asked for. The policymaker needs to give an honest account of what the sacrifice is for, why it is necessary, and what is gained. This approach involves trusting that those who are asked will respond reasonably, not purely selfishly, which is in turn a way of respecting them as equal citizens.

—Second, sacrifices need to be publicly honored and acknowledged. This requirement means, in part, that policymakers cannot secure popular support for a solution by demonizing those who will suffer losses. Instead, policymakers have to begin by acknowledging past and present sacrifices of those being asked, and be prepared and willing to honor future ones.

—Finally, sacrifice must be evenly distributed. Such an outcome requires an honest accounting of who has already sacrificed for whom.[19]

In the heat of the debate around public pensions, policymakers generally have not done a good job of structuring a fair process. They have rarely started a conversation by acknowledging that public employees sustain our society: they make sure that roads work, fires are put out, laws enforced, records kept, and children taught. In some instances, public employees may have already sacrificed to keep taxes low and other government activities funded. And rarely have public employees been assured that the distribution of sacrifice from pension reform will be shared equally among current and future taxpayers as well as the employees themselves. If changes are to be made successfully in the public arena—especially in states where underfunding is a serious problem—all parties

18. Allen (2004, pp. 28–29).
19. Laden (2011).

need to believe that they will be treated with respect and fairness. Rhode Island provides an example of how much progress can be made when the process is perceived as fair.

Fairness Works—The Case of Rhode Island

In November 2011, Rhode Island's General Assembly passed, by an overwhelming majority, legislation that moved the state-administered pension system toward a firm financial footing. The reforms suspended the COLA until the funded level reaches 80 percent, raised the retirement age, and replaced the existing defined benefit plan with a hybrid. In dollar terms, the legislation cut the plan's unfunded liability by $3 billion (from $7 billion to $4 billion) and reduced state expenses over the next twenty-five years by $4 billion.

The reform process was led by the state treasurer, Gina Raimondo, a 40-year-old progressive Democrat who had taken office in January. Although she was a political rookie, she had an impressive educational background (Harvard, Oxford, Yale Law School) and twelve years in venture capital. She had learned as a venture capitalist that the successful CEOs were the ones who confronted and solved problems in their organizations. She had the quantitative skills to understand pension math and she had no political baggage.

When Raimondo took office in January 2011, the Employees' Retirement System of Rhode Island (ERSRI), which covers state employees, teachers, and some municipal employees, had an unfunded liability of $6.8 billion (assuming a 7.5 percent discount rate) and a funded ratio of 48 percent. Rhode Island had the highest unfunded liability per capita of any state in the nation. The system had a good chance of running out of money between 2019 and 2023.

Instead of focusing on budget shortfalls, however, Raimondo immediately identified the problem as an issue of retirement security. She recognized that the state had a twofold responsibility: first, to provide its public employees with a level of replacement income that would ensure a dignified retirement; and second, to structure a retirement system that could be sustained by the state for generations to come. If the system failed, all citizens of Rhode Island would suffer.

As a first step, the Treasurer released "Truth in Numbers," a publication that set out the dimensions of the pension problem and the implications of doing nothing. The portion of each taxpayer dollar going to pensions had tripled to 10 percent by 2009 and was headed to 20 percent by 2018. Rhode Island is a relatively poor state with high unemployment and very high taxes, so increasing revenues was not a realistic alternative. If such a large share of the budget went to pensions, money would not be available for good schools, safe streets, strong infrastructure, and support services for vulnerable citizens. By delineating what would be lost, public employees understood what they were being asked to sacrifice for and regular citizens learned what was at stake.

The focus of discussion was on the math and the magnitude of the problem. Public officials did not engage in finger-pointing; no one blamed public employees. Current underfunding was attributed to a poorly designed system and the failure of appointed and elected officials for decades to follow the advice of the actuaries to set appropriate contribution levels for both the employer and the employee.

Delineating the problem set the stage for a campaign for reform. A broad coalition argued that the pension system needed to be changed so that Rhode Islanders could receive the services they needed to prosper. The treasurer established a twelve-person task force of experts, politicians, and labor representatives.[20] The task force held five meetings, open to the public, to define the problem and explore alternative solutions. The discussion began with setting the percentage of pre-retirement income needed to maintain living standards in retirement. The focus was always long term—not how to make next year's pension payment but how to establish a secure retirement system for public employees with predictable and affordable costs for taxpayers for decades to come. Throughout the summer and fall of 2011, the treasurer and lawmakers traveled the state, meeting with hundreds of groups to explain the problem and discuss possible solutions.

In the end, the legislation affected everyone. Retirees saw their COLA suspended until the funded level rises to 80 percent. Even when that happens, the amount of the COLA will depend on the plan actually earning the 7.5 percent return assumed in the cost estimates. Current employees also saw their defined benefit plan replaced by a hybrid defined benefit/defined contribution plan and their expected work life lengthened as the retirement age gradually rises to mirror that of Social Security. Future taxpayers also took a hit, underwriting a package to extend the amortization period for the current unfunded liability from nineteen years to twenty-five years.

The changes applied to current workers and retirees, not just future ones. Those involved in the process generally viewed this distribution of burden as fair. Nevertheless, it has been difficult for some current state and local workers to accept the outcome. In fact, the reforms are being challenged in court. In the meantime, the provisions have taken effect, so any reversal would require a large repayment from the state to public employees. The state is unlikely to have that kind of money. More important, as noted in the legal constraints discussion, changes can be justified when needed to save the financial health of the state. So the reforms are likely to stick.

The Rhode Island story shows that government can work when citizens engage and leaders are seen as looking for a fair solution. So fairness is not the

20. The author served as a member of this task force.

sole purview of philosophers but is central to the task of solving the nation's pension challenges.

Parity between the Public and Private Sectors

No matter what reforms are made in state and local plans, pressure to cut benefits will continue as long as public plans provide more generous benefits than the private sector plans. "Pension envy" was particularly evident in the wake of the 2008 financial crisis, when taxpayers with depleted 401(k) plans were being asked to pay higher taxes or adjust to fewer services to finance the defined benefit commitments made to public employees. Such a perspective suffers from two flaws, however.

The first problem is that a focus on pensions alone is not the appropriate basis for comparing public and private sector pay. Virtually every study shows that, on average, public sector workers earn lower wages than their private sector counterparts, taking account of education and experience. In other words, public sector employees pay for their higher benefits by accepting lower wages. If anything, taxpayers should be concerned that cutting pensions without raising wages will create an inadequate compensation package to attract the kind of people that they would like to teach their children.

The second issue is even more important. The private sector has an inadequate retirement system. It is too small and too risky. With the decline of defined benefit pensions, most private sector workers will end up with Social Security and the balances in their 401(k) plan. Social Security is the backbone of the retirement system for both private and, in most cases, public sector employees. But the program will provide less relative to pre-retirement income in the future for a number of reasons. First, as the age for collecting full benefits moves from 65 to 67, those retiring at age 65 will face a larger actuarial reduction. Second, Medicare premiums, which are deducted before the Social Security payment is made, will claim an increasing share of the benefit. And third, taxation of Social Security benefits under the personal income tax will apply to an increasing number of households as incomes rise above unindexed thresholds in the law. As a result of these three factors, Social Security benefits as a percentage of pre-retirement earnings will decline from 41 percent in 2002 to 29 percent in 2030.[21] At the same time, 401(k) plans will become the only other source of retirement income, and the balances in these plans are small. In 2010, according to the Federal Reserve's *Survey of Consumer Finances*, the median 401(k)/IRA holdings for a household approaching retirement (age 55–64) was $120,000. (IRA balances are included because the bulk of the assets in these accounts have been rolled

---

21. Author's updates based on Munnell (2003).

Figure 8-3. *New Tier of Retirement Saving*

Replacement rate (percent)

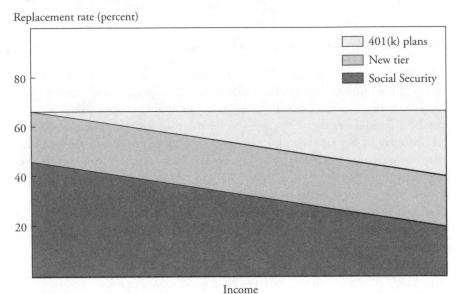

Source: Author's illustration.

over from 401(k) plans.) Assuming the purchase of an annuity, $120,000 will produce a monthly income of $575.[22] Not surprisingly, the National Retirement Risk Index maintained by the Center for Retirement Research at Boston College projects that 51 percent of today's working households will not be able to maintain their standard of living once they stop working.

The private sector needs an additional tier of retirement saving on top of Social Security and below 401(k) plans (see figure 8-3). This new tier should be universal, contributory, and not too risky; replace about 20 percent of pre-retirement income; and provide benefits at retirement in the form of an annuity. It would have to be a government initiative because it is unlikely to happen on its own, but it should be managed by the private sector.

A recent proposal by the National Conference on Public Employee Retirement Systems builds on the public sector infrastructure to provide a plan for private sector workers that meets many of the goals of a new tier.[23] The plan—a

22. This figure, from ImmediteAnnuities.com, assumes a joint-and-survivor annuity for a male age 64 and a female age 62.

23. National Conference on Public Employee Retirement Systems (NCPERS) (2011). NCPERS is a public plan trade association comprising a network of public trustees, administrators,

cash balance defined benefit plan—is a hybrid between the conventional defined benefit plan in which the employer bears all the risk and the 401(k) in which all the risk rests with the employee. Participants would be guaranteed their contributions plus earnings credited at the yield on the ten-year Treasury bill rate, but to the extent that investment returns exceed this rate, they could share in some of the upside. Importantly, the plan takes advantage of the public sector's economies of scale to deliver investment results in a cost-effective manner and of its ability to pool mortality risk over a large number of participants to provide annuities at retirement.

The most interesting aspect of the proposal is that public employees recognize that their future security hinges on their counterparts in the private sector having access to a retirement system that ensures adequate retirement income. And it would be a positive development if the public sector infrastructure could serve as the basis for helping private sector workers get an adequate retirement system. The alternative of trying to cut public employees' retirement plans down to the private sector level would just ensure that most Americans face a bleak old age.

Conclusion

The story of state and local pensions is big and complicated. It cannot be reduced to a single mantra such as discounting liabilities by the riskless rate or limiting union power. It's a story of states with different histories, different resources, and different political cultures. Most states and localities have provided reasonable benefits and put aside money to pre-fund their commitments, but a few have simply behaved irresponsibly. Whatever differences existed before 2008 were magnified by the financial crisis and the ensuing recession.

Even the good states, however, face three major challenges. First, many plans have too much of their portfolio invested in risky assets. Such an allocation undermines funding given the asymmetry in the treatment of deficits and surpluses that results from abnormally high or low returns. Year after year of higher-than-assumed returns inevitably leads to reduced contributions or benefit expansions, so surpluses are not there when the lean years arrive. Reducing equity holdings will mean lower returns and the need to levy higher taxes or pay lower benefits over the long term, but it will make public sector plans more secure and equitable.

The second major challenge is to establish compensation packages that will attract the best candidates for public sector jobs. This goal has been jeopardized by large cuts in pension benefits for new employees. Given that compensation

---

public officials, and investment professionals. Initiating such a plan would require an amendment to ERISA permitting each state to set up a "Secure Choice Pension," which as a public-private enterprise would serve those who currently do not have a pension.

in the public and private sectors was roughly comparable before the cuts, it must now be lower for new employees. Many of the changes in the pension benefits—such as extending the age for full benefits—reflect good policy, but the cuts need to be offset by higher wages to avoid eroding the public sector's ability to compete in the labor market.

The third major challenge is to alleviate legal constraints so that public officials can change *future* benefits for current employees. Change is feasible given that only a few states have established protections in their state constitutions; in most states, the protections are in statutes or derived from case law. The goal should be for public sector workers to have the same protections that ERISA provides those in the private sector—namely, benefits earned to date cannot be taken away, but sponsors can amend the plan going forward to adjust to changing circumstances. An ERISA standard could be achieved under the contract theory, which protects most public sector benefits, by establishing that the contract is created when the employee performs the service. Allowing officials to change future benefits for current employees would make it much easier for public plans to adapt to changing economic tides.

In addition to the three challenges facing all plans, some states have plans that are very expensive and only marginally funded. Without changes, these plans could well require 15 percent of state and local revenues, driving out expenditures for education, health, and infrastructure. The question is how to proceed. Some have sought to demonize public employees and shame them into concessions. Such an approach might seem expedient, but is unlikely to be effective in the long run. A successful strategy must be fair. The need for benefit cuts for public employees or retirees must be broadly understood; employees need to be publicly honored and acknowledged; and the cuts need to be distributed evenly among public employees and between employees and taxpayers. Rhode Island is an example where a fair process brought about dramatic reform, which, if upheld in court, should move the state toward a permanent solution.

In the end, even if states and localities solve all the financing issues around their pension systems, public plans will remain a source of controversy. They simply provide more retirement income than do 401(k)s in the private sector. And critics often forget that public employees pay for these more generous benefits with substantial contributions and the acceptance of lower wages. But the goal should not be to bring public sector workers down to the inadequate standards of the private sector; instead, it should be to enhance the retirement system for private sector workers. If public sector pension infrastructure can be used to achieve that goal, so much the better.

References

Agency for Healthcare Research and Quality. Various years. *Medical Expenditure Panel Survey*. Washington: U.S. Department of Health and Human Services.

Agnew, Julie, Pierluigi Balduzzi, and Annika Sundén. 2003. "Portfolio Choice and Trading in a Large (401)k Plan." *American Economic Review* 93, no. 1: 193–215.

Allegretto, Sylvia A., and Jeffrey Keefe. 2010. "The Truth about Public Employees in California: They Are Neither Overpaid Nor Overcompensated." Policy Brief. Center on Wage and Employment Dynamics at the University of California, Berkeley.

Allen, Danielle S. 2004. *Talking to Strangers: Anxieties of Citizenship since Brown v. Board of Education*. University of Chicago Press.

Almeida, Beth, and William B. Fornia. 2008. "A Better Bang for the Buck: The Economic Efficiencies of Defined Benefit Pension Plans." Washington: National Institute of Retirement Security.

American Federation of State, County and Municipal Employees (AFSCME). 2007. "State Pension Threat Levels." Washington.

Amir, Eli, Yanling Guan, and Dennis Oswald. 2010. "The Effect of Pension Accounting on Corporate Pension Asset Allocation." *Review of Accounting Studies* 15, no. 2: 345–66.

Arizona State Retirement System. 2011. *2011 Comprehensive Annual Financial Report*. Phoenix and Tucson.

Arrow, Kenneth J., and Robert C. Lind. 1970. "Uncertainty and the Evaluation of Public Investment Decisions." *American Economic Review* 60, no. 3: 364–78.

Ashenfelter, Orley. 1971. "The Effect of Unionization on Wages in the Public Sector: The Case of Fire Fighters." *Industrial and Labor Relations Review* 24, no. 2: 191–202.

Bader, Lawrence N., and Jeremy Gold. 2003. "Reinventing Pension Actuarial Science." *Pension Forum* 15, no. 1: 1–13.

————. 2007. "The Case against Stock in Public Pension Funds." *Financial Analysts Journal* 63, no. 1: 55–62.

Banks, James, Richard Blundell, and Sarah Tanner. 1998. "Is There a Retirement-Savings Puzzle?" *American Economic Review* 88, no. 4: 769–88.

Barclays Capital. Various years. *Barclays U.S. Treasury 10-year Term Index.* New York.

Barclays Global Investors. 2004. "The Retirement Benefits Crisis: A Survival Guide." *Barclays Global Investors Investment Insights* 7, no. 5: 1–33.

Barsky, Robert B., F. Thomas Juster, Miles S. Kimball, and Matthew D. Shapiro. 1997. "Preference Parameters and Behavioral Heterogeneity: An Experimental Approach in the Health and Retirement Study." *Quarterly Journal of Economics* 112, no. 2: 537–79.

Bellante, Don, and Albert N. Link. 1981. "Are Public Sector Workers More Risk Averse Than Private Sector Workers?" *Industrial and Labor Relations Review* 34, no. 3: 408–12.

Belman, Dale, and John S. Heywood. 1989a. "Establishment Size, Public Administration and Government Wage Differentials." *Economics Letters* 29, no. 1: 95–98.

————. 1989b. "Government Wage Differentials: A Sample Selection Approach." *Applied Economics* 21, no. 4: 427–39.

————. 1997. "Changes in the Relative Provision of Public-Sector Pensions." *Public Finance Review* 25, no. 4: 426–41.

————. 2004. "Public-Sector Wage Comparability: The Role of Earnings Dispersion." *Public Finance Review* 32, no. 6: 567–87.

Belman, Dale, John S. Heywood, and John Lund. 1997. "Public Sector Earnings and the Extent of Unionization." *Industrial and Labor Relations Review* 50, no. 4: 610–28.

Benartzi, Shlomo, and Richard H. Thaler. 2001. "Naive Diversification Strategies in Defined Contribution Saving Plans." *American Economic Review* 91, no. 1: 79–98.

————. 2002. "How Much Is Investor Autonomy Worth?" *Journal of Finance* 57, no. 4: 1596–1616.

Bender, Keith A., and John S. Heywood. 2010. "Out of Balance? Comparing Private and Public Sector Compensation Over 20 Years." Washington: Center for State and Local Government Excellence and National Institute on Retirement Security.

Benner, Katie. 2009. "The Public Pension Bomb." *CNN Money* (May 12).

Benninga, Simon. 2008. *Financial Modeling.* MIT Press.

Bernheim, B. Douglas, Jonathan Skinner, and Steven Weinberg. 2001. "What Accounts for the Variation in Retirement Wealth among U.S. Households?" *American Economic Review* 91, no. 4: 832–57.

Beshears, John, James J. Choi, David Laibson, and Brigitte C. Madrian. 2011. "Behavioral Economic Perspectives on Public Sector Pension Plans." Working Paper 16728. Cambridge, Mass: National Bureau of Economic Research.

Biggs, Andrew G. 2010. "An Options Pricing Method for Calculating the Market Price of Public Sector Pension Liabilities." Working Paper 164. Washington: American Enterprise Institute.

————. 2011a. "Do Public Employees Actually Have More Job Security?" Blog post in *The Enterprise Blog* (http://blog.american.com) (September 22). Washington: American Enterprise Institute.

————. 2011b. "The Value of Public Sector Job Security." Blog post in *The Enterprise Blog* (http://blog.american.com) (July 28) Washington: American Enterprise Institute.

————. 2011c. "Lining Up for Government Jobs." Blog post in *The Enterprise Blog* (http://blog.american.com) (February 28). Washington: American Enterprise Institute.

Black, Fischer. 1989. "Should You Use Stocks to Hedge Your Pension Liability?" *Financial Analysts Journal* 45, no. 1: 10–12.

Bleakney, Thomas P. 1972. *Retirement Systems for Public Employees.* University of Pennsylvania Press.

Blinder, Alan. 1973. "Wage Discrimination: Reduced Form and Structural Estimates." *Journal of Human Resources* 8, no. 4: 436–55.

Block, Peter, and Robin Prunty. 2008. "Time May Be Ripe for a POB Revival." *Standard & Poor's Ratings Direct* (January 23).

Bloomberg L. P. 2011. "Municipal Bonds." Bloombergonline.com [accessed October 20]. New York.

Bloomberg Online Service. Various years. Proprietary bond data. New York.

Bodie, Zvi, Robert Merton, and David Cheeton. 2008. *Financial Economics.* Upper Saddle River, N.J.: Prentice Hall.

Bohn, Henning. 1997. "Social Security Reform and Financial Markets." In *Social Security Reform: Links to Savings, Investment, and Growth,* edited by Steven Sass and Robert Triest. Boston, Mass.: Federal Reserve Bank of Boston.

————. 2011. "Should Public Retirement Plans Be Fully Funded?" *Journal of Pension Economics and Finance* 10, no. 2: 195–219.

Bohn, Henning, and Robert P. Inman. 1996. "Balanced-Budget Rules and Public Deficits: Evidence from the U.S. States." *Carnegie-Rochester Conference Series on Public Policy* 45, no. 1: 13–76.

Borenstein, Daniel. 2009. "'Spiking' of Public Pensions Is Costing Taxpayers." *Contra Costa Times* (August 11).

Borjas, George J. 2002. "The Wage Structure and Sorting of Workers into the Public Sector." Working Paper 9313. Cambridge, Mass.: National Bureau of Economic Research.

Braconi, Frank. 2011. "Municipal Employee Compensation in New York City." New York: Office of New York City Comptroller John. C. Liu.

Brown, Jeffrey R., and David Wilcox. 2009. "Discounting State and Local Pension Liabilities." *American Economic Review Papers and Proceedings* 99, no. 2: 538–42.

Brown, Jeffrey R., Robert Clark, and Joshua Rauh. 2011. "The Economics of State and Local Pensions." *Journal of Pension Economics and Finance* 10, no. 2: 161–72.

Bulow, Jeremy I. 1982. "What Are Corporate Pension Liabilities?" *Quarterly Journal of Economics* 97, no. 3: 435–52.

Burnham, James B. 2003. "Risky Business? Evaluating the Use of Pension Obligation Bonds." *Government Finance Review* 19, no. 3: 12–17.

Business Wire. 1994. "Massachusetts Man Pleads Guilty to Federal Charges." (December 13).

Calabrese, Thad. 2009. "Public Pensions, Public Budgets, and the Use of Pension Obligation Bonds." Presented at the 2009 Public Pension Fund Symposium, Society of Actuaries. Chicago, Ill.

California Public Employees' Retirement System. 2005. "The Myths and Realities of Defined Benefit and Defined Contribution Plans." Research Brief. Sacramento, Calif.
————. 2009. "A History of CALPERS Benefits." *California Retirement Dialogue 2010.* Sacramento, Calif.

California State Teachers' Retirement System. 2008. "Defined Benefit Program–2008 Actuarial Valuation." West Sacramento, Calif.

Campbell, John Y., and Luis M. Viceira. 2001. "Who Should Buy Long-Term Bonds?" *American Economic Review* 91, no. 1: 99–127.

Carmichael, Jeffrey, and Robert Palacios. 2003. "A Framework for Public Pension Fund Management." Washington: World Bank.

Carroll, Thomas J., and Greg Niehaus. 1998. "Pension Plan Funding and Corporate Debt Ratings." *Journal of Risk and Insurance* 65, no. 3: 427–43.

Center for Retirement Research at Boston College. 2008a. "Why Does Funding Status Vary among State and Local Plans?" Issue in Brief SLP-6. Chestnut Hill, Mass.: Published jointly with the Center for State and Local Government Excellence.
————. 2008b. "Why Have Some States Introduced Defined Contribution Plans?" Issue in Brief SLP-3. Chestnut Hill, Mass.: Published jointly with the Center for State and Local Government Excellence.
————. 2010a. "Valuing Liabilities in State and Local Plans." Issue in Brief SLP-11. Chestnut Hill, Mass.: Published jointly with the Center for State and Local Government Excellence.
————. 2010b. "The Impact of Public Pensions on State and Local Budgets." Issue in Brief SLP-13. Chestnut Hill, Mass.: Published jointly with the Center for State and Local Government Excellence.
————. 2010c. "Pension Obligation Bonds: Financial Crisis Exposes Risks." Issue in Brief SLP-9. Chestnut Hill, Mass.: Published jointly with the Center for State and Local Government Excellence.
————. 2010d. "Problems with State-Local Final Pay Plans and Options for Reform." Issue in Brief SLP-12. Chestnut Hill, Mass.
————. 2011a. "Can State and Local Pensions Muddle Through?" Issue in Brief SLP-15. Chestnut Hill, Mass.
————. 2011b. "The Funding of State and Local Pensions in 2010." Issue in Brief SLP-17. Chestnut Hill, Mass. Published jointly with the Center for State and Local Government Excellence.
————. 2011c. "How Would GASB Proposals Affect State and Local Pension Reporting?" Issue in Brief SLP-23. Chestnut Hill, Mass.
————. 2011d. "An Update on Locally-Administered Pension Plans." Issue in Brief SLP-18. Chestnut Hill, Mass.
————. 2011e. "The Impact of Pensions on State Borrowing Costs." Issue in Brief SLP-14. Chestnut Hill, Mass.: Published jointly with the Center for State and Local Government Excellence.
————. 2011f. "How Prepared Are State and Local Workers for Retirement?" Working Paper 2011-15. Chestnut Hill, Mass.

————. 2011g. "Unions and Public Pension Benefits." Issue in Brief SLP-19. Chestnut Hill, Mass.: Published jointly with the Center for State and Local Government Excellence.

————. 2011h. "Comparing Compensation: State-Local versus Private Sector Workers." Issue in Brief SLP-20. Chestnut Hill, Mass.: Published jointly with the Center for State and Local Government Excellence.

————. 2011i. "Comparing Wealth in Retirement: State-Local versus Private Sector Workers." Issue in Brief SLP-21. Chestnut Hill, Mass.

————. 2012a. "The Funding of State and Local Pensions: 2011–2015." Issue in Brief SLP-24. Chestnut Hill, Mass.: Published jointly with the Center for State and Local Government Excellence.

————. 2012b. "Legal Constraints on Pension Changes." Issue in Brief. Chestnut Hill, Mass.

Center for State and Local Government Excellence. 2011. *State and Local Government Workforce: 2011 Realities*. Washington.

Chaney, Barbara A., Paul A. Copley, and Mary S. Stone. 2002. "The Effect of Fiscal Stress and Balanced Budget Requirements on the Funding and Measurement of State Pension Obligations." *Journal of Accounting and Public Policy* 21, no. 4–5: 287–313.

Choi, James J., David Laibson, Brigitte C. Madrian, and Andrew Metrick. 2004. "For Better or for Worse: Default Effects and 401(k) Savings Behavior." In *Perspectives on the Economics of Aging*, edited by David A. Wise. University of Chicago Press.

Clark, Robert L., and Melinda Morrill. 2011a. "Health Insurance for Active and Retired State Employees: California, North Carolina and Ohio." Washington: Center for State and Local Government Excellence.

————. 2011b. *Retiree Health Plans in the Public Sector: Is There a Funding Crisis?* Northampton, Mass.: Edward Elgar.

Cloud, Whitney. 2011. "State Pension Deficits, the Recession, and a Modern View of the Contracts Clause." Comment. *Yale Law Journal* 120, no. 8: 2199–2212.

Coggburn, Jerrell D. 2010. "How Local Governments Are Addressing Retiree Health Care Funding." Washington: Center for State and Local Government Excellence.

Congressional Budget Office. 2010. *Supplemental Data for the Congressional Budget Office's Long-Term Budget Outlook*. Washington.

Coronado, Julia, Olivia S. Mitchell, Steven A. Sharpe, and S. Blake Nesbitt. 2008. "Footnotes Aren't Enough: The Impact of Pension Accounting on Stock Values." Working Paper 13726. Cambridge, Mass.: National Bureau of Economic Research.

Costrell, Robert M., and Michael Podgursky. 2009. "Peaks, Cliffs, and Valleys: The Peculiar Incentives in Teacher Retirement Systems and their Consequences for School Staffing." *Education Finance and Policy* 4, no. 2: 175–211.

Daley, Lane Allen. 1984. "The Valuation of Reported Pension Measures for Firms Sponsoring Defined Benefit Plans." *Accounting Review* 59, no. 2: 177–98.

Davis, E. Philip, Sybille Grob, and Leo de Haan. 2007. "Pension Fund Finance and Sponsoring Companies: Empirical Evidence on Theoretical Hypotheses." Working Paper 158. Amsterdam, Netherlands: Nederlandsche Bank.

Davis, Roger L. 2006. "Pension Obligation Bonds and Other Post-Employment Benefits." New York: Orrick, Herrington & Sutcliffe LLP.

Davis v. Michigan Dept. of Treasury, 489 U.S. 803 (1989).

De Nederlandsche Bank. 2011. *Supervisory Data on Pension Funds.* Amsterdam, Netherlands.

Dhaliwal, Dan S. 1986. "Measurement of Financial Leverage in the Presence of Unfunded Pension Obligations." *Accounting Review* 61, no. 4: 651–61.

Diamond, Peter A. 1997. "Macroeconomic Aspects of Social Security Reform." *Brookings Papers on Economic Activity* no. 2: 1–87.

Employees Retirement System of Texas (Texas ERS). 2007–10. *Actuarial Valuation.* Austin, Tex.

Engen, Eric M., William G. Gale, and Cori E. Uccello. 1999. "The Adequacy of Retirement Saving." *Brookings Papers on Economic Activity,* no. 2: 65–187.

Farber, Henry S. 2005. "Union Membership in the United States: The Divergence between the Public and the Private Sectors." Working Paper 503. Industrial Relations Section, Princeton University.

Federal Reserve Bank of St. Louis. 2005–10. *Treasury Constant Maturity.* Saint Louis, Mo.

Fehr, Stephen C. 2010. "Election Adds Pressure to Change Public Pensions." *Stateline* (November 4).

Financial Accounting Standards Board. 1980. "Accounting and Reporting by Defined Benefit Pension Plans." Statement 35. Norwalk, Conn.

———. 1985. "Employers' Accounting for Pensions." Statement 87. Norwalk, Conn.

———. 2006. "Employers' Accounting for Defined Benefit Pension and Other Postretirement Plans—An Amendment of FASB Statements 87, 88, 106 and 132(R)." Statement 158. Norwalk, Conn.

Florida Retirement System. 2009. "Actuarial Valuation as of July 1, 2009." Tallahassee, Fla.

Fogel, Walter, and David Lewin. 1974. "Wage Determination in the Public Sector." *Industrial and Labor Relations Review* 27, no. 3: 410–31.

Fore, Douglas. 2001. "Going Private in the Public Sector." In *Pensions in the Public Sector,* edited by Olivia S. Mitchell and Edwin C. Hustead. University of Pennsylvania Press.

Frazier, Trish. 2010. "Pension Issues Heat Up." Oklahoma City, Okla.: Oklahoma Public Employees Association.

Freeman, Richard B. 1986. "Unionism Comes to the Public Sector." Working Paper 1452. Cambridge, Mass.: National Bureau of Economic Research.

———. 1988. "Contraction and Expansion: The Divergence of Private Sector and Public Sector Unionism in the United States." *Journal of Economic Perspectives* 2, no. 2: 63–88.

Freeman, Richard B., and James L. Medoff. 1984. "What Do Unions Do?" *Industrial and Labor Relations Review* 38, no. 2: 244–63.

Freeman, Richard B., and Robert G. Valletta. 1988. "The Effect of Public Sector Labor Laws on Labor Market Institutions and Outcomes." In *When Public Sector Workers Unionize,* edited by Richard Freeman and Casey Ischniowski. University of Chicago Press.

Friedberg, Leora. 2011. "Labor Market Aspects of State and Local Retirement Plans: A Review of Evidence and a Blueprint for Future Research." *Journal of Pension Economics and Finance* 10, no. 2: 337–60.

Gale, William G., J. Mark Iwry, and Peter R. Orszag. 2005. "The Automatic 401(k): A Simple Way to Strengthen Retirement Saving." Working Paper 2005-1. Washington: Brookings Institution, Retirement Security Project.

GFOA Advisory. March 2005. "Evaluating the Use of Pension Obligation Bonds (1997 and 2005) (DEBT & CORBA)." Washington: Government Finance Officers Association.

Gittleman, Maury, and Brooks Pierce. 2011. "Compensation for State and Local Government Workers." *Journal of Economic Perspectives* 26, no. 1: 217–42.

Gold, Jeremy. 2000. "Assumed Rates of Discount for Valuations of Publicly Sponsored Defined Benefit Plans." Working Paper 2001-6. Philadelphia, Pa.: Pension Research Council at the University of Pennsylvania.

———. 2002. "Risk Transfer in Public Pension Plans." Working Paper 2002-18. Philadelphia, Pa.: Pension Research Council.

———. 2005. "Retirement Benefits, Economics and Accounting: Moral Hazard and Frail Benefit Designs. *North American Actuarial Journal* 9, no. 1: 88–111.

———. 2009. "Response to Invitation to Comment: Pension Accounting and Financial Reporting." Issued to Governmental Accounting Standards Board (GASB). Norwalk, Conn.: GASB.

Gold, Jeremy, and Gordon Latter. 2008. "The Case for Marking Public Plan Liabilities to Market." In *The Future of Public Employee Retirement Systems*, edited by Gary Anderson and Olivia S. Mitchell. Oxford University Press.

Golembiewski, Pat, Gary Bornholdt, and Timothy Jones. 1999. "Allocation and Accounting Regulations for Arbitrage Bonds." Continuing Professional Education Exempt Organizations Technical Instruction Program for FY 1999 Training 4277-050: 135–52.

Gollier, Christian. 2001. *The Economics of Risk and Time.* MIT Press.

———. 2008. "Intergenerational Risk-Sharing and Risk-Taking of a Pension Fund." *Journal of Public Economics* 92, no. 5–6: 1463–85.

Gottlieb, Jenna. 2005. "Defined Contribution: Alaska Puts New Hires in 401(a) Plan; Looking to Succeed Where California So Far Has Not." *Pensions & Investments* (May 30).

Governmental Accounting Standards Board. 1986. "Disclosure of Pension Information by Public Employee Retirement Systems and State and Local Governmental Employers." Statement 5. Norwalk, Conn.

———. 1994a. "Financial Reporting for Defined Benefit Pension Plans and Note Disclosures for Defined Contribution Plans." Statement 25. Norwalk, Conn.

———. 1994b. "Accounting for Pensions by State and Local Governmental Employers." Statement 27. Norwalk, Conn.

———. 2011a. "Proposed Statement of the Governmental Accounting Standards Board: Financial Reporting for Pension Plans, an Amendment of GASB Statement 25." Norwalk, Conn.

————. 2011b. "Proposed Statement of the Governmental Accounting Standards Board: Accounting and Financial Reporting for Pensions, an Amendment of GASB Statement 27." Norwalk, Conn.

GovMonitor. 2010. "Michigan to Reform State Employee and Public School Retirement Systems" (March 12).

Graham, Avy D. 1988. "How Has Vesting Changed since Passage of Employee Retirement Income Security Act?" *Monthly Labor Review* 111, no. 8: 20–25.

Greenhut, Steven. 2010. "Vallejo's Painful Lessons in Municipal Bankruptcy." *Wall Street Journal* (March 27).

Gustman, Alan L., and Thomas L. Steinmeier. 1999. "Effects of Pensions on Saving: Analysis with Data from the *Health and Retirement Study*." Working Paper 6681. Cambridge, Mass.: National Bureau of Economic Research.

Gyourko, Joseph, and Joseph Tracy. 1988. "An Analysis of Public- and Private-Sector Wages Allowing for Endogenous Choices of Both Government and Union Status." *Journal of Labor Economics* 6, no. 2: 229–53.

Hakim, Danny. 2012. "Deficits Push N.Y. Cities and Counties to Desperation." *New York Times* (March 10).

Hirsch, Barry T., and David A. Macpherson. 1983–2010. *Union Membership and Coverage Database* (www.unionstats.com).

Hitchcock, David G., and Robin Prunty. 2009. "No Immediate Pension Hardship for State and Local Governments, but Plenty of Long-Term Worries." *Standard & Poor's Ratings Direct* (June 8).

Hryshko, Dmytro, Maria Jose Luengo-Prado, and Bent E. Sorensen. 2011. "Childhood Determinants of Risk Aversion: The Long Shadow of Compulsory Education." *Quantitative Economics* 2, no. 1: 37–72.

Hurd, Michael, and Susann Rohwedder. 2003. "The Retirement Consumption Puzzle: Anticipated and Actual Declines in Spending at Retirement." Working Paper 9586. Cambridge, Mass.: National Bureau of Economic Research.

Hustead, Edwin. 1998. "Qualified Pension Plans and the Regulatory Environment." *Benefits Quarterly* 14, no. 4: 29–35.

Ibbotson Associates. 2011. *Ibbotson SBBI Classic Yearbook.* Chicago, Ill.: Morningstar, Inc.

Illinois Municipal Retirement Fund. 1999. "The Defined Benefit versus Defined Contribution Debate: The $250 Million Question." Oak Brook, Ill.

————. 2009. "Annual Actuarial Valuation Report: December 31, 2009." Oak Brook, Ill.

Jin, Li, Robert Merton, and Zvi Bodie. 2004. "Do a Firm's Equity Returns Reflect the Risk of Its Pension Plans?" Working Paper 10650. Cambridge, Mass.: National Bureau of Economic Research.

Kansas PERS (Kansas Public Employees Retirement System). 2008–10. *Valuation Report.* Topeka, Kan.

Katz, Lawrence F., and Alan B. Krueger. 1991. "Changes in the Structure of Wages in the Public and Private Sectors." Working Paper 3667. Cambridge, Mass.: National Bureau of Economic Research.

Keefe, Jeffrey. 2010. "Debunking the Myth of the Overcompensated Public Employee: The Evidence." Briefing Paper. Washington: Economic Policy Institute.

———. 2011. "Are Wisconsin Public Employees Over-Compensated?" Washington: Economic Policy Institute.

Keegan, Frank. 2012. "Commentary: Actuaries Ponder 'Pension Funding to Avoid Ruin.'" Blog post in *State Budget Solutions* (www.statebudgetsolutions.org/) (March 26).

Klas, Mary Ellen. 2011. "Scott Tells Legislators Pension Plan 'Doesn't Go Far Enough.'" *Tampa Bay Times* (April 12).

Kohlmeier, Louis M. 1976. *Conflicts of Interest: State and Local Pension Fund Management.* New York: Twentieth Century Fund.

Kortleve, Niels, and Eduard H. M. Ponds. 2010. "How to Close the Funding Gap in Dutch Pension Plans? Impact on Generations." Issue in Brief 10-7. Chestnut Hill, Mass.: Center for Retirement Research at Boston College.

Krueger, Alan B. 1988. "Are Public Sector Workers Paid More Than Their Alternative Wage? Evidence from Longitudinal Data and Job Queues." In *When Public Sector Workers Unionize,* edited by Richard B. Freeman and Casey Ichniowski. University of Chicago Press.

Kruse, Douglas L. 1995. "Pension Substitution in the 1980s: Why the Shift toward Defined Contribution?" *Industrial Relations* 34, no. 2: 218–41.

Kutter, Robert, and Timothy Blake. 2004. "Moody's State Rating Methodology." New York: Moody's Investors Service.

Lachance, Marie-Eve, and Olivia S. Mitchell. 2002. "Guaranteeing Defined Contribution Pensions: The Option to Buy Back a Defined Benefit Promise." Working Paper 8731. Cambridge, Mass.: National Bureau of Economic Research.

Laden, Anthony. 2011. Presentation at the IGPA State Summit 2011: A Bold New Dialogue on Public Pensions. Chicago, Ill., October 3–4.

Landsman, Wayne. 1986. "An Empirical Investigation of Pension Fund Property Rights." *Accounting Review* 61, no. 4: 662–91.

Lav, Iris J., and Elizabeth McNichol. 2011. "Misunderstandings Regarding State Debt, Pensions, and Retiree Health Costs Create Unnecessary Alarm: Misconceptions Also Divert Attention from Needed Structural Reforms." Washington: Center on Budget and Policy Priorities.

Law Enforcement and Custodial Officer Supplemental Retirement Fund of the Employees Retirement System of Texas (Texas LECOS). 2007–10. *Actuarial Valuation.* Austin, Tex.

Lazear, Edward P. 1985. "Incentive Effects of Pensions." In *Pensions, Labor, and Individual Choice,* edited by David A. Wise. University of Chicago Press.

Liang, Nellie, and Scott Weisbenner. 2002. "Investor Behavior and the Purchase of Company Stock in 401(k) Plans—The Importance of Plan Design." Working Paper 9131. Cambridge Mass.: National Bureau of Economic Research.

Liljenquist, Daniel R. 2010. "New Public Employees' Tier II Contributory Retirement Act." S.B. 63. Salt Lake City: Utah State Legislature.

Little Hoover Commission. 2011. *Public Pensions for Retirement Security.* Sacramento, Calif.

Lucas, Deborah, and Stephen P. Zeldes. 2009. "How Should Public Pension Plans Invest?" *American Economic Review* 99, no. 2: 527–32.

Luenberger, David G. 1997. *Investment Science.* Oxford University Press.

Macchia, David. 2007. "Interview with Dallas Salisbury: President & CEO of EBRI Offers Fascinating Historical Perspective on Today's Retirement Security Challenges; Reveals Preference for Mandatory, National Retirement Savings Program in Addition to Social Security." Blog post in *David Macchia Blog* (http://david macchiablog.com/).

Madrian, Brigitte C., and Dennis F. Shea. 2001. "The Power of Suggestion: Inertia in 401(k) Participation and Savings Behavior." *Quarterly Journal of Economics* 116, no. 4: 1149–87.

Maher, John J. 1987. "Pension Obligations and the Bond Credit Market: An Empirical Analysis of Accounting Numbers." *Accounting Review* 62, no. 4: 785–98.

Mas-Colell, Andreu, Michael D. Whinston, and Jerry Green. 1995. *Microeconomic Theory.* Oxford University Press.

Massachusetts Retirement Law Commission. 1976. *Report of the Funding Advisory Committee and the Retirement Law Commission to the Governor and General Court of Massachusetts.* Boston, Mass.

Mattoon, Richard H. 2006. "State and Local Government Public Pension Forum: A Conference Summary." Chicago Fed Letter 226a. Chicago, Ill.: Federal Reserve Bank of Chicago.

McArdle, Frank, Amy Atchison, Dale Yamamoto, Michelle Kitchman Strollo, and Tricia Neuman. 2006. "Retiree Health Benefits Examined: Findings from the Kaiser/Hewitt 2006 Survey on Retiree Health Benefits." Washington: Kaiser Family Foundation and Hewitt.

McGill, Dan M. 1978. Statement by Dan M. McGill. Hearings on Public Employee Retirement Income Security Act of 1978, H.R. 14138, before the Subcommittee on Labor Standards of the House Committee on Education and Labor, 95th Congress, 2nd session. Washington: U.S. Government Printing Office.

McGill, Dan M., Kyle N. Brown, John J. Haley, and Sylvester J. Schieber. 2005. *Fundamentals of Private Pensions,* 8th ed. Oxford University Press.

McGill, Dan M., Kyle N. Brown, John J. Haley, Sylvester J. Schieber, and Mark Warshawsky. 2010. *Fundamentals of Private Pensions,* 9th ed. Oxford University Press.

McNichol, Elizabeth, Phil Oliff, and Nicholas Johnson. 2012. "States Continue to Feel Recession's Impact." Washington: Center on Budget and Policy Priorities.

Michigan Association of School Boards. 2010. "Retirement Reform: An Analysis of Public Act 75 of 2010—MPSERS Reform." Lansing, Mich.

Michigan House Fiscal Agency. 2009. "Converting MPSERS from a Defined Benefit (DB) to a Defined Contribution (DC) System." Memorandum. Lansing, Mich.

———. 2010. "A Summary of Senate Bill 1227 as Enacted." Lansing, Mich.

Mitchell, Olivia S., and Gary W. Anderson, eds. 2009. *The Future of Public Employee Retirement Systems.* Oxford University Press.

Mitchell, Olivia S., and Edwin C. Hustead, eds. 2001. *Pensions in the Public Sector.* University of Pennsylvania Press.

Mitchell, Olivia S., and Ping-Lung Hsin. 1997. "Public Sector Pension Governance and Performance." In *The Economics of Pensions: Principles, Policies and International Experience,* edited by Salvador Valdes Prieto. Cambridge University Press.

Mitchell, Olivia S., James M. Poterba, Mark J. Warshawsky, and Jeffrey R. Brown. 1999. "New Evidence on the Money's Worth of Individual Annuities." *American Economic Review* 89, no. 5: 1299–1318.

Monahan, Amy B. 2010. "Public Pension Plan Reform: The Legal Framework." *Education Finance and Policy* 5, no. 4: 617–46.

Moody's Investors Service. Various years. "Moody's Proprietary Data." New York.

Moore, William J., and John Raisian. 1991. "Government Wage Differentials Revisited." *Journal of Labor Research* 12, no. 1: 13–33.

Mumford, Terry A. M., and Mary Leto Pareja. 1997. "The Employer's (In)Ability to Reduce Benefits in the Public Sector." ALI-ABA Course Study. Washington and Philadelphia, Penn.: American Law Institute and American Bar Association.

Munnell, Alicia H. 2003. "The Declining Role of Social Security." Just the Facts on Retirement Issues 6. Chestnut Hill, Mass.: Center for Retirement Research at Boston College.

———. 2012. "401(k) Plans in 2010: An Update from the SCF." Issue in Brief 12-13. Chestnut Hill, Mass.: Center for Retirement Research at Boston College.

Munnell, Alicia H., Jean-Pierre Aubry, Josh Hurwitz, and Laura Quinby. 2012. "How Would GASB Proposals Affect State and Local Pension Reporting?" *Journal of Government Financial Management* 61, no. 2: 18–22.

Munnell, Alicia H., Jean-Pierre Aubry, and Laura Quinby. 2011. "Public Pension Funding in Practice." *Journal of Pension Economics and Finance* 10, no. 2: 247–68.

Munnell, Alicia H., Francesca Golub-Sass, and Dan Muldoon. 2009. "An Update on 401(k) Plans: Insights from the 2007 SCF." Issue in Brief 9-5. Chestnut Hill, Mass.: Center for Retirement Research at Boston College.

Munnell, Alicia H., Francesca Golub-Sass, and Anthony Webb. 2011. "How Much to Save for a Secure Retirement." Issue in Brief 11-13. Chestnut Hill, Mass.: Center for Retirement Research at Boston College.

Munnell, Alicia H., and Mauricio Soto. 2007. "Why Are Companies Freezing Their Pensions?" Working Paper 2007-22. Chestnut Hill, Mass.: Center for Retirement Research at Boston College.

Munnell, Alicia H., Mauricio Soto, Jerilyn Libby, and John Prinzivalli. 2006. "Comparing Investment Returns: Defined Benefit vs. 401(k)." Issue in Brief 52. Chestnut Hill, Mass.: Center for Retirement Research at Boston College.

National Association of State Budget Officers. 2008. "Budget Processes in the States." Washington.

National Bureau of Economic Research. Various years. *Collective Bargaining Law Dataset*. Cambridge, Mass.

National Conference of State Legislatures. 2008–12. "Pensions and Retirement Plan Enactments in 2008–2010 Legislatures." Washington.

———. 2011. "State Pensions and Retirement Legislation 2011." Washington.

National Conference on Public Employee Retirement Systems (NCPERS). 2007. "State Constitutional Protections for Public Sector Retirement Benefits." Washington.

———. 2010. "State Protections for Retirement Benefits." Washington.

———. 2011. "The Secure Choice Pension: A Way Forward for Retirement Security in the Private Sector." Washington.

National League of Cities v. *Usery*, 426 U.S. 833 (1976).

Nebraska Public Employees' Retirement Systems. 2002. *Retirement Roundup* 17, no. 5.

Novy-Marx, Robert, and Joshua D. Rauh. 2008. "The Intergenerational Transfer of Public Pension Promises." Working Paper 14343. Cambridge, Mass.: National Bureau of Economic Research.

———. 2011a. "The Revenue Demands of Public Employee Pension Promises." Working Paper. Chicago, Ill.: Kellogg School of Management, Northwestern University.

———. 2011b. "Policy Options for State Pension Systems and Their Impact on Plan Liabilities." *Journal of Pension Economics and Finance* 10, no. 2: 173–94.

———. 2011c. "Public Pension Promises: How Big Are They and What Are They Worth?" *Journal of Finance* 66, no. 4: 1211–49.

Oaxaca, Ronald. 1973. "Male-Female Wage Differentials in Urban Labor Markets." *International Economic Review* 14, no. 3: 693–709.

Ontario Teachers' Pension Plan. 2011. "Leading the Way: 2011 Annual Report." Toronto, Canada.

Palmer, Bruce A. 2008. "2008 GSU/AON RETIRE Project Report." Research Report Series 08-1. Atlanta: J. Mack Robinson College of Business, Georgia State University.

Paul, Mark, and Micah Weinberg. 2010. "Public Affluence, Private Squalor: California's Duel Pension Crisis." Washington: New America Foundation.

Peng, Jun. 2004. "Public Pension Funds and Operating Budgets: A Tale of Three States." *Public Budgeting & Finance* 24, no. 2: 59–73.

———. 2009. *State and Local Pension Fund Management.* Boca Raton, Fla.: Auerbach Publications, Taylor & Francis Group.

Pennacchi, George, and Mahdi Rastad. 2011. "Portfolio Allocation for Public Pension Funds." *Journal of Pension Economics and Finance* 10, no. 2: 221–45.

"The Pension Protection Act of 2006." Public Law 109-280. Washington, DC: U.S. Government Printing Office.

Peskin, Michael. 2001. "Asset/Liability Management in the Public Sector." In *Pensions in the Public Sector*, edited by Olivia Mitchell and Edwin Hustead. University of Pennsylvania Press.

The Pew Center on the States. 2012. "The Widening Gap Update." Issue Brief. Washington.

Plan Member Financial Corporation. 2010. "Employer Retirement Plan Comparison Chart: 403(b), 401(k) and 457(b) Plans." Carpinteria, Calif.

Plan Sponsor Council of America. 2011. *54th Annual Survey of Profit Sharing and 401(k) Plans.* Chicago, Ill.

Police and Firemen's Retirement System of New Jersey. 2009. "Annual Report of the Actuary: Prepared as of July 1, 2009." Trenton, N.J.

Ponds, Eduard H. M., and Bart van Riel. 2007. "The Recent Evolution of Pension Funds in the Netherlands: The Trend to Hybrid DB-DC Plans and Beyond." Working Paper 2007-9. Chestnut Hill, Mass.: Center for Retirement Research at Boston College.

Poterba, James M., and Kim S. Rueben. 1994. "The Distribution of Public Sector Wage Premia: New Evidence Using Quantile Regression Methods." Working Paper 4734. Cambridge, Mass.: National Bureau of Economic Research.

Preston, Darrell, and Dunstan McNichol. 2010. "Nevada Switch to 401(k)-Style Pension Adds $1.2 Billion Cost, Study Says." *Bloomberg News* (December 16).

Public Plans Database. 2000–10. Center for Retirement Research at Boston College and Center for State and Local Government Excellence. Chestnut Hill, Mass., and Washington.

Puchalski, Richard J. 2002. "Circuit Court Decides Pension Spike Case." Carol Stream, Ill.: Illinois Public Pension Fund Association.

Quinn, Joseph F. 1982. "Pension Wealth of Government and Private Sector Workers." *American Economic Review* 72, no. 2: 283–87.

Rauh, Joshua D. 2009. "Are State Public Pensions Sustainable?" Presented at "Train Wreck: A Conference on America's Looming Fiscal Crisis," sponsored by Urban-Brookings Tax Policy Center and the USC-Caltech Center for the Study of Law and Politics. Los Angeles, Calif., January 15, 2010.

Rawls, John. 1999. "Justice as Fairness." In *Collected Papers*, edited by Samuel Freeman. Harvard University Press.

Reinke, Gavin. 2011. "When a Promise Isn't a Promise: Public Employers' Ability to Alter Pension Plans of Retired Employees." *Vanderbilt Law Review* 64, no. 5: 1674–1710.

Retirement Systems of Minnesota. 2011. "Retirement Plan Design Study: Minnesota Public Retirement Systems." St. Paul, Minn.

Richwine, Jason, and Andrew Biggs. 2011. "Are California Public Employees Overpaid?" Working Paper. Washington: Heritage Foundation.

Sass, Steven A. 1997. *The Promise of Private Pensions: The First Hundred Years.* Harvard University Press.

Scanlan, Matthew H., and Carter M. Lyon. 2006. "The Retirement Benefits Crisis: A Survival Guide." *Journal of Investing* 15, no. 2: 26–41.

Scheer, Peter. 2008. "Vallejo's Bankruptcy Might Have Been Prevented." *Huffington Post* (May 9).

Schieber, Sylvester J. 2011. "Political Economy of Public Sector Retirement Plans." *Journal of Pension Economics and Finance* 10, no. 2: 269–90.

Schmidt, Daniel. 2011. "2010 Comparative Study of Major Public Employee Retirement Systems." Madison, Wisc.: Wisconsin Legislative Council.

Schmitt, John. 2010. "The Wage Penalty for State and Local Government Employees." Washington: Center for Economic and Policy Research.

Schmitt, Raymond. 1976. *Retirement Systems of State and Local Governments: Dimensions of the Pension Problem.* Washington: U.S. Government Printing Office.

Schneider, Marguerite, and Fariborz Damanpour. 2002. "Public Choice Economics and Public Pension Plan Funding: An Empirical Test." *Administration & Society* 34 no. 1: 57–86.

Scholz, John Karl, Ananth Seshadri, and Surachai Khitatrakun. 2004. "Are Americans Saving 'Optimally' for Retirement?" Working Paper 10260. Cambridge, Mass.: National Bureau of Economic Research.

Schotland, Roy A. 1978. Statement by Roy A. Schotland. *Hearings on Public Employee Retirement Income Security Act of 1978, H.R. 14138*, before the Subcommittee on Labor Standards of the House Committee on Education and Labor, 95th Congress, 2nd session. Washington: U.S. Government Printing Office.

The Segal Company. 2010. "Public Employees' Retirement System of the State of Nevada: Analysis and Comparison of Defined Benefit and Defined Contribution Retirement Plans." Greenwood Village, Colo.

Sharpe, William, Gordon J. Alexander, and Jeffrey W. Bailey. 2003. *Investments*. Upper Saddle River, N.J.: Prentice Hall.

Shelton, Alison M. 2010a. *Social Security: The Government Pension Offset*. Washington: Library of Congress, Congressional Research Service.

————. 2010b. *Social Security: The Windfall Elimination Provision*. Washington: Library of Congress, Congressional Research Service.

Simko, Darryl B. 1996. "Of Public Pensions, State Constitutional Contract Protection, and Fiscal Constraint." *Temple Law Review* 69, no. 1: 1059–79.

Slack, Donovan, and Walter V. Robinson. 2008. "U.S. Probes Firefighter Disability Abuse: FBI Issues Subpoenas for Past and Current Members of Boston Department." *Boston Globe* (April 17).

Smith, Sharon. 1976. "Pay Differentials between Federal Government and Private Sector Workers." *Industrial and Labor Relations Review* 29, no. 2: 179–97.

Special Commission to Study the Massachusetts Contributory Retirement System. 2009. "Final Report of the Special Commission to Study the Massachusetts Contributory Retirement System." Boston, Mass.

Staman, Jennifer. 2011. *State and Local Pension Plans and Fiscal Distress: A Legal Overview*. Report R41736. Washington: Congressional Research Service.

Standard & Poor's Index Services. Various years. *S&P 500 Monthly Returns*. New York.

State Employees' Retirement System of Illinois. 2009. "Annual Actuarial Valuation as of June 30, 2009." Springfield, Ill.

State of Wisconsin Retirement Research Committee. 1996. "1996 Comparative Study of Major Public Employee Retirement Systems." Staff Report 82. Madison, Wisc.

State Universities Retirement System of Illinois. 2009. "Actuarial Valuation Report as of June 30, 2009." Champaign, Ill.

Steffen, Karen. 2001. "State Employee Pension Plans." In *Pensions in the Public Sector*, edited by Olivia S. Mitchell and Edwin C. Hustead. University of Pennsylvania Press.

Steyer, Robert. 2010. "New DC Plan among Connecticut Governor's Ideas." *Pensions & Investments* (September 8).

Summers, Adam. 2009. "California Needs to Stop Defined-Benefit Pensions." Washington: Reason Foundation.

The Associated Press. 2012. "Court: NH Can't Raise Vested Workers' Pension Rate." (February 2.)

The Tax Foundation. 2005–10. *State Individual Income Tax Rates, 2000–2010*. Washington.

Teacher Retirement System of Texas (Texas TRS). 1999 and 2007–10. *Actuarial Valuation Report*. Austin, Tex.

Teachers' Pension and Annuity Fund of New Jersey. 2009. "June 30, 2009 Actuarial Valuation Report." Trenton, N.J.

Teachers Retirement System of Georgia (Georgia TRS). 2010. *Comprehensive Annual Financial Report for Fiscal Year Ended June 30, 2011*. Atlanta, Ga.

Teachers' Retirement System of the State of Illinois. 2009. "Actuarial Valuation: June 30, 2009." Springfield, Ill.

Tennessee Consolidated Retirement System. 2010. *Comprehensive Annual Financial Report for Fiscal Year Ended June 30, 2010*. Nashville.

Texas Municipal Retirement System. 2007–10. *Actuarial Valuation Report*. Austin, Tex.

Thompson, Jeffrey, and John Schmitt. 2010. "The Wage Penalty for State and Local Government Employees in New England." Center for Economic and Policy Research and the Political Economy Research Institute at the University of Massachusetts, Amherst.

Thomson Reuters. Various years. *SDC Platinum Municipal Bonds Dataset*. New York.

Towers Watson. 2009. "Employer Commitment to Retirement Plans in the United States." Washington.

Troy, Leo, and Neil Sheflin. 1985. "Union Sourcebook: Membership, Finances, Structure, Directory." West Orange, N.J.: Industrial Relations Data and Information Services.

University of Michigan. Various years. *Health and Retirement Study*.

———. Various years. *The Panel Study of Income Dynamics*.

U.S. Board of Governors of the Federal Reserve System. Various years. *Flow of Funds Accounts of the United States*. Washington.

———. 2007. *Survey of Consumer Finances*. Washington.

U.S. Bureau of Economic Analysis. 2011. *National Income and Product Accounts*. Washington: Department of Commerce.

U.S. Bureau of Labor Statistics. Various years. *Employer Costs for Employee Compensation*. Washington: U.S. Government Printing Office.

———. Various years. *Consumer Expenditure Survey*. Washington: U.S. Government Printing Office.

U.S. Census Bureau. 2005–09. *State and Local Government Finances*. Washington.

———. Various years. *State and Local Public-Employee Retirement Systems*. Washington.

———. 2007. *Statistical Abstract: 2007 Edition*. Washington.

———. 2009. *Quarterly Summary of State and Local Government Tax Revenue*. (Table 1). Washington.

———. 2010a. "Annual Estimates of the Resident Population by Sex and Age for States and for Puerto Rico: April 1, 2000 to July 1, 2008." Washington.

———. 2010b. *Annual Public Employment Survey*. Washington.

U.S. Census Bureau and the U.S. Department of Labor. Various years. *Current Population Survey*. Washington.

U.S. Congress. 1978. *Pension Task Force Report on Public Employee Retirement Systems*. House Committee on Education and Labor, Subcommittee on Labor Standards. 95th Congress, 2nd session. Washington: U.S. Government Printing Office.

———. 1980. *Hearings on the Public Employee Retirement Income Security Act of 1980, H.R. 6525*. House Committee on Education and Labor, Task Force on Welfare and Pension Plans of the Subcommittee on Labor-Management Relations. 96th Congress, 2nd session. Washington: U.S. Government Printing Office.

U.S. Department of Labor. *Annual Return/Report Form 5500 Series for Plan Years 1980, 1990–2006, and 2008*. Washington: U.S. Government Printing Office

———. Various years. *Current Employment Statistics*. Washington.

U.S. General Accounting Office. 1985. *Budget Issues: State Balanced Budget Practices*. Washington: U.S. Government Printing Office.

———. 1993. *Balanced Budget Requirements: State Experiences and Implications for the Federal Government*. Washington: U.S. Government Printing Office.

U.S. Government Accountability Office. 2008. *State and Local Government Retiree Benefits: Current Funded Status of Pension and Health Benefits*. GAO-08-223. Washington: U.S. Government Printing Office.

———. 2009. *State And Local Government Retiree Health Benefits: Liabilities Are Largely Unfunded, But Some Governments Are Taking Action*. GAO-10-61. Washington: U.S. Government Printing Office.

———. 2010. *Social Security Administration: Management Oversight Needed to Ensure Accurate Treatment of State and Local Government Employees*. GAO-10-938. Washington: U.S. Government Printing Office.

U.S. Securities and Exchange Commission. 2004. "Report on Transactions in Municipal Securities." Washington.

Vanguard Group. 2011. "How America Saves 2011—A Report on Vanguard's 2010 Defined Contribution Plan Data." Valley Forge, Pa.

Venti, Steven. 1987. "Wages in the Federal and Private Sectors." In *Public Sector Payrolls*, edited by David A. Wise. Cambridge, Mass.: National Bureau of Economic Research.

Waring, M. Barton. 2004a. "Liability-Relative Investing." *Journal of Portfolio Management* 30, no. 4: 8–20.

———. 2004b. "Liability-Relative Investing II." *Journal of Portfolio Management* 31, no. 1: 40–53.

Watson Wyatt Worldwide. 2006. *Survey of Actuarial Assumptions and Funding: Pension Plans with 1,000 or More Participants*. Washington.

Weber, Jonathan. 2011. "For Vallejo, Bankruptcy Isn't Exactly a Fresh Start." *New York Times* (January 22).

Weller, Christian E., Mark A. Price, and David M. Margolis. 2006. "Rewarding Hard Work: Give Pennsylvania Families a Shot at Middle Class Retirement Benefits." Washington: Center for American Progress.

Whaley, Sean. 2012. "National Group Calls on Nation's Governors to Freeze Defined Benefit Pensions for Public Workers." Nevada News Bureau (February 20).

Wiles, Gregory. 2006. "Why Are There Any Public Defined Contribution Plans?" Undergraduate Thesis. Chestnut Hill, Mass.: Boston College.

Williams, Erica. 2012. "Strengthening State Fiscal Policies for a Stronger Economy." Washington: Center on Budget and Policy Priorities.

Williams Walsh, Mary. 2011. "Two Rulings Find Cuts in Public Pensions Permissible." *New York Times* (June 30).

Wyoming Retirement System. 2005. *Comprehensive Annual Financial Report for Fiscal Year Ended December 31, 2005*. Cheyenne, Wyo.

Yang, Tongxuan (Stella), and Olivia S. Mitchell. 2005. "Public Pension Governance, Funding, and Performance: A Longitudinal Appraisal." Working Paper 2005-2. Philadelphia, Pa.: Pension Research Council.

Zax, Jeffrey S. 1985. "Municipal Employment, Municipal Unions, and Demand for Municipal Services." Working Paper 1728. Cambridge, Mass.: National Bureau of Economic Research.

Zorn, Paul. 1990–2000. *Survey of State and Local Government Retirement Systems: Survey Report for Members of the Public Pension Coordinating Council.* Chicago, Ill.: Government Finance Officers Association.

Index

ABO (accumulated benefit obligation), 50–51, 58, 113

Accounting methods/standards: annual earnings, 49–50; constitutional issues, 37–38; cost allocation, 49, 51–54; discount selection, 49, 54–57, 64–68, 73–74; regulatory history, 17–18, 32; revisions/proposals, 57–58, 68–73, 76–77, 179

Accrual rates, and defined contribution plan introductions, 194–95

Accumulated benefit obligation (ABO), 50–51, 58, 113

Actuarial cost methods: in budget allocation analysis, 117–18; for cost allocation question, 49, 51–55; in fund status comparisons, 82, 85–87

Administrative costs, defined benefit plans, 176–77, 190

Age of plan, in fund status comparisons, 85

Age statistics, state/local government employees, 141

Alabama, bankruptcy case, 1, 3

Alaska, 123, 192, 195–96, 219

Allen, Danielle, 224

Annual required contribution (ARC): discount rate impact, 61–62; and equities investments, 67–68; in fund status comparisons, 78–87, 89–91; in GASB's accounting standards, 18, 57, 73; local vs. state-administered plans, 89–91; payment patterns, 5, 79–84, 89–91, 101–02, 179–80. *See also* Budget allocation, pension spending

Annuities, 15, 31, 55, 206

Anti-spiking provisions, pension calculations, 185–86

ARC. *See* annual required contribution (ARC)

Arizona, contract protections, 219

Asset-benefit payment ratios, 108–12. *See also* Funded ratios/fund status

Asset totals, 5, 22. *See also* Funded ratios/fund status

Asset valuation. *See* accounting methods/standards

Auto escalation and automatic enrollment, 189

Automatic enrollment, 401(k) plans, 188–89

Bankruptcy filings, city governments, 1, 3

Benefit provisions. *See specific topics, e.g.,* Accounting methods/standards; Compensation packages, public/private comparisons; Defined benefit plans; Pension plans, overview; Unions